Henry Allon, Henry John Gauntlett

The Congregational Psalmist

Henry Allon, Henry John Gauntlett

The Congregational Psalmist

ISBN/EAN: 9783337812201

Printed in Europe, USA, Canada, Australia, Japan

Cover: Foto ©Lupo / pixelio.de

More available books at **www.hansebooks.com**

THE

Congregational Psalmist.

THE
Congregational Psalmist:

A COMPANION TO

ALL THE NEW HYMN-BOOKS;

PROVIDING

TUNES, CHORALES, AND CHANTS,

FOR

THE METRICAL HYMNS AND PASSAGES OF SCRIPTURE CONTAINED IN THOSE BOOKS.

FIRST SECTION. TUNES AND CHORALES.

Compressed Score Edition.

EDITED BY

HENRY ALLON, D.D.,

AND

HENRY JOHN GAUNTLETT, Mus. Doc.

LONDON:
HODDER AND STOUGHTON, 27, PATERNOSTER ROW;
NOVELLO, EWER & CO., BERNERS STREET, OXFORD STREET, AND QUEEN STREET, CHEAPSIDE, E.C.

1884.

PREFACE TO THE ENLARGED EDITION.

THE first edition of the "Congregational Psalmist" was published in 1858. In 1868 fifty-three tunes were added to the book. The copious additions to the hymnody of the Church, both of Hymns and Tunes, which have since been made, necessitate a further enlargement, in order that the Churches may possess for their worship such compositions as the manifold gifts of holy men in all sections of the Church continue to supply. Finality in the provision for the Service of Song is as impossible as it were fatal. While each generation inherits what is most precious from the past, it will, so long as the Church is a living Church, bring its own contribution of fresh Hymns and Tunes—the exact expression of its own distinctive life.

The revolt of hymn writers from the cramped and meagre Iambic forms, to which in England we have chiefly been restricted, is in every way a great gain to Church Song. Trochaic and other metres give variety and richness to hymns, which not only gratify the taste, and fill the imagination, but like all forms of beauty directly minister to feeling. Just now, perhaps, this diversity is in danger of becoming excessive and eccentric; but it is only a passing phase, a not unnatural reaction from stiff traditional forms. Nothing that is merely odd endures.

It is indicative, that of the hundred and seventeen additional tunes in this edition, nearly eighty are for metres, or for hymns, hitherto unprovided for in the book; provision for which has become imperative through the general acceptance which the hymns have found.

It is matter for great satisfaction that we are no longer contented to sing a hymn to any tune for which its metre may be practicable. We demand that the music shall be the best possible expression of the distinctive sentiment of the hymn. Hence some hymns of ordinary metres, demand tunes exclusively for themselves, e.g., the hymns to which the tunes 453, 469, 478, 479, and 488 are respectively set. Music is the eloquence of a hymn; and the difference of devotional inspiration between an expressive and a mere mechanical setting is very great. In the Old Psalters, as in the *Choralbücher* of Germany, each hymn has its own inalienable tune; and to this I hope we are returning.

The character of tune demanded by trochaic metres such as are here chiefly provided for, differs widely from the traditional iambic tune of the Old Psalters. The question, "what is a Church Tune?" is not therefore to be answered by antiquarian or ecclesiastical traditions. That is the best Church Tune which gives the most religious and devotional expression to the hymn to which it is set? Hence in this additional selection I have cared but little for traditional forms; I have not sought in Gregorian Psalters models for trochaic or anapæstic metres. Avoiding everything unseemly in character or undesirable in association, I have freely appropriated whatever seemed to give the most precise and fervent expression to the religious feeling of a hymn, and to provide for it a genuine melody, and not a mere musical phrase.

Some of the finest tunes of the Church have been derived from secular sources; the "Conditor alme" of Ambrose was a heathen offer-song. Several of the grandest of the Lutheran melodies were street ballads. Some of the most devotional airs of Handel's Oratorios were originally written for his Operas. The only legitimate or sensible test of a tune is its practical fitness.

The same principle has determined my use of the old or the new. As a rule neither great hymns nor great tunes can be written to order. They are inspirations which come as the breath of God comes—their authors know not how. The best hymnal will be that which collects the best hymns and tunes of all generations. I have sought, therefore, to procure the use of such tunes as experience has commended, rather than to provide a large number of new compositions. The conditions of effectiveness are sometimes very subtle; they can neither be forecast by genius, nor calculated from its untried products. Just as the hymns of the greatest poets have failed, while those of comparatively prosaic men have become the possession and joy of the Church—so it is with tunes.

I have not rejected excerpts and adaptations from the works of the great masters; although in their justification there is perhaps nothing theoretically to be said. Practically all depends upon the way in which they are made. All that I can say is, that those included in this collection have been made by others, in some instances by very competent authorities. I have found, not made them; and have simply been unable to resist the strong temptation to enrich worship-song by their inspiration and beauty.

When the first edition of this work was compiled, the fine old Latin, and Psalter Tunes, and the grand Chorales of Germany, were but very little known to the English Churches. One of my chief objects was to help to make them known, that their use might supersede the inferior and worthless tunes of the preceding century. To this end the book largely contributed; some of the fine Tunes and Chorales now in common use were introduced to the English Churches in it. A large proportion of the tunes added in 1868 were modern English tunes, chiefly after the old models. The present addition is of an element different from both: which has been determined chiefly by the metres of the hymns for which provision had to be made.

Objection has been taken to the old psalter form of a double note at the beginning and end of each line. In some iambic tunes this is almost essential; its advantages in enabling congregations to sing steadily rapid tunes are very great. But if in any instance, or by any congregation it be thought undesirable, nothing is easier than for the organist or choir practically to disregard it, and to sing the initial and terminal semibreves as minims. In some instances the best effect may be produced by singing two lines of a verse at one strain, in others the entire verse. In trochaic tunes the old iambic form is of course incongruous.

Diversity of opinion prevails about the use of the "Amen" at the end of hymns. Intrinsically, as a simple affirmation of assent, it must be as congruous as at the end of a prayer. There are few hymns so destitute of pious expression and aspiration as to make such assent unsuitable. It is matter of simple option. I have thought it best to provide it for those who prefer to use it, others can omit it.

The first edition of the "Congregational Psalmist" consisted of only 330 Tunes. In the Preface to that edition it is said, "In the preparation of this work I am responsible for the selection of the Tunes, for the Introductory Notices, and for the general arrangement of the book; Dr. Gauntlett's responsibility being restricted to his arrangements of the Tunes put into his hands. The same division of responsibility applies to the companion volume of Chants." Inasmuch as two considerable additions to the work, amounting to 170 Tunes, have since been made' it is only right to say that for these I alone am responsible; as I am also for the substitution in later editions of new Tunes for the numbers 18, 21, 27, 45, 47, 49, 61, 64, 94, 99, 101, 113, 114, 170, 217, 222, and 264.

My grateful thanks are due alike to those who have generously given me permission to insert their compositions, and to those who have permitted me to purchase it.

For the contribution of new tunes written for this selection, I am under obligation to the Rev. J. B. Dykes, M.A., Mus. Doc., Mr. Arthur Sullivan, Mr. E. Prout, B.A., Mr. T. M. Mudie, Mr. Samuel Smith, Mr. Hancock, Mus. Bac., Mr. Richard Payne, Mr. A. Legge, and Mr. C. W. Poole.

And for permission to use tunes previously published, to the Rev. J. B. Dykes, M.A., Mus. Doc., Mr. Arthur Sullivan, J. Stainer, Mus. Doc., Rev. L. G. Hayne, Mus. Doc., S. S. Wesley, Mus. Doc., Mr. Arthur H. Brown, Mr. W. B. Gilbert, Mus. Bac., Rev. T. R. Matthews, Mr. John Gill, Mr. James Watson, Rev. R. Brown-Borthwick, Messrs. Burns and Oates, the Rev. Sir H. W. Baker, Bart., and the proprietors of "Hymns Ancient and Modern." Also to the proprietors of "Psalms and Hmyns for Public Worship;" "Church Hymns and Tunes" of the Society for Promoting Christian Knowledge, edited by Arthur Sullivan; the "Sarum Hymnal;" the "Hymnary;" the "Supplemental Hymn and Tune Book," by Rev. R. Brown-Borthwick; Mercer's "Church Hymn Book and Psalter;" Chope's "Congregational Hymn and Tune Book;" "Hymns of the Eastern Church;" "Crown of Jesus Music;" the representatives of the late Mr. Wm. Bayley; "The London Church Choir Association." &c.

If I select for the expression of special gratitude the names of the Rev. Dr. Dykes, Mr. James Watson (Messrs. Nisbet), publisher of "Psalms and Hymns for Public Worship," Mr. Arthur Sullivan, and the Rev R. Brown-Borthwick, it is because their generous kindness far exceeded any request that I should have felt at liberty to prefer, and indeed any advantage of it that I could take; although, as will be seen, I have been very largely indebted to it.

HENRY ALLON

Canonbury, April, 1875.

PREFACE TO THE FIRST EDITION OF THE COMPRESSED SCORE.

THE rapid sale of fifty-two thousand copies of the "Congregational Psalmist" is a gratifying indication of the interest felt in popular Psalmody, as well as of the adaptation of this work to meet the want which occasioned its compilation.

The object of the Editor was to render available for worshipping use the finest chorals of every age and of every section of the church. Gifts of poetry and of song have been bestowed upon every generation, and upon none, perhaps, more richly than our own. Hence the canon of Church song can never be completed; additions will continuously be made to the richness of the worship of the Church, and to the joy of its spiritual life. It were, therefore, an egregious folly and loss, either to refuse the precious inheritance of the past, or to exclude ourselves from the fresh contributions to it that from time to time are proffered. The past is commended to us by the test of successive generations, the present by contemporary form and feeling; the old that remains to us has filtered out of much that has perished, and the new that is proffered to us is doubtless destined to undergo the same process. It is simple pedantry to restrict the music of the Church to either any particular age or any particular school. Like a hymn-book, a tune-book should provide for various tastes and degrees of capacity; the ruling canon of its compilation should be, not conformity to dogmatic rules, but practical fitness for devotional use. Whatever contributes to worshipping reverence and joy—so long as it is free from incongruous associations—is both legitimate and desirable. In the "Congregational Psalmist," both tunes and harmonies of various periods, and of various schools will be found; of the chorals of the Latin Church, from Ambrose to Luther, it contains twenty-five; from the rich choral treasures of the German Protestant Churches, ninety-five have been selected; the limited Psalmody of the French Protestant Church has furnished seven; from the English and Scottish Psalters of the sixteenth and seventeenh centuries, thirty-four have been taken; living composers of various churches and schools have contributed seventy-six; the rest have been gathered from various writers of the last two centuries. It is scarcely too much to say that no existing English compilation contains so large and so Catholic a representation of the worship-song of "the Holy Church throughout the world."

The varying capacities of congregations have also been considered; while the great bulk of the tunes are such as the least advanced may use, some tunes are inserted which only the cultured can sing.

To the Catholic character of the book, to the imperishable qualities of the grand chorals which have come down to us from past generations, and to the variety of taste and capacity for which it provides, its large success is doubtless owing.

The present Edition contains fifty-three additional tunes. These are added, partly, to supply such deficiencies as the practical use of the book had revealed, partly to add some tunes of unquestionable excellence which had been overlooked, and partly, to enable the use of tunes which have appeared since this work was published, and which, from various causes have become popular. Permission to use the latter has in every instance been most readily and generously given, and is hereby most gratefully acknowledged.

HENRY ALLON.

Canonbury, April, 1867.

ALPHABETICAL INDEX.

* Indicates Tunes inserted by permission from the Rev. W. J. Blew's "Church Hymn and Tune Book."
† Words inserted by permission from Mendelssohn's "St. Paul."
‡ Words inserted by permission from Mendelssohn's "Lobgesang."
§ Inserted by permission from "Twelve Chorals," arranged by Sir H. Bishop.
‖ Adaptation of a German Melody by permission from Rev. Wm. Mercer's "Church Psalter."
** Words by permission from Rev. Wm. Mercer's "Church Psalter."

				No.
ABBEY	C.M.	Andro Hart's Psalter, No. 10, 1615		233
ABRIDGE	C.M.	Isaac Smith, 1770		156
ADVENT	46.64.64.64.	J. Baptiste Calkin		485
ADVENT EVENING HYMN	L.M.	Old Latin, "Conditor almæ siderum," 4th Cent.		35
AGATHA	66.66.66.66.	Weber		470
AJALON	77.77.77.	R. Redhead		376
ALBION	664.6664.	Henry Carey, d. 1743		326
ALLA TRINITA	87.87.87.87.	Laudi Spirituali, 1545		125
ALSACE	L.M.	Beethoven, d. 1827		275
ALTONA†	L.M.	Clauderi Psalmodia, 1630		93

(Herr Jesu Christ, meines Lebens Licht.)

| ALTORF ‖ | 8336.8336. | Johann Georg Ebeling, 1666 | | 382 |

(Warum sollt' ich mich denn grämen?)

AMBROSE	777.5.	Dr. Gauntlett, 1844		69
ANATOLIUS	76.76.88.	Arthur H. Brown		434
ANGELS' HYMN	L.M.	Dr. Orlando Gibbons, 1623		85
ANGELUS	L.M.	J. Scheffler		442
ANTIOCH	888.888.	Old Latin, "Veni, Sancte Spiritus," adapted by Luther, 1524		314
APOLLOS	7s—10 lines	Arranged from Beethoven		417
ARIMATHEA	77.77.77.77.	Latin Melody, "Resonet in Laudibus" 14th Cent.		318
ARMSTADT	77.77.	J. S. Bach, d. 1750		256

(Nicht so traurig, nicht so sehr.)

| ARNHEIM | C.M. | Adam Krieger, 1666 | | 343 |

(Nun sich der Tag geendet hat.)

ALPHABETICAL INDEX.

№

ARNO . . . 76.76.76.76. (pec. acc.) or 8 lines 7s, Old Latin Melody,
"Patris sapientia" 148
ARNOLD . . . C.M. . . . . . Dr. S. Arnold, d. 1791 251
ARNSBERG . . 887.887. . . . . Freylinghausen, 1704 206
(Agni pugna et draconis.)
ASAPH . . . 87.87.77., or 8.7.4. . . Henry Purcell, d. 1695 260
(O, Thou art my God.)
ASCALON. . . 668.668. . . . . Crusaders' Melody 126
(Schönster Herr Jesu.)
ASLACTON . . 87.87.47. . . . . Dr. Gauntlett, 1856 205
ASPIRATION . . 64.64.664. . . . . Arthur Sullivan 422
AUGSBURG . . 87.87.87.87. Töpler's "Alte Choral Melodien," 1850 282
(Sollt ich meinem Gott nicht singen?)
AUGUSTINE . . 66.66.66. . . . . Recueil de Berne 457
AURELIA. . . 76.76.76.76. . . . . Dr. S. S. Wesley 415
AYNHOE . . . S.M. . . Dr. Nares, Ashworth's Collection, 1766 46
BABYLON. . . I.M. . Dr. T. Campion, 1600, "Book of Sacred Airs" 297
(By the Waters of Babylon.)
BADEN . . . 88.88.7. J. Pachelbel (?), "Nürnbergisches Gesang-
buch," 1690 172
(Was Gott thut, das ist wohlgethan.)
BALLERMA . . C.M. . . . . Spanish Melody of 10th Cent. 99
BANIAS . . . L.M.—8 lines . . . . Meyer Lutz 500
BARNABAS . . 76.76.77.76. C. Damantius (?) Marot & Beza's
Psalms, Ps. 75, 1562 16
BARTHOLOMEW . 1010.1010. Goudimel, Marot & Beza's Psalms, Ps.
124, 1562 302
BARTON . . . 76.76. . . . . . J. H. Knecht 440
(Der niedern Menschheit Hülle.)
BATTISHILL . . 77.77. . . . . . J. Battishill, d. 1801 299
BAUN . . . 87.87. . . . . Beethoven, d. 1827 162
BAVARIA. . . L.M. . . . . . Mozart, d. 1791 249
BEDFORD. . . C.M. . W. Wheall, Mus. Bac., Wilkin's Psalmody,
1699 163
BEERSHEBA . . 1111.1111. . . . . August Störl 398
(O Jesu, wann soll ich erlöset.)
BELMONT . . C.M. . . Adapted from Mozart by S. Webbe 49
BEMERTON . . 65.65. . . . . Dr. Fred. Filitz, 1846 357
(Wem in Leidenstagen.)
BENEVENTO . . 77.77.77.77. . . . . S. Webbe, d. 1816 246

ALPHABETICAL INDEX. xiii

			No.
Berlin	L. M.	Graun, d. 1759	250
Berne	L. M.	ascribed to Beethoven	490
Bethabara	6610.6610.	Dr. Gauntlett, 1866	370
Bethany	C. M.	Gregorian Melody	166
Bethel	76.76.77.	H. A. Wedd, 1859	320
Bethlehem	87.87.	Latin Melody, "Quem Pastores," 14th Cent.	106
Bethsaida	610.610.	Dr. Gauntlett, 1866	362
Beulah	64.64.6664.	Dr. Lowell Mason 1859	396
Beverley	87.87.88.	Pergolesi's Stabat Mater, "Quando corpus morietur"	278
Bexley	C. M.	"Sacred Harmony," 1760	211
Biberach	77.77.	J. H. Knecht, 1797	339
(Ohne Rast und unverweilt.)			
Birkenhead	87.87.	Dr. Gauntlett, 1857	4
Bishopsthorpe	C. M.	Jeremiah Clarke, d. 1707	255
Bohemia	L. M.	George Rhau's "Neue deutsche geistliche Gesänge, Wittenberg," 1544	34
(Nun läst uns den Lieb begraben.)			
Bonchurch	76.76.76.76.	Beethoven, d. 1827	224
Bonifacr	888.6.	(Trochaic). Darmstadt Gesangbuch, 1698 "Jesu clemens pie Deus"	345
(Seelenfreund! hier liegt ein Herze.)			
Boston	L. M.	Dr. Lowell Mason	207
Boylston	S. M.	Dr. Lowell Mason	219
Bozrah	1110.11 6.	Johann Crüger 1640	395
(„Herzliebster Jesu, was hast du verbrochen.")			
Brandenburg	77.77.77.	Johann Crüger 1653	353
(Jesus, meine Zuversicht.)			
Bremen	s. m.—8 lines	J. B. Woodbury	70
Broadlands	66.66.66.66.	"Recueil Français des Eglises de la Confession d'Augsbourg," Paris, 1846	364
Brunswick	C. M.	Handel, d. 1759	263
Budleigh	64.64.1010.	T. M. Mudie	407
Burford	C. M.	attr. to H. Purcell, d. 1695	252
Burmah	C. M.		323
Burnham	66.66.88.	Dr. Croft, d. 1727	212
Byzantium	C. M.	Jackson, d. 1781	285
Caernarvon	66.66.88.	Handel, c. 1742	280
(Fitzwilliam Museum MS.)			
Cana	L. M.—6 or 8 lines	Beethoven	475

				No.
CANITZ	. .	847.847. . . .	Marot and Beza's Psalms	444
		(„Seele bu mußt munter werden.")		
CANNONS	. .	L.M.	Handel, c. 1742	287
		(Fitzwilliam Museum MS.)		
CANON	. .	L.M. . .	Tallis, Parker's Psalter, No. 8, 1561	12
CANONBURY	. .	L.M.	. R. Schumann	27
CANTERBURY	. .	S.M. .	Ravenscroft's "Whole Booke of Psalms,"	
			Ps. 25, 1621	271
CAPE TOWN	. .	777.5.	. Dr. Filitz	412
CAPERNAUM	. .	77.77.	. R. Redhead	341
CAREY	. .	L.M.—6 lin's	H. Carey, 1730	184
CARINTHIA	. .	77.77.	Froylinghausen, 1704	199
		(Gott sei Dank in aller Welt.)		
CARMEL	. .	L.M.	. John Bishop, 1700	267
CARROW	. .	84.84.84.	. Arthur Sullivan	496
CASSEL	. .	77.77.77.77. . .	. Brüderchoralbuch, 1784	213
		(„O gesegnetes Regieren.")		
CASTOR	. .	C.M.	. Philip Hart, 1689	198
CHERITH	. .	C.M.	Dr. Louis Spohr, d. 1859	374
CHERWELL	. .	C.M.	. J. Turle	367
CHESHUNT	. .	44.776.	Christoph Peter	384
		(O Traurigkeit! O Herzeleid!)		
CHESTER	. .	C.M. .	J. Dowland, Este's Psalter, Ps. 146,	
			1592	143
CHICHESTER	. .	87.87.87.87. . . .	. S. Wesley, d. 1837	182
CHRISTCHURCH	. .	S.M.	. S. Wesley, d. 1837	159
CHRISTMAS CHORAL	L.M.	.	Luther, "Klug's Gesangbuch," 1535	66
		(Vom Himmel hoch, da komm ich her.)		
CHRISTUS CONSOLATOR	85.83.	. . . . .	. . .	468
CLARENCE	. .	77.77.	. Arthur Sullivan	453
CLARENS	. .	65.65.65.65. . . .	. Carl August Groos	433
CLIFTON	. .	888.4. . .	(Metrical Chant) W. L. Reynolds	432
COBLENTZ	.	86.86.44.88. . . .	. Maximilian Stadler	418
COBURG	. .	87.87.887	Luther, "Walther's Gesangbuch," 1525	176
		(Aus tiefer Noth schrei ich zu Dir.)		
COLCHESTER	. .	C.M.	. . .	247
COMPTON	. .	104.104.	. Richard Payne	403
CONSTANCE	. .	L.M. . .	Gothäischen Cantional, 1651	124
		(Herr Jesus Christ, dich zu uns wend'.)		
CONWAY	. .	664.664. . . .	Freylinghausen, 1704	155
		(Mein Jes^u der du mich.)		

				No.
COPPET	65.—12 lines		Rev. Cæsar Malan, D.D.	456
CORINTH	87.87.87.87.	S. Webbe, d. 1816 "Tantum Ergo," from "Short Masses"		137
CORSICA	77.77.		Gluck, d. 1787	65
COURLAND	L.M.		Haydn, d. 1809	300
COVENEY	C.M.		T. M. Wood, 1866	355
COVERDALE	888.888.	Luther, "Walther's Gesangbuch," 1525		288

(Es spricht der Unweisen Mund wohl.)

CROYLAND*	888.6		Dr. Gauntlett, 1852	37
CRUCIFER (Bethany)	87.87.87.87.		Henry Smart	497
CULROSS	C.M.	Andro Hart's Psalter, No. 13, 1635		115
CUTHBERT*	77.77.77.		Dr. Gauntlett, 1852	116
CYPRUS	77.77		Mendelssohn, d. 1847	378
CYRIL	85.83.		A. R. Reinagle	21
DALKEITH	1010.1010.		T. Hewlett	230
DAMASCUS	888.		Bohemian Brethren	388

(Betracht'n wir heut zu dieser Frist.)

DANUBE	L.M.—6 lines		Mendelssohn, d. 1847	244
DARMSTADT	87.87.87.	Briegel's "Darmstadt Cantional," 1687 attr. to Joachim Neander		301

(Jesu, meines Lebens Leben.)

DETTINGEN	87.87.887	Melody of the 15th Century, Luther's "Eight Spiritual Songs," 1524		240

(Es ist das Heil uns kommen her.)

DIJON	77.77.		German Volkslied	91
DISMISSION	87.87.87.87.		S. Webbe, 1792	330
DONCASTER	S.M.		S. Wesley, d. 1837	122
DOVERSDALE	L.M.		Stanley, d. 1786	225
DRESDEN **	5555.1011.1110		J. G. Ebeling, 1666	180

(Die güld'ne Sonne.)

DUMAH †	888.664.88		J. Prätorius (?) Nicolai's "Freudenspiegel des ewigen Lebens" Frankfort, 1599	32

(Wachet auf! ruft uns die Stimme.)

DUNFERMLINE	C.M.	Andro Hart's Psalter, No. 8, 1615		9
DURHAM (St. Agnes)	C.M.		Rev. J. B. Dykes, Mus. Doc.	414
DUSSELDORF	777.5		Crüger's "Praxis Pietatis," 1656	209

(Heiliger Geist, du Tröster mein.)

EASTER HYMN	77.77		"Lyra Davidica," 1708	242
ECKINGTON	87.87.47.	Giovanni Martini. "Scuola d'Organo," 1804		5

ALPHABETICAL INDEX.

			No.
EISENACH	. L.M. . . . . . J. Hermann Schein, 1628	131
	(Mad's mit mir, Gott, nach beiner Güt.)	
EISLEBEN	. . 87.87.887 . . Luther, "Klug's Gesangbuch," 1535	102
	(Es ist gewißlich an der Zeit.)	
ELAH	. . . 65—12 lines . . . . . From Haydn	491
ELBERFELDT	. . 87.87.87.87. . . . Johann Crüger, 1649	232
	(Schmücke bich, o liebe Seele.)	
ELIM	. . . C.M.—8 lines (irreg.) . . W. H. Calcott, 1866	375
ELLA	. . . L.M. . . . . From Mendelssohn	94
ELLERKER	. . 87.87. . . . . . J. B. König, 1738	8
	(Ringe recht, wenn Gottes Gnade.)	
ELLERS .	. . 1010.1010 . . . . E. J. Hopkins	424
ELY	. . . L.M . . . . . Goudimel, Ps. 140, 1562	48
EMMANUEL	. . C.M. . . . . Beethoven	75
EMMAUS .	. . C.M.	93
ENON	. . . 65.65 . . . . Fielden	438
EPHESUS .	. . L.M.—6 lines Luther, "Erfurt Enchiridion," 1.	306
	(Ach Gott, vom Himmel sieh barein.)	
EPHRATAH	. . L.M.—6 lines "Veni, veni, Emmanuel," 12th Cent	372
ERNAN .	. . L.M. . . . . Dr. Lowell Mason	459
EUDOXIA	. . (Met. Chant, irreg.) Dr. W. Hayes, Adap. by Troyte	493
EUROCLYDON .	. . 1010.1010 . . . . E. R. B.	483
EVAN	. . . C.M. . . . . Rev. W. H. Havergal, M. A.	87
EVENTIDE	. . 1010.1010 . . . . W. H. Monk	358
EXETER .	. . C.M. Ravenscroft's "Whole Booke of Psalms," Ps. 110	307
FARRANT	. . C.M. . . . . From Richard Farrant, d. 1585	105
FELIX .	. . C.M. . . . . . . Mendelssohn, d. 1847	241
FERRIBY .	. . 6664.884 . . . . Old Melody	61
FLANDERS	. . 87.87.87.87. . . . . . J. Schop, 1641	262
	(Sollt ich meinem Gott nicht singen?)	
FLAVIAN .	. . C.M. . . . . . Barber's Psalm Tunes, 1686	467
FLEMMING	. . 1111.115 . Fred. Ferd. Flemming, "Integer Vitæ"	393
FLORENCE	. . 87.87.87.87. . . . . . Italian Melody	472
FRANCONIA	. . S.M. . . . . . . Lutheran Melody 1720	160
FRANKFORT	. . 87.87. . . . . Peter Von Winter, d. 1825	6
FRENCH .	. . C.M. ("Norwich") Andro Hart's Psalter, No. 5, 1615	1
FULDA .	. . L.M. . . . . . . From Beethoven, d. 1827	127
GALILEE .	. . L.M. . . . . Old Latin, "Crudelis Herodes"	295
GENEVA .	. . 65.65 . . . . Old Latin	170

ALPHABETICAL INDEX. xvii

				No.
GENNESARET	Irregular		P. P. Bliss	466
GETHSEMANE	77.77.77.		Latin Melody, " In natali Domini," 14th Cent.	144
GHENT	66.66.88.			253
GIBBONS	C.M.		Dr. Orlando Gibbons, 1623	68
GIBRALTAR	L.M.		C. W. Poole, 1867	63
GILDAS	S.M.	Peter Abelard,	"Mittit ad Virginem," 1120	321
GILEAD	1010.1010	(Metrical Chant)	Handel	416
GLASGOW	C.M.	Andrew Hart's Psalter, No. 29, alt., 1615		188
GLASTONBURY	L.M.	Old Carol, from Chetham's Psalmody		243
GLOUCESTER	C.M.		Ravenscroft's Psalter, 1621	317
GOLGOTHA	L.M.		Rev. J. B. Dykes, Mus. Doc.	338
GOSHEN	65.65.65.65.			458
GOTHA	77.77.77.		List's Choralbuch	191
(Christus, der uns selig macht.)				
GOTTINGEN	77.77.77.		Michael Weiss, 1531	337
(Gottes Sohn ist kommen.)				
GREENLAND	76.76.76.76		Lausanne Psalter	476
GREGORY	L.M.		Gregorian	83

HAARLEM	L.M.		Handel, d. 1759	197
HALLE	87.87.887		Hans Kugelmann, 1540	154
(Allein Gött in der Höh' sei Ehr'.)				
HAMBURG	87.87.88.77		"Darmstädter Cantional," 1687	196
(„Alle Menschen müssen sterben.")				
HAMPTON	S.M.			183
HANFORD	888.4.		Arthur Sullivan	486
HANOVER	10 10.11 11.	Dr. Croft, Wilkin's Psalmody, 1699		103
HARRINGTON	C.M.		Dr. Harrington, d. 1816	177
HAWTHORNDEN	S.M		J. Watson	426
HAYNE	L.M.		Rev. L. G. Hayne, Mus. Doc.	217
HEBER	1112.1210		Dr. Gauntlett, 1858	123
HEBRON	65.65.65.65.		"Laus tibi Christe,"	
(O wir armen Sünder.)			15th Cent.	379
HEIDELBERG	76.76. or C.M.		M. Vulpius, 1609	23
(„Christus, der ist mein Leben.")				
HEINLEIN	77.77.		Paul Heinlein, 1677	349
(Aus der Tiefen rufe ich.)				
HEMINGFORD	10 4.10 4			404
HEREFORD	886.886		Dr. William Boyce, 1745	268

b

		No.
HERMON . . . 664.6664. . . . . . . Braun, 1675		129
(„Ave Maria zart.")		
HERNHUTT . . 998.998.664.88. . . . Conrad Kocher		428
(Heiligster Jesu.)		
HEXHAM. . . 1111.1111.. . . . Mendelssohn, d. 1847		369
HIGHBURY . . 66.86.47 . . . Dr. Gauntlett, 1860		238
Hallelujah by C. F. Witt, "Psalmodia Sacra," 1715.		
(Sollt es gleich bisweilen scheinen.)		
HILARY . . . 668.668. . Marot and Beza's Psalms. Ps. 3, 1561		316
HOLLEY . . . L.M. . . . . . . George Hews		409
HOLLINGSIDE . . 77.77.77.77. . . Rev. J. B. Dykes, Mus. Doc.		354
HOLSTEIN . . S.M.—8 lines . . . . J. S. Bach, d. 1750		235
HOLY CROSS* . . 68.64 . . . . Dr. Gauntlett, 1852		15
HOLYROOD . . 77.77 . . . . . Romberg, d. 1821		237
HOLYWELL . . L.M. . . . . . . Gluck, d. 1787		213
HOREB . . . 64.66 . . . . . . Henry Smart		386
HOSANNAH . . L.M. . . . . H. G. Nägeli		471
HOUGHTON . . 1010.1111.. . . . . Dr. Gauntlett, 1860		246
HULL . . . 886.886. . . . . . . Old Melody		291
HUNTINGDON . . L.M.—6 lines . . . Dr. Gauntlett, 1858		75
ILALA . . . 1010.1010.. . . . . From La Feuillée		423
INCARNATION . . L.M.—8 lines Beethoven, "Six Sacred Songs," 1800		257
INNSPRUCK . . 886.886 . . . . Henry Isaac, 1490		7
(„O Welt, ich muß dich lassen.)		
INTERCESSION . 75.75.75.75.88. . . . W. H. Calcott, 1866		366
INTERLACHEN . . 88.88.88. (Trochaic) . . . . Ferd. Laur		443
INVITATION . C.M. (with Coda) . . . . T. Hastings		202
IONA . . . 66.66.88. . . . Rev. W. H. Havergal, M.A.		327
IRENE . . . 87.87.87., or 87.87.47. Dr. Louis Spohr, d. 1859		296
IRISH . . . C.M. . . Isaac Smith, Ashworth's Collection, 1776		187
ISLINGTON . . 557.557.1010 . . . . Richard Payne		405
JARROW . . . C.M.—6 lines . . , . . Joseph Haydn		488
JENA . . . L.M.—6 lines . . . Ancient Melody, adapted		
by Luther, Walther's Gesangbuch, 1525		310
(Christ lag in Todesbanden.)		
JERUSALEM . . 86.86.86. . . . . . Johann Crüger, 1653		294
(Wie soll ich dich empfangen?)		
KIDRON . . . 886.886. . . . . . . Handel, c. 1742		266
(Fitzwilliam Museum MS.)		

ALPHABETICAL INDEX. xix

			No.
KELSO	1010.1010.	Dr. Gauntlett, 1858	112
KETTERING	77.77.	Dr. Boyce, d. 1779	90
KIEL	77.77.	Andreas Romberg, 1802	79
KING'S COLLEGE	66.66.88	Henry Lawes, 1637	226
KIRKELLA	C.M.—8 lines	C. F. Rungenhagen	389
LABRADOR	65.65.65.65.	Heinrich Oswald	481
LALEHAM	64.64.664.	Dr. Gauntlett, 1858	220
LAMBETH	1311.1312. (irr.)	Dr. Gauntlett, 1860	258
LANCASTER	C.M.	Dr. Howard, 1762	287
LEBANON	86.86.88.	Dr. Louis Spohr, d. 1859	272
LEDFORTH	86.86.66.66.	From Mehul	64
LEEDS	888.6.	Dr. Lowell Mason	269
LEICESTER	888.4., or 888.6.	Kocher's "Zionsharfe"	305

(Jn's Feld geh', zähle alles Gras.)

| LEIPSIC | 77.77.77., or 8 lines | J. Schop, 1642 | 290 |

(Werbe munter, mein Gemüth.)

LEOMINSTER	S.M.—8 lines	Arr. by Arthur Sullivan	493
LEONI	6684.6684.	Old Hebrew Melody	132
LEVEN	76.76.	Dr. Gauntlett, 1852	161
LIGURIA	77.77. "Veni Redemptor gentium," Ambrose, d. 397		195
LINCOLN	C.M.	Allison's Psalter, Ps. 142, 1599	62
LINDEN	76.76.77.	J. Crüger	462

(Schwing dich auf zu beinem Gott.)

LITANY	777.6., or 77.77.	John Hatton	277
LIVERPOOL	C.M.	Dr. Wainwright, d. 1782	96
LIVONIA	76.76.77.	Knödel	463

(Blühen, welken.)

| LONDON NEW | C.M. | Andro Hart's Psalter, No. 22, 1635 | 95 |
| LUBECK | L.M.—6 lines Luther, "Kophl's Gesangbuch," 1537 | | 189 |

(Vater unser im Himmelreich.)

| LUCERNE. | 888.888. | "Strasburg Gesangbuch," 1525 | 210 |

(O Mensch, bewein deine Sünde groß.)

LUDLOW	S.M. "Ravenscroft's "Whole Booke of Psalms," Ps. 45, 1621		179
LUDWIG	66.66.	Sigillus. Goth. Cant., 1657	101
LUGANO	777.	Giovani Maria Nanini (Stabat Mater)	390

(Sag, was hilft alle Welt.)

| LUSATIA | 76.76.76.76. | Johann Crüger, 1640 | 356 |

(Von Gott will ich nicht lassen.)

| LUTTERWORTH | 87.87.47. | Ancient Melody | 214 |

ALPHABETICAL INDEX.

			No.
LUTZEN	76.76.76.76. Hans Leo Hasler's "Lustgarten," 1601		119
	(O Haupt voll Blut und Wunden.)		
LUX BENIGNA	10 4.10 4.1010. . . Rev. J. B. Dykes, Mus. Doc.		411
LUX CRUCIS	87.87.87.87. . . . . Sir John Goss		495
LYONS	87.87.87.87. . . . Goudimel, Ps. 42, 1562		171
LYTE	S.M. . . . . J. B. Wilkes		342
MACCABEUS	L.M. . . . . . . From Handel, d. 1759		261
MAGDALA	86.84. . . . Rev. J. B. Dykes, Mus. Doc.		351
MAGDALEN COLLEGE	L.M. Dr. Rogers, "Te Deum Patrem colimus," 1695		265
MAIDSTONE	77.77.77.77 or 6 lines W. B. Gilbert, Mus. Bac.		435
MAINZER	L.M. . . . . Dr. Mainzer		400
MALAGA	L.M. . . . . H. A. Wedd, 1857		55
MALDON	888.6. (Trochaic) . . Dr. Gauntlett, 1858		88
MAMRE	L.M. . . . . . From Handel, d. 1759		223
MANCHESTER	C.M. . . . . . Dr. Wainwright, d. 1782		190
MANNHEIM	87.87.87., or 87.87.47. German Choral, arranged by		
	Dr. Lowell Mason		380
MANSFELD	L.M.—6 lines Luther, "Walther's Gesangbuch," 1525		80
	(Christ, unser Herr, zum Jordan kam.)		
MARINERS	87.87. . . . . . . Sicilian Melody		293
MARTYRDOM	C.M. . . . . Hugh Wilson		71
MARTYRS	C.M. . . . Andro Hart's Psalter, No. 14, 1615		6
MASBURY, or TIVERTON	C.M. . . . . . . Grigg, d. 1768		41
MEAUX ABBEY	C.M. . . . . . Johann Crüger, 1658		153
	(Nun danket All' und bringet Ehr.)		
MECKLENBURG	L.M. . . . . J. S. Bach, 1736		130
	(Das walt Gott Vater und Gott Sohn.)		
MELANCTHON	L.M.—6 lines Luther, "Eight Spiritual Songs," 1524		304
	(Nun freut euch, liebe Christen g'mein.)		
MELANESIA	L.M. . . . . Samuel Smith		478
MELCOMBE	L.M. . . S. Webbe, "O salutaris hostia," 1800		78
MELITA	L.M.—6 lines . . Rev. J. B. Dykes, Mus. Doc.		346
MELTON	77.77. . . . . . Dr. Gauntlett, 1858		107
MIDIAN	65.65.65.65. . . . . John A. P. Schulz		454
MIGDOL	666.666. . . . . Theme from Haydn		399
MILAN	77.77. . . . . Ancient "Stabat Mater"		117
MILES' LANE	C.M. . . . . Shrubsole		215
MINDEN	87.87. . . . . . Heinrich Albert, 1644		158
	(Gott des Himmels und der Erden.)—alt.		
MISSIONARY	76.76.76.76. . . . . Dr. Lowell Mason		286

ALPHABETICAL INDEX.   xxi

				No.
MIZPAH	. .	55511.D . .	. . Rev. J. B. Dykes, Mus. Doc.	391
MODENA	. .	L.M. . .	. . . . Mediæval Melody	40
MONKLAND	.	1112.1210.	. . Rev. J. B. Dykes, Mus. Doc.	348
MONTGOMERY	.	L.M.	. . . . . . S. Stanley, 1810	92
MORAVIA	.	98.98.88. .	. . . Ch. Neumark, 1657	147

(Wer nur den lieben Gott läßt walten.)

MORIAH	. .	5511.5511.	. . . . Dr. Gauntlett, 1860	276
MORNING HYMN		L.M. . .	. . . F. H. Barthelemon, d. 1788	151
MORNING STAR §		887.887.412 8.	Melody probably by P. Nicolai, 1597,	
			harm. by Scheidemann, 1604	25

(Wie schön leucht't der Morgenstern.)

MOSCOW	. .	87.87.47. .	. . . . Lvoff	274
MOUNT ZION	.	77.77.77. .	. . . . . Arthur Sullivan	451
MULHAUSEN	.	78.78.88 or 77.77.	. John Rudolph Ahle, 1664	227

(Liebster Jesu, wir sind hier.)

| MUNICH | . . | 76.76.76.76. | . . . . Goth. Cant., 1715 | 165 |

(O Gott, du frommer Gott.)

NAIN	. .	64.64.	. . . . . Dr. Lowell Mason	108
NAPLES	. .	L.M. .	. . . . . . Italian Melody	234
NARENZA	.	S.M. .	. . . . . Cologne Choralbuch	45
NASSAU	. .	77.77.77. .	. . . . . Rosenmüller, 1655	56

(Straf mich nicht in deinem Zorn.)

NATIVITY	.	77.77.77.77.	. Latin Melody, "In dulce jubilo,"	
			13th Cent.	322
NAVARRE	.	98.98.98.98.	. . . Goudimel, Ps. 66, 1562	169
NAZARETH	.	87.87.47. .	. . . . . J. Banister, 1866	360
NEANDER	.	668.668.3366.	. . . . J. Neander, 1680	460

(Wunderbarer König.)

| NEAPOLIS | . | L.M. . | . . . . . . Haydn, d. 1809 | 139 |
| NEBO | . . | 87.87.77.77. | . . . . J. Rosenmüller | 484 |

(Welt ade! ich bin dein müde.)

NEWLAND	.	S.M. .	. . . . . . Dr. Gauntlett, 1857	58
NICEA	. .	L.M.	Old Latin, "Lucis Creator," 7th or 8th Cent.	315
NOEL	. .	C.M.—8 lines	. Old Melody, arr. by Arthur Sullivan	431
NORLAND	.	S.M. .	. . . .	228
NORMANDY	.	87.87.87.87.	Ami Bost, from "Chants Chrétiens"	109
NORMINSTER	.	78.78.77. .	. . . . Julius Grove	464
NORTHAMPTON		C.M. .	. . . . . . Dr. Croft, d. 1727	194
NORTH COATES		65.65.	. . . . T. R. Mathews	436
NORWICH	.	C.M.—8 lines	. . Day's Psalter, Ps. 137 1563	328

ALPHABETICAL INDEX.

			No.
NUREMBURG .	. 886.886.	Hans Sachs, 1552	152
	(Warum betrübst du dich, mein Herz?)		
OBERLIN .	. . 88.886.	Magdeburg Choralbuch, 1540	383
	(O Lamm Gottes, unschuldig.)		
OLDENBERG .	. 1111.1111.	T. Selle, 1655	150
	(O Ursprung des Lebens, o ewiges Licht.)		
OLD HUNDREDTH (SAVOY) L.M	. Guillaume Franc., 1565	363
OLD WINCHESTER . c.m. . . .	Este's Psalter, Ps. 84, 1592	133
OLIVET . . . 664.6664.	. Dr. Lowell Mason	39
OLMUTZ . . . 85.84.	.	420
OLNEY . . . 66.66.88.	. Rev. J. Darwell	44
OPHEL . . . 1111.1111.	. Metrical Chant	447
ORIEL . . . 104.104.1010. . . .	Wm. Birtwhistle	331
OXFORD . . . 66.66. (Trochaic) . . .	J. B. König, 1738	231
	(Den die Engel droben.)		
PADERBORN .	. 886.886. . .	Dr. William Hayes, 1780	43
PALESTINE .	. L.M. .	E. Directoris Guidetti, "Jam lucis orto	
		sidere," 7th Cent.	47
PALESTRINA .	. L.M.—6 lines	Palestrina, d. 1594	208
PARADISE .	. 86.86.6666.	. John Gill	474
PARAN . .	. 87.87.47., or 87.87.77. .	Joachim Neander, 1680	371
	(Unser Herscher, unser König.)		
PARIS . .	. 98.98.88.	. J. B. Delaborde	427
PASCAL . .	. L.M.	. Mozart, d. 1791	10
PASTON, or CANTERBURY C.M.	Este's Psalter, Ps. 4, 1592 (altered by	
		Playford)	14
PASTOR BONUS	. 66.66.88.	Samuel Smith	494
PATMOS . .	. L.M. Latin Melody, "Splendor Paternæ," 7th Cent.	347
PENIEL . .	. 75.75.75.75.	. H. G. Nageli	413
PENTECOST .	. L.M	Ambrose, "Veni Creator,"	
		adapted by Luther, 1524	186
PERGAMOS .	. L.M. . .	Old Latin, "Tristes erant Apostoli"	319
PETERSHAM .	. c.m.—8 lines	. C. W. Poole	482
PHILADELPHIA .	. L.M.	.	201
PHILIPPI .	. c.m.	. S. Wesley, d. 1837	279
PLEYEL . .	. 77.77.	Pleyel, d. 1831	138
PORTUGUESE .	. 1111.1111. John Reading, "Adeste Fideles," 1760	292
POTSDAM. .	. s.m.	. From Bach	192
PRAGUE . .	. s.m.	. L. West, 1795	104
PRAISE . .	. 77.77.77.77. Mendelssohn's "Fest Gesang," d. 1847	26
PROVENCE .	. 77.77.77.77. . .	. Old Provençal Melody	284
PYRTON . .	. L.M.	.	221

ALPHABETICAL INDEX.   xxiii

				No.
Ramah	87.87.47.		Old Hebrew Melody	72
Ramleh	s.m.		Dr. Gauntlett, 1852	336
Ramoth	65.—10 lines		R. Schumann	439
Ratisbon	77.77..		Old Litany	38
Ravenna	l.m.	Old Latin, "A solis ortus cardine," 4th Cent. adapted by Luther, 1525		329
Ravenshaw	86.86.88.86.		J. H. Schein, 1627	350
	(Wie lieblich sind die Wohnung' bein.)			
Ravensworth	777.5.		Dr. Gauntlett, 1859	168
Redemptor	664.6664.		Joseph Schnabel	430
Refuge	77.77.77.77.	Andreas Hammerschmidt, 1646		28
	(Freut euch, ihr Christen alle.)			
Regent Square	87.87.47.		Henry Smart	385
Rephidim	1110.1110.		Lvoff	489
Rest	l.m.,—6 lines		Dr. Stainer	477
Requiem	46.46.46.46.		J. Barnby	492
Riston	87.87.87.87.	Latin Melody, "In media vitæ," 10th Cent., adapted by Luther, 1525		164
Rochester	l.m.		Day's Psalter, 1562	50
Rockingham, or Caton	l.m.		Dr. Miller, c. 1787	19
Rutherford	76.76.76.76.	D'Urhan, from "Chants Chrétiens"		473
Ruth	65.65.65.65.		Samuel Smith	452
St. Aëlred	888.3	Rev. J. B. Dykes, Mus. Doc.		408
St. Agnes	77.77.77.77.		Beethoven, d. 1827	333
St. Andrew *	77.87.77.87.		Dr. Gauntlett, 1852	121
St. Ann	c.m.	Dr. Croft, Suppt. to New Version of the Psalms, 1703		54
St. Basil	87.87., or l.m.	Ambrosian Melody, "O lux beata Trinitas," 7th Cent., ad. by Schein, 1627		36
St. Bernard *	86.886.		Dr. Gauntlett, 1852	118
St. Bride	s.m.		Dr. Howard Riley's Ps. 1762	81
St. David	c.m.	Ravenscroft's "Whole Booke of Psalms," Ps. 95, 1621 (alt. by Playford)		97
St. Dunstan	66.66		Dr. Hayne	392
St. George	c.m.		Nicholas Hermann, 1560	135
	(„Lobt Gott, ihr Christen alle gleich.")			
St. James	c.m.		R. Courteville, 1680	51
St. John	66.66.88.		Handel, d. 1759	216
St. Leonard	c.m.		Henry Smart, 1866	365
St. Magnus (Nottingham)	c.m.		J. Clarke, 1707	181
St. Margaret	c.m.		J. Turle	361

ALPHABETICAL INDEX.

			No.
St. Mary . .	c.m. . . .	. Archd. Prys' Book of Psalms, 1621	141
St. Matthew .	c.m.—8 lines	. Dr. Croft, Suppt. to New Version of the Psalms, 1703	167
St. Michael .	s.m. . . .	. Guillaume Franc, Marot's Psalter, Ps. 101, 1543	2
St. Paul .	l.m.	. Dr. Greene, d. 1755	245
St. Peter .	c.m.	. . A. Reinagle	332
St. Stephen .	c.m.	Rev. Wm. Jones, d. 1800	42
St. Thomas .	888.6	. Dr. Gauntlett, 1858	52
St. Vincent* .	86.86.88. . . .	. Dr. Gauntlett, 1852	20
Salem . .	76.76.76.76. . .	. A. Ewing	346
Salisbury	c.m. . . .	Ravenscroft's "Whole Booke of Psalms," Ps. 54, 1621	200
Salvator .	l.m.—6 lines . . .	. Melchior Vulpius	401
(Lobt Gott ben Herrn, ihr Heiden all'.)			
Samson .	l.m.	. From Handel	24
Salzburg .	87.87.87.87. .	. Mozart "Ave verum corpus"	128
Samaria . .	l.m.,—6 lines . .	. . Beethoven	450
Sanctuary .	77.77.77.77. (Trochaic)	. . Schubert	446
Sardis . .	87.87. . . .	. . From Beethoven	113
Sarnen . .	1212.1212. . .	. . L. Cherubini	421
Sarum . .	888.4. . .	Hymnarium Sarisburiense, arranged by J. Hullah	325
Savoy, or Old Hundredth, l.m.	. .	. Guillaume Franc, 1565	363
Saxony . .	88.88.88.88. (Anapæstic)	. . Lutheran	67
Scopas . .	87.87.87.87. .	. C. Hancock, Mus. Bac.	479
Sculcoates .	77.77. . . .	. . . Pleyel	455
Seraphim .	10 9.10 9.10.10.810.10 8.	. . Schubert	448
Serbal . .	s.m. . . .	. Mendelssohn. d. 1847	381
Shalford .	76.76.76.76.66.86 .	. J. A. E. Schultze	487
(Wir pflügen.)			
Sharon . .	77.77.77.77. .	. G. J. Elvey, Mus. Doc.	373
Sheba . .	1110.1110. . .	. . J. Sörenson	394
Sherborne .	l.m. . . .	. . Old Latin	31
Sherbrooke .	87.87.77. . .	. W. Schulthes	410
Sherwood .	86.86.86 . .	. Dr. Gauntlett, 1859	134
Shiloh . .	76.76.76.76. .	. . S. Salvatori	222
Shore . .	77.77. . .	. From Weber, d. 1826	273
Silchester .	s.m. . .	. Rev. Cæsar Malan, D.D., d. 1865	309
Silesia . .	76.76.76.76. .	. Hans Sachs, 1526	142
("Wacht auf, ihr Christen alle.")			
Siloam . .	l.m.—6 lines . . .	. W. H. Monk	352

ALPHABETICAL INDEX.   xxv

			No.
SILSOE	66.66.88.	Dr. Gauntlett, 1857	13
SION*	887.887.	Dr. Gauntlett, 1852	33
SMYRNA	L.M.	Old Latin " Jesu Redemptor omnium "	313
SOHO	C.M.	Old Chant	146
SOLDAU	L.M.	From a German Melody,	

"Nun bitten wir," 13th Cent., adapted by Luther, 1525   175
(„Nun bitten wir den heil'gen Geist.")

SOLICITUDE	77.77.	J. Daniell	76
SOLOMON	C.M.	From Handel	100
SONNING	S.M.	Dr. Gauntlett, 1856	3
SOUTHGATE	64.64.1010.	Fred. B. Benefen	387
SOUTHMINSTER	77.77.	Dr. Orlando Gibbons, 1623	204
SOUTHWELL	S.M.	Denham's Psalter, Ps. 70, 1588	84
SOUTHWOLD*	C.M.	Dr. Gauntlett, 1852	110
SPIRE	55.88.55	Adam Drese, 1680	60

(Seelenbräutigam.)

STELLA	L.M.,—6 lines		441
SPANDAU	86.84.	C. H. Graun	419
STEPNEY	87.87.77.	W. Bayley	449
STRASBURG	1110.1110. (Anapæstic) J. Rudolph Ahle, d. 1673	298

(„Liebster Immanuel, Herzog der Frommen."

| STUKELEY | C.M. | Mendelssohn, d. 1847 | 173 |
| STUTTGART | 87.87.87.87. | J. Rosenmüller, 1650 | 335 |

(Siegesfürst und Ehrenkönig.)

| STYRIA | 446.446., or L.M. | Vopelius, 1682 | 157 |

(„Ach Gott und Herr.")

| SUABIA | S.M.—8 lines | Elzevier'schen Psalmbuch, 1646 | 174 |

(„Herzlich thut mich erfreuen.")

SUCCOUR	1212.1212.	Arthur Sullivan	481
SUDELEY	C.M.	Dr. Stainer	461
SUTTON	L.M.—6 lines	Bernard Klein	429
SWANLAND*	S.M.	Dr. Gauntlett, 1857	74
SYLVESTER	87.87.88.88.	Rev. J. Dykes, Mus. Doc.	445
TABOR	76.76.76.76.	H. Kugelmann, 1540	368

(Nun lob', mein Seel', den Herren.)

TALLIS	C.M. "Veni Creator," Archbp. Parker's Psalter, 1561	59
THANET	83.36	Rev. J. Jowett, " Musæ Solitariæ," 1823	77
THAXTED	78.78	Dr. Gauntlett, 1859	136
THEODORA	99.99	Alfred Legge	499

ALPHABETICAL INDEX.

			No
THURINGIA	L.M.—8 lines	Luther, "Klug's Gesangbuch," 1543	32⁴
	(„Es wollt uns Gott gnädig sein.")		
TIBERIAS	77.77.77.	Conrad Kocher, 1855	344
	(Treuer Heiland, wir sind hier.)		
TIRZAH	S.M.	Henry Purcell, d. 1695	230
TOTTENHAM	C.M.	T. Greatorex, d. 1831	283
TRINITY	664.6664:	F. Giardini, 1760	11
TRIUMPH*	87.87.87., or 8.7.4.	Dr. Gauntlett, 1852	29
TROYTE	1010.1010.	A. H. D. Troyte, d. 1859	359
TRURO	L.M.	Dr. Burney, d. 1814	82

UPSAL ‖	84.84.88.84.	Johann Crüger, 1664	178
	(Schmücke dich, o liebe Seele.)		

VESPER	87.87.47.	Sir J. Stephenson (?)	270
VEVAY	777		480
VIA CRUCIS	7.6. (Irregular).	Rev. J. B. Dykes, Mus. Doc.	406
VIENNA	87.87.87.87.	Haydn, d. 1809	111
VOX ANGELICA	1110.1110.9 11.	Rev. J. B. Dykes, Mus. Doc.	18
VOX DILECTI	C.M.—8 lines	Rev. J. B. Dykes, Mus. Doc.	469

WALDECK	L.M.	Rinck, d. 1846	120
WALTHAM, or BRAYLESFORD	87.87.87.	Dr. Gauntlett	264
WALSAL	C.M.	Wilkin's Psalmody, 1699, attr. to H. Purcell	303
WAREHAM	L.M.	William Knapp, d. 1768	22
WARRINGTON	L.M.	R. Harrison, d. 1810	236
WARTBURG	L.M.	Luther, "Klug's Gesangbuch," 1543	145
	(Erhalt uns, Herr, bei deinem Wort.)		
WATERFORD	76.76.76.76.	Melchior Teschner, 1613	140
	(Valet will ich dir geben.)		
WATFORD	96.96.96.96. Ger. Chorale, arr. by Rev.P.Maurice, D.D.		377
WEARMOUTH	C.M.—8 lines	Day's Psalter, Ps. 81, 1562	308
WEIMAR	77.77.77.77.	Vulpius, 1609	86
	(Jesu Leiden, Pein und Tod.)		
WELLS	77.77.77.	D. Bortnianski, d. 1826	30
WELTON	88.88. (Anap.)	Dr. Gauntlett, 1858	53
WERBURG	1010.1111.	Ravenscroft's "Whole Booke of Psalms," Ps. 104, 1621	311
WESTENHANGER	S.M.	C. W. Poole, 1860	289

ALPHABETICAL INDEX.   xxvii

				No.
WESTMINSTER .	. C.M. .	. . . . . . Dr. Nares, d. 1783	259
WESTPHALIA .	. 86.86.86., or 8 lines	Luther, "Walther's Gesang- buch," 1525	312

("Mit Fried und Freud' fahr ich dahin.")

WHITCHURCH .	. S.M. .	. . . . . . Handel, d. 1759	149
WILLERBY .	. 84.84.888.	. . . . E. Prout, B. A.	402
WILLINGHAM .	. 1110.1110.	. . . . Franz Abt	397
WILTSHIRE .	. C.M.	. . . Sir G. Smart, d. 1867	254
WINCHESTER .	. L.M.	Musical Handbook of Spiritual Melodies, Hamburg, 1690	57

(Wer nur den lieben Gott läßt walten.)

WINCHESTER, OLD .	C.M.	. . . Este's Psalter, Ps. 84, 1592	133
WINDSOR .	. C.M. ("Dundee")	Este's Psalter, Ps. 116, 1592	203
WIRKSWORTH .	. L.M. .	. . M. Greene, Mus. Doc., d. 1755	185
WITTEMBURG†	. 67.67.66 66.	. . . . Johann Crüger, 1653	80

(Nun danket Alle Gott.)

| WITTON, or ROGATION 7.7.7. | . . . . Dr. Gauntlett, 1861 | 114 |
| WORMS, or FORTRESS§ | 88.88.66.668. Luther, 1530, "Klug's Gesangbuch," 1535 | 17 |

("Ein feste Burg ist unser Gott.")

| WYCLIFFE . | . L.M.—6 lines . | . . . Johann Schop, 1641 | 73 |

("O Ewigkeit, du Donnerwort!")

| YORK . . | . C.M. ("Stilt") | Andro Hart's Psalter, No. 7, 1615 | 98 |

| ZURICH . . | . 888.888. . | . . . . . Swiss Melody | 229 |
| ZWEISIMMEN . | . 66.66.66.66. | . . . Thuringian Volkesweise | 425 |

METRICAL INDEX.

S.M.

	No.
Aynhoe	46
Boylston	219
Canterbury	271
Christchurch	159
Doncaster	122
Franconia	160
Gildas	321
Hampton	183
Hawthornden	426
Ludlow	179
Lyte	342
Narenza	45
Newland	58
Norland	228
Potsdam	192
Prague	104
Ramleh	336
St. Bride	81
St. Michael	2
Serbal	381
Silchester	309
Sonning	3
Southwell	84
Swanland	74
Tirzah	230
Westenhanger	289
Whitchurch	149
Wirksworth	185

S.M., 8 LINES.

	No.
Bremen	70
Holstein	235
Leominster	498
Suabia	174

C.M.

	No.
Abbey	233
Abridge	156
Arnheim	343
Arnold	251
Ballerma	99
Bedford	163
Belmont	49
Bethany	166
Bexley	211
Bishopsthorpe	255
Brunswick	263
Burford	252
Burmah	323
Byzantium	285
Castor	198
Cherith	374
Cherwell	367
Chester	143
Colchester	247
Coveney	355
Culross	115
Dunfermline	9
Durham (St. Agnes)	414
Emmanuel	465
Emmaus	193
Evan	87
Exeter	307
Farrant	105
Felix	241
Flavian	467
French	1
Gibbons	68
Glasgow	188
Gloucester	317
Harrington	177
Heidelberg	23
Invitation	202
Irish	187
Lancaster	281
Lincoln	62
Liverpool	96
London New	95
Manchester	190
Martyrdom	71
Martyrs	8
Masbury	41
Meaux Abbey	153
Miles' Lane	215
Northampton	194
Old Winchester	133
Paston	14
Philippi	279
St. Ann	54
St. David	97
St. George	135
St. James	51
St. Leonard	365
St. Magnus	181
St. Margaret	361
St. Mary	141
St. Peter	332
St. Stephen	42
Salisbury	200
Soho	146
Solomon	100
Southwold	110
Stukeley	173
Sudeley	461
Tallis	59
Tottenham	283
Walsal	303
Westminster	259
Wiltshire	254
Windsor	203
York	98

METRICAL INDEX.

C.M., 6 LINES.
	No.
Jerusalem	294
Sherwood	134
Westphalia	312

C.M., 8 LINES.
	No.
Elim (Irreg.)	375
Jarrow	488
Kirkella	389
Noel	431
Norwich	328
Petersham	482
St. Matthew	167
Vox Dilecti	469
Wearmouth	308
Westphalia	312

L.M.
	No.
Advent Evening Hymn	35
Alsace	275
Altona	93
Angels' Hymn	85
Angelus	442
Babylon	297
Bavaria	249
Berlin	250
Berne	490
Bohemia	34
Boston	207
Cannons	287
Canon	12
Canonbury	27
Carmel	267
Christmas Choral	66
Constance	124
Courland	300
Doversdale	225
Eisenach	131
Ella	94
Ely	48
Ernan	459
Fulda	127
Galilee	295
Gibraltar	63
Glastonbury	243
Golgotha	338
Gregory	83
Haarlem	197
Haync	217

	No.
Holley	409
Holywell	213
Hosanna	471
Maccabæus	261
Magdalen College	265
Mainzer	400
Malaga	55
Mamre	223
Mecklenburg	130
Melanesia	478
Melcombe	78
Modena	40
Montgomery	92
Morning Hymn	151
Naples	234
Neapolis	139
Nicea	315
Old Hundredth	363
Palestine	47
Pascal	10
Patmos	347
Pentecost	186
Pergamos	319
Philadelphia	201
Pyrton	221
Ravenna	329
Rochester	50
Rockingham	19
Samson	24
Savoy, or Old Hundredth	363
Sherborne	31
Smyrna	313
Soldau	175
St. Basil	36
St. Paul	245
Styria	157
Truro	82
Waldeck	120
Wareham	22
Warrington	236
Wartburg	145
Winchester	57

L.M., 6 LINES.
	No.
Antioch (Triplets)	314
Cana	475
Carey	184
Coverdale (Triplets)	288
Danube	244
Ephesus	306

	No.
Ephratah	372
Huntingdon	75
Jena	310
Lubeck	189
Lucerne (Triplets)	210
Mansfield	80
Melancthon	304
Melita	346
Moravia	147
Palestrina	208
Rest	477
Salvator	401
Samaria	450
Siloam	352
Stella	441
Sutton	429
Wycliffe	73
Zurich (Triplets)	229

L.M., 8 LINES.
	No.
Banias	500
Cana	475
Incarnation	257
Thuringia	324

446.446.
	No.
Styria	157

447.76.
	No.
Cheshunt	334

46.46.46.46.
	No.
Requiem	492

46.64.64.64.
	No.
Advent	485

5555.1011.1110.
	No.
Dresden	180

55511.55511.
	No.
Mizpah	391

557.557.1010.
	No.
Islington	405

55.88.55.
	No.
Spire	60

5511.5511.
	No.
Moriah	276

METRICAL INDEX.

64.64.
	No.
Nain	108

64.64.664.
Aspiration	422
Laleham	220

64.64.6664.
Beulah	396

64.64.1010.
Budleigh	407
Southgate	387

64.66.
Horeb	386

65.65.
Bemerton	357
Enon	438
Geneva	170
North Coates	436

65.65.65.65.
Clarens	433
Coppett (12 lines)	456
Elah (12 lines)	491
Goshen	458
Hebron	379
Labrador	437
Midian	454
Ramoth (10 lines)	439
Ruth	452

664.664.
Conway	155

664.6664.
Albion	326
Hermon	129
Olivet	39
Redemptor	430
Trinity	11

6664.884.
Ferriby	61

66.66.
Ludwig	101
Oxford (Trochaic)	231
St. Dunstan	392

666.666.
	No.
Augustine	457
Migdol (12 lines)	399

66.66.66.66.
Agatha	470
Broadlands	364
Zweisimmen	425

66.66.88.
Burnham	212
Caernarvon	280
Ghent	253
Iona	327
King's College	226
Olney	44
Pastor Bonus	494
Silsoe	13
St. John	216

66.77.77.
Ajalon	376

6684.6684.
Leoni	132

66.86.47.
Highbury	238

668.668.
Ascalon	126
Hilary	316

668.668.3366.
Neander	460

6610.6610.
Bethabara	370

67.67.66.66.
Wittemberg	80

68.64.
Holy Cross	15

610.610.
Bethsaida	362

75.75.75.75.
Peniel	413

75.75.75.75.88.
Intercession	366

76.76.
Barton	440
Heidelberg	23

	No.
Leven	161

76.76.76.76.
Arno (Pec. Acc.)	148
Aurelia	415
Bonchurch	224
Greenland	476
Lusatia	356
Lutzen	119
Missionary	286
Munich	165
Rutherford	473
Salem	340
Shiloh	222
Silesia	142
Tabor	368
Via Crucis (Irregular)	406
Waterford	140

76.76.76.76.66.86.
Shalford	487

76.76.77.
Bethel	320
Linden	462
Livonia	463

76.76.77.76.
Barnabas	16

76.76.88.
Anatolius	434

777.
Lugano	390
Vevay	480
Witton, or Rogation	114

777.5.
Ambrose	69
Cape Town	412
Dusseldorf	209
Ravensworth	168

777.6.
Litany	277

77.77.
Armstadt	200
Battishill	299
Biberach	339
Capernaum	341
Carinthia	199

METRICAL INDEX.

	No.
Clarence	453
Corsica	65
Cyprus	378
Dijon	91
Easter Hymn	242
Heinlein	349
Holyrood	237
Kettering	90
Kiel	79
Liguria	195
Litany	277
Melton	107
Milan	117
Mulhausen	227
Pleyel	138
Ratisbon	38
Sculcoates	455
Shore	273
Solicitude	76
Southminster	204

77.77.77.

Ajalon	376
Brandenburg	353
Cuthbert	116
Gethsemane	144
Gotha	191
Göttingen	337
Leipsic	290
Maidstone	435
Mount Zion	451
Nassau	56
Tiberias	344
Wells	30

77.77.77.77.

Apollos (or 10 lines)	417
Arimathea	318
Arno	148
Benevento	248
Cassell	218
Göttingen	337
Hollingside	354
Leipsic	290
Maidstone	435
Nativity	322
Praise	26
Provence	284
Refuge	28
St. Agnes	333
Sanctuary (Trochaic)	446

	No.
Sharon	373
Weimar	86

77.87.77.87.

St. Andrew	121

78.78.

Thaxted	136

78.78.77.

Brandenburg	353
Norminster	464

78.78.88.

Mulhausen	227

83.36.

Altorf	382
Thanet	77

847.847.

Canitz	444

84.84.84.

Carrow	496

84.84.888.

Willerby	402

84.84.8884.

Upsal	178

85.83.

Christus Consolator	468
Cyril	21

86.84.

Magdala	351
Olmutz	420
Spandau	419

86.86.44.88.

Coblentz	418

86.86.66.66.

Ledforth	64
Paradise	474

86.86.88.

Lebanon	272
St. Vincent	20

86.86.8886.

Ravenshaw	350

86.886.

St. Bernard	118

87.87.

	No.
Baun	162
Bethlehem	106
Birkenhead	4
Ellerker	334
Frankfort	6
Mariners	293
Minden	158
Paran	371
Sardis	113

87.87. (Iambic).

St. Basil	36

87.87.47.

Asaph	260
Aslacton	205
Darmstadt	301
Eckington	5
Irene	296
Lutterworth	214
Mannheim	380
Moscow	274
Nazareth	360
Paran	371
Ramah	72
Regent's Square	385
Stuttgart	335
Triumph	29
Vesper	270

87.87.77.

Asaph	260
Paran	371
Sherbrooke	410
Stepney	449

87.87.7777.

Nebo	484

87.87.87., or 87.87.47.

Aslacton	205
Darmstadt	301
Eckington	5
Irene	296
Mannheim	380
Paran	371
Stuttgart	335
Triumph	29
Waltham, or Braylesford	264

87.87.87.87.

Alla Trinita	125
Augsburg	282

METRICAL INDEX.

	No.
Chichester	182
Corinth	137
Crucifer	497
Dismission	330
Elberfeldt	232
Flanders	262
Florence	472
Leipsic	290
Lux Crucis	495
Lyons	171
Normandy	109
Riston	164
Salzburg	128
Scopas	479
Stuttgart	335
Vienna	111

87.87.88.
Beverley	278

87.87.887.
Coburg	176
Dettingen	240
Eisleben	102
Halle	154

87.87.88.77.
Hamburg	196

87.87.88.88.
Sylvester	445

886.886.
Hereford	268
Hull	291
Innspruck	7
Kedron	266
Nuremberg	152
Paderborn	43

887.887.
Arnsberg	206
Sion	33

887.887.4128.
Morning Star	25

888.
Damascus	388

888.3.
St. Aëlred	408

888.4.
Clifton	432

	No.
Hanford	486
Leicester	305
Sarum	325
Troyte	359

888.6.
Croyland	37
Leeds	269
Leicester	305
St. Thomas	52

888.6. (Trochaic).
Boniface	345
Maldon	88

888.664.88.
Dumah	32

8888. (Anapæstic).
Welton	53
Saxony (8 lines)	67

8888.6.
Oberlin	383

88.88.66.668.
Worms	17

88.88.7.
Baden	172

88.88.88. (Trochaic.)
Interlachen	443

96.96.96.96.
Watford	377

98.98.88.
Moravia	147
Paris	427

98.98.98.98.
Navarre	169

998.998.66.488.
Dumah	32
Hernhutt	428

99.99.
Theodora	499

10 4.10 4.
Compton	403
Hemingford	404

10 4.10 4.10 10.
Lux Benigna	411
Oriel	331

1010.1010.
	No.
Bartholomew	302
Dalkeith	239
Ellers	424
Euroclydon	483
Eventide	358
Gilead	416
Ilala	423
Kelso	112
Troyte	359

1010.1111.
Hanover	103
Houghton	246
Werburg	311

1110.116.
Bozrah	395

1110.1110.
Rephidim	489
Sheba	394
Strasburg	298
Willingham	397

1110.1110.911.
Vox Angelica	18

1111.115.
Flemming	393

1111.1111.
Beersheba	398
Hexham	369
Oldenburg	150
Ophel	447
Portuguese	292

1112.1210.
Heber	123
Monkland	348

1212.1212.
Sarnen	421
Succour	481

1311.1312.
Lambeth	258

Irregular.
Seraphim	448
Gennesaret	460
Eudoxia	493

Note to Supplement.

Since the completion of the "Congregational Psalmist," Supplements to several Hymnals in general use have been published. These contain an unusual number of hymns peculiar in metre, or in expression—how large their number may be inferred from the tunes necessary to provide for them. Opportunity has been taken of adding a few tunes which have become popular.

My grateful thanks are due to the following contributors of original tunes—Samuel Smith, Esq., for *Allhallows*, 506; *Newfield*, 520; *Curfew*, 551; *Invocation*, 552; *Amor*, 571; *Lynmouth*, 577. Charles Hancock, Mus. Doc., for *Tranquillity*, 553; *Trust*, 597; *Adoration*, 602; *Consecration*, 604; *Sacrifice*, 612. Prof. W. H. Monk, Mus. Doc., for *Autumnus*, 519; *Shadows*, 523; *Benison*, 607; *Amor Jesu*, 622. Ebenezer Prout, B.A., for *Paraclete*, 609. Fountain Meen, Esq., for *Compassion*, 537; *Spencer*, 581. W. C. Filby, Esq., for *Sandringham*, 636. J. D. Macey, Esq., for *Finchley*, 559. Erskine Allon, for *Sunderland*, 533; *Caversham*, 613. Also for the offer of a large number of new tunes, of which the exigencies of space and the special object of this supplement have prevented the use.

I very gratefully acknowledge permission to use copyright tunes, both to those by whom it has been generously given, and to those of whom it has been purchased—the former are distinguished by an asterisk (*).

To the * Rev. W. Pulling, and the Proprietors of " Hymns Ancient and Modern," who, with unstinted and characteristic generosity, have added to former obligations by permitting the use of *Pilgrims*, 504; *Pax Dei*, 514; *Vigilate*, 526; *Alford*, 540; *Quam Dilecta*, 563; *Irons (Southwell)*, 638; *Chalvey*, 640; "*Come unto Me*," 642; *Dies Iræ*, 647; *Laudes Domini*, 648. * Messrs. Nisbet and Co., for *Præneste*, 501; *Lancashire*, 585, from "Psalms and Hymns for Divine Worship." The Proprietors of the "Sarum Hymnal," *St. Philip*, 546. * The Proprietors of "Congregational Church Music," for *Clarewood*, 566.

NOTE TO SUPPLEMENT.

The Proprietors of the "Psalmist," for *Inglewhite*, 548 ; *Roseneath*, 610. Mr. F. Morgan, and the Proprietors of the " Bristol Tune Book," for *Morgenlied*, 549 ; *Arley*, 564 ; *Dalehurst*, 645. *G. H. Baines, Esq., *Greatham*, 570. *H. Baker, Esq., *Hesperus*, 531*. *Rev. E. H. Bickersteth, *Pax Tecum*, 558 ; *Laybach*, 572 ; *Visio Domini*, 637 ; from the "Hymnal Companion to the Book of Common Prayer." *Rev. W. J. Blew, *St. Fulbert*, 547 ; *St. Albinus*, 554. *The Proprietors of the "Bradford Tune Book," for *Bradford*, 502 ; *Beatitude*, 591. A. H. Brown, Esq., *St. Keverne*, 519. *Rev. E. W. Bullinger, D.D., *Bullinger*, 592. *Rev. E. S. Carter, *Slingsby*, 605. *Rev. R. R. Chope, *St. Godric*, 568 ; *St. Drostane*, 594 ; *St. Oswald*, 618 ; from "Congregational Hymn and Tune Book." *Rev. F. Dale, Mus. Doc., *St. Catherine*, 562. *Rev. Thomas Darling, *Lux Eoi*, 595 ; from "Hymns for the Church of England, with Proper Tunes." *Andrew Deakin, Esq., *Saltburn*, 589. *Mrs. Deane, *Sorrento*, 639. A. Elliott, Esq., *Day of Rest*, 632. *W. C. Filby, Esq., *Brabourne*, 575 ; *Epiphany*, 617 ; *Chiselhurst*, 624. *Lady Victoria Evans Freke, *Westerham*, 545 ; *Jesu Magister Bone*, 611 ; *Crepusculum*, 630 ; from the "Song of Praise." Alfred R. Gaul, Mus. Doc., *Filius Dei*, 535 ; *St. Cyprian*, 596 ; *Holy City*, 598 ; *Edgbaston*, 603 ; *Winterslow*, 643. *Rev. L. G. Haynes, Mus. Doc., *Bergen*, 550 ; *Mistley*, 616. E. J. Hopkins, Esq., *Temple*, 619. *Miss Havergal, *Hermas*, 529. *H. Lahee, Esq., *St. Serf*, 544. *James Langran, Esq., *Deerhurst*, 504 ; *Tottenham*, 576. *The Right Rev. Dr. Maclagan, Bishop of Lichfield, *Showers of Blessing*, 511. *Miss Maurice, *Springfield*, 509 ; *Tarsus*, 580 ; from "Choral Harmony." *Rev. W. Mercer, *Nocturn*, 560 ; from "Church Psalter and Hymn Book." Messrs. Novello and Co., *St. Gertrude*, 512 ; *Safe Home*, 579 ; *Nachtlied*, 635 ; from the "Hymnary." Prof. Sir Herbert Oakley, Mus. Doc., *Abends*, 557 ; *Edina*, 629. *Rev. Sir F. A. G. Ouseley, Bart., *Tenbury*, 530. *Mrs. Reinagle, *Milman*, 601. Messrs. Shaw and Co., *Audite audientes me*, 641. *Arthur Sullivan, Mus. Doc., *Shalom*, 508 ; *Mar Saba*, 539 ; *Milicent*, 543 ; from the "Church Hymn and Tune Book."

HENRY ALLON.

Canonbury, March 12, 1883.

Index of Metres.

METRE.	TUNE.	NO.	METRE.	TUNE.	NO.
S.M.	Roumania	561	66.66.66.66.3.	Allhallows	506
	Shawmut	599	66.66.77.	Saltburn	589
S.M.D.	Clarewood	566	66.66.88.	St. Godric	568
	Chalvey	640		Safe Home	579
C.M.	St. Fulbert	547	66.84.	Shawmut	599
	Bergen	550	66.86.86.86.	Spencer	581
	Horsley	565	66.86.88.	Departure	623
	Irons (Southwell)	638	66.86.10.12.	Inglewhite	548
	Dalehurst	645	66.97.	Benison	607
(Irregular)	Teman	588	75.75.75.75.	Newfield	520
C.M.D.	Gabriel	507	76.76.	Formosa	620
	Filius Dei	535	76.76.76.76.	Ellacombe	516
	Bethlm.Ephratah	538		New York	527
	Edgbaston	603		Fairford	534
	Audite audientes me	641		St. Catherine	562
				Lancashire	585
C.M. (12 lines)	Consecration	604		Holy City	598
L.M.	Hesperus	531*		Jesu, Magister Bone	611
	Santa Trinita	555		Day of Rest	632
	Abends	557		"Come unto Me"	642
	Matins	593		Eden	644
	St. Drostane	594		Atonement	646
L.M.D.	St. Serf	544	76.76.76.76.76.76.	Sabbath	600
4.10.10.10.4.	Bluntisham	628		Norman	614
54.54.54.	St. Cyprian	596	76.76.77.	Romsdal	556
55.55.65.65.	Tenbury	530	76.76.77.77.	Wimbourne	536
557.557.55.55.	Adoration	602	76.86.76.86.	Alford	540
55.88.55.	Tranquillity	553	77.4.	Millicent	543
	Eandringham	636	777.3.	Vigilate	526
64.64.	Amor	571	777.5.	Shalom	508
64.64.64.64.	Stockholm	524	777.6.	Lebbeus	633
64.64.664.	Mistley	616		Montreux	634
65.65	Clewer	517	77.77.3.	Caversham	613
65.65.65.65.	Miriam	567	77.77.4.	Anastasis	625
	Edina	629		Leyden	626
65.65.65.65.65.	St. Gertrude	512	77.77.	Tarsus	580
	Hermas	529	77.77.77.77.	Sorrento	639
65.65.66.65. (Iambic)	Sunderland	533	77.77.77.77.77.	Nocturn	560
666.4.	Rosneath	610	77.77.85.85.	Shadows	523
66.66.	Quam Dilecta	563	77.77.88.	Mar Saba(Hebron)	539
	Salonica	582	77.78.88.	Milman	601
66.66.66.	Sacrifice	612	78.78.	St. Albinus	554
	Laudes Domini	648			

INDEX OF METRES.

Metre	Tune	No.
78.78.77	Sneyd Park	542
78.87	Beatitude	591
84 84.888.4	Evensong	521
	Curfew	551
	Temple	619
85.83	Bullinger	592
86.86.88	Amsterdam	608
86.86.88.6	Beth-peor	583
87.84	Oriens	584
87.87	Slingsby	605
	St. Oswald	618
87.87.3	Showers of Blessing	511
87.87.77.77	Mayflower	522
	Clevedon	541
87.87.87	Baveno	525
87.87.87.7	Hardanger	586
87.87.87.87	Deerhurst	504
	Rosenthal	505
	Mentone	518
	Lux Eoi	595
(Iambic)	Luneberg	621
	Exsultans	631
87.87 87.87.87.87	Morgenlied	549
87.87.88 77	Mayflower	522
87.88.7	Lynmouth	577
88.4	Pietas	569
884.884	Misericordia	606
887.887	Bradford	502
	Prætorium	510
	Finchley	559
888.4	Supplication	587
	Crepusculum	630
888.4.888.4	Chiselhurst	624
888.6	Winterslow	643
88.88.88	Dies Iræ	647
	Burwell	649
98.98.88	Friburg	615
99.97.99. (Irregular)	Compassion	537

Metre	Tune	No.
10.4.10.4	Trust	597
10.6.10.6. (Irregular)	Laybach	572
	Langdon	573
	Amor Jesu	622
10.7.10.7	Invocation	552
10.8.10.8.98	Manger	627
10.10	Pax Tecum	558
10.10.4.6 10.10.4.6	Brabourne	575
10.10.7	Autumnus	515
10.10.10.4	St. Philip	546
10.10.10.10	Præneste	501
	Pax Dei	514
	Westerham	545
	Tottenham	576
10.10.10.10.4	St. Keverne	519
10.10.10.10.10 10	Yorkshire	528
	Greatham	570
	Nachtlied	635
10.10.11.11.10.10 11.11	Hope	590
10.11.11.11.12.11.10.11	Epiphany	617
11.10.11.10	Springfield	509
	Paraclete	609
	Visio Domini	637
11 10.11.10.9.11	Pilgrims	503
11.10 11.10.10.10	Arley	564
11.11.11.5	Merton	578
11.11.11.11	Corton	513
11. (8 lines, Irregular)	Woodword	574

METRICAL CHANTS.

St. Keverne		519
Endless Alleluia		531
The Strain Upraise		532
Laybach		572
Langdon		573
Edgbaston		603
Bluntisham		628

First Lines of Hymns.

	No.
Abide with me, fast falls the eventide...	576
A few more years shall roll	640
Angels assist to sing	589
Angels holy, high and lowly	577
Another year has fled, renew	583
Arm of the Lord! awake! awake!	594
Art thou weary, art thou languid	592
As much have I of worldly good	608
Awake, my soul, and with the sun	593
Baptized into Thy name, most holy	615
Beloved, let us love!	571
Breast the wave, Christian	530
By cool Siloam's shady rill	550
Christ is risen! Hallelujah!	549
Christ, the Lord, is risen again! ... 625,	626
"Christian! seek not yet repose"	526
Christians, awake, salute the happy morn	528
Come, labour on	623
Come, sing with holy gladness	516
Come to the Saviour now!	506
"Come unto Me," ye weary	642
Darkly rose the guilty morning	510
Day by day, we magnify Thee	605
Day of wrath! O day of mourning	647
Depth of mercy! can there be	639
Draw near, ye weary, bowed and brokenhearted	564
Dropping, dropping, dropping	607
Ere God had built the mountains	585
Eye hath not seen Thy glory 572,	573
Father, by Thy love and power	560
Father, here we dedicate	520
Father, in high heaven dwelling ... 502,	559
Father, while the shadows fall	523
Fear no more the clanking chain	591
Fierce was the wild billow	524

	No.
For all the saints, who from their labours rest	546
Friend after friend departs	623
From the recesses of a lowly spirit	578
Go, bear the joyful tidings	614
God is gone up with a merry noise	588
God that madest earth and heaven 521,	551
Golden harps are sounding	529
Gracious Saviour, holy Shepherd	525
Great Giver of all good, to Thee again...	515
Hark! a thrilling voice is sounding	595
Hark! hark, my soul, angelic songs are swelling	503
Hark, the sound of holy voices	504
Hark! the voice of Jesus crying	518
Hear Thy children, heavenly Father	505
Heavenly Father, all creation..........522,	541
Heavenward still our pathway tends	542
I do not ask, O Lord, that life may be...	597
I heard the voice of Jesus say	641
I saw Him leave His Father's throne	606
I was a wandering sheep	566
It is not death to die	561
It passeth knowledge, that dear love of Thine	519
I've found a Friend; oh, such a Friend!	621
Jerusalem, my happy home 547,	638
Jesu, from Thy throne on high	633
Jesu, still lead on	636
Jesus, Immanuel	610
Jesus lives! no longer now	554
Jesus, we are far away	634
Just as I am—without one plea	643
Lamb of God, whose bleeding love	646
Let no tears to-day be shed	543
Lift your glad voices in triumph on high	617
Lord, I hear of showers of blessing	511

	No.
Light hath arisen, we walk in its brightness	509
Lord, we sit and cry to Thee	601
Mighty Quickener, Spirit blest	536
My God, is any hour so sweet	624
My God, my Father, while I stray	587
No shadows yonder!	596
Not Thy garment's hem alone	556
Now the labourer's task is o'er	539
O had I, my Saviour, the wings of a dove	513
O Jesus, I have promised	611, 632
O Jesus, Thou art standing	562
O Master, at Thy feet	548
O most merciful! O most bountiful	552
O what a lonely path were ours	645
Of the Father's love begotten	586
Oh! for the peace which floweth as a river	609
One sole baptismal sign	568
One sweetly solemn thought	582
Onward, Christian Soldiers	512
Peace, doubting heart, my God's I am	649
Peace, perfect peace, in this dark world of sin	558
Praise the Redeemer, almighty to save	574
Round the throne of glory seated	631
Safe across the waters	567
Safe home, safe home in port	579
Safe in the arms of Jesus	600
Saviour, again to Thy dear name we raise	514
Saviour, blessed Saviour	629
Saviour, now receive him	517
Show pity, Lord, for we are frail and faint	501
Sinful, sighing to be blest	530
Sing Alleluia forth in duteous praise	531
Soon, and for ever, such promise our trust	590
Stand up before your God	581
Stand up, stand up for Jesus	527
Star of Morning, brightly shining	584

	No.
Sun of my soul, Thou Saviour dear	557
Sweet the moments, rich in blessing	618
Take up thy cross, the Saviour said	531*
Ten thousand times ten thousand	540
The day is gently sinking to a close	570, 635
The radiant morn hath passed away	630
The Son of God goes forth to war	535
The spacious firmament on high	544
The strain upraise of joy and praise, Alleluia	532
The voice that breathed o'er Eden	644
The year is swiftly waning	620
There is a green hill far away	565
There is no love like the love of Jesus	622
There were ninety and nine that safely lay	537
Thou didst leave Thy throne, and Thy kingly crown	627
Though the night be very long	613
Thy life was given for me	612
'Tis the Church triumphant singing	619
To Thee, O Comforter Divine	569
To thee, O dear, dear country	598
Walking with Thee, my God	616
Weary of earth, and laden with my sin	545
We cannot praise Thee now, Lord	534
We love Thee, Lord, yet not alone	603
We love the place, O God	563
We praise, we bless Thee	602
We would see Jesus; for the shadows lengthen	637
When I had wandered from His fold	604
When morning gilds the skies	648
When shall we meet again	533
When the day of toil is done	508
While shepherds watched their flocks by night	507, 538
Who, as Thou, makes blest	553
With broken heart and contrite sigh	555
With the sweet word of peace	599
"Yet there is room!" the Lamb's bright hall of song	575

INDEX OF TUNES AND HYMNS.

epared for the assistance of those who are not sufficiently familiar with
ge of their fitness for particular hymns. The hymns selected are those
Congregational Hymn Book and Supplement, and in Dr. Allon's
l Hymns. The Hymns in the latter and not in the former are
an asterisk.

	NO.	TUNE.	NO.	HYMN.	NO.	TUNE.	NO.
rith	222	...Durham	414	And am I born to die	497	...St. Bride	81
e...	1000	...Augustine	457	*And dost thou fast ...	158	...Southwold	110
		Kelso	112	And is there, Lord, a	650	...Gregory	83
t...	941	{ Eventide	358	And is this life pro- ...	489	...Manchester	190
		Troyte	359	And must this body ...	738	...Tirzah	230
cre-	48	...Castor	199	And will the great eter-	884	...Ely	48
, O	723	...Rochester	50	Angels from the realms	343	...Aslacton	205
ra-	865	...Cherwell	367	Another six days' work	753	...Holley	409
ave	566	...Serbal	381	Another year has fled	1267	...St. Bernard	118
.....	1173	...Leominster	498			(repeating first two lines.)	
.....	1191	...Holley	409	Approach, my soul, the	802	...St. Stephen	42
day	760	...Bartholomew	302	Are we the soldiers of	623	...Salisbury	200
t is	396	...St. John	216	Arise, my soul, my joy-	663	...Old Winchester	133
Sa-	576	...St. Mary	141	Arise, my tenderest ...	907	...Berlin	250
.....	1224	...Angelus	442	Arise, O King of grace	218	...Emmanuel	465
God	412	...King's College	226	Arm of the Lord, awake	918	...Mainzer	400
r of	414	{ Miles Lane	215	Art thou weary	1164	{ Christus Cons.	468
		Old Winchester	133			Cyril	21
it...	392	...Iona	327	As helpless as a child	1130	...Kirkella	389
...	172	...Burnham	212	As high as the heavens	49	...Welton	53
.....	215	...Altorf	382	As much have I of.....	348	...St. Vincent	20
.....	153	...Savoy	363	As pants the hart for...	57	...Cherith	374
ag-	681	...Mamre	223	Assembled at thy great	913	...Soldau	175
sin	574	...Philippi	279	As with gladness	1029	...Tiberias	341
hee	2	...Göttingen	337	At even, ere the sun...	1193	{ Angelus	442
e...	186	...Carinthia	199			Hayne	217
...	217	...Byzantium	285	At Thy command, our	863	...Berne	490
...	375	...Moriah	276	Author of faith, eter-	540	{ Angelus	442
ear	1376	...Berne	490			Malaga	55
f ...	101	...Northampton	194	Awake and sing the ...	339	{ Gildas	321
word	790	...Bedford	163			Prague	104
ose	284	...Rockingham	19	*Awake, awake, O Zion	201	...Waterford	140
God	271	...Narenza	45	Awake, my heart, arise	694	...Harrington	177
my	482	...Babylon	297	Awake, my soul, and	929	...Morning Hymn	151
the	972	...Carmel	267	Awake, my soul, in ...	366	...Constance	124
.....	1059	...Ellaker	334	Awake, my soul, stretch	617	{ York	98
re-	51	...Martyrs	8			Philippi	279

C

INDEX OF TUNES AND HYMNS.

HYMN.	NO.	TUNE.	NO.
Awake, my zeal, awake	618	Mainzer	400
Awake, our souls	616	Soldau	175
Awake, ye saints, awake	758	Ghent	253
Away from every mor-	769	Pyrton	221
		Mainzer	400
Backward with hum-	476	Irish	187
*Bear thou my burden	110	Itala	423
Before Jehovah's awful	152	Savoy	363
Begin, my tongue, some	269	Emmanuel	465
Begone, unbelief, my	608	Hanover	103
		Werburg	311
Behold a stranger at	509	St. Paul	245
Behold how glorious is	749	Morning Star	25
Behold, One cometh	1034	Cana	475
		Thuringia	324
Behold, O Lord, before	994	Martyrs	8
Behold the amazing	377	Swanland	74
Behold, the blind their	350	Ravenna	329
*Behold the eternal	184	Hayne	217
Behold the expected	909	Melcombe	78
Behold the glories of	303	Old Winchester	133
Behold the grace ap-	342	Doncaster	122
		Ramleh	336
*Behold the Lamb of	251	Ferriby	61
Behold the lofty sky	19	Hampton	183
Behold the morning	19	Gildas	324
Behold the mountain	925	Gloucester	317
Behold the Saviour of	373	Arnheim	343
		Martyrs	8
Behold the sure found-	187	St. Peter	332
Behold the throne of	801	Potsdam	192
Behold the woman's	346	Fulda	127
Behold what wondrous	556	Newland	58
*Be known to us	238	St. Peter	332
Beset with snares on	967	Holley	409
		Doversdale	225
Beyond, beyond that	264	Sherwood	134
Beyond the bounds	1168	Innspruck	7
Beyond the glittering	339	Lincoln	62
Birds have their quiet	1126	Bethsaida	362
Bless, O my soul, the	160	Carmel	267
Bless, O Lord, the	953	Solicitude	76
*Bless'd are the pure	78	Boylston	219
Blessed are the sons	557	Göttingen	337
Blessed be God, our	1026	Gilead	416
*Blessed Jesus, at Thy	159	Mulhausen	227
*Blessed Lord, Thy	166	Mulhausen	227
Blessed Redeemer, how	582	Angels' Hymn	85
Blest are the humble	630	Montgomery	92
Blest are the sons of	222	Prague	104
Blest are the souls that	129	Salisbury	200
Blest are the undefiled	190	Gibbons	68
Blest be the dear unit-	847	St. Peter	342
Blest be the everlast-	737	Old Winchester	133

HYMN.	NO.	TUNE.	NO.
Blest be the Father	448	Mainzer	400
		Wareham	22
Blest be the Lord, who	36	Wareham	22
Blest be the wisdom	298	Dunfermline	9
*Blest be Thy love	77	Franconia	160
Blest is the man, for	41	Courland	300
Blest is the man who	1	Salisbury	200
Blest is the man whom	55	Angels' Hymn	85
Blest is the tie that	832	Franconia	160
Blest morning, whose	755	Meaux Abbey	153
Blest work, the youth-	974	London New	95
Blow ye the trumpet	923	Silsoe	13
Bowed with a sense of	526	Gregory	83
Bread of heaven,	867	Ajalon	376
		Mount Zion	451
Bread of the world	1237	Navarre	169
Brethren, let us join to	314	Biberach	339
Brief life is here	1171	Salem	340
Bright as the sun's	910	Montgomery	92
Brightest and best	1028	Hexham	369
		Strasburg	298
Bright King of glory	308	Holywell	213
Bright Source of ever-	977	Wiltshire	254
Broad is the road that	645	Pentecost	186
Brother in Christ, and	841	Neapolis	139
Buried in shadows of	479	Glastonbury	243
By Christ redeemed	1241	Clifton	432
Calm me, my God	1123	Flavian	407
Captain and Saviour	1250	Sudeley	461
*Captain of our sal-	303	Wycliffe	73
Captain of Thine en-	921	Melcombe	78
Chief Shepherd of Thy	894	French	1
Children of the heaven-	630	Carinthia	199
Christ and His cross is	501	Coveney	355
		St. James	51
Christ is made	1253	Mannheim	380
*Christ the Lord is	30	Biberach	339
Christ the Lord is	385	Arimathea	318
		Easter Hymn	242
Christ, whose glory	1198	Maidstone	435
Christian, dost thou	1163	Midian	454
*Christian, let not	284	Nebo	484
Christian, seek not yet	1102	Ambrose	69
Christians, awake	1027	Bartholomew	302
		Sheba	394
Churches of Christ, by	905	Stella	441
Come, all harmonious	393	Hampton	183
Come, and let us	1243	Nassau	56
Come, dearest Lord	674	Truro	82
Come, Father, Son	859	Rockingham	19
Come, gracious Spirit	436	Eisenach	131
Come, happy souls	498	Bishopsthorpe	255
		Linoln	62
Come hither, all ye	507	Warrington	236

INDEX OF TUNES AND HYMNS.

HYMN.	NO.	TUNE.	NO.	HYMN.	NO.	TUNE.	NO.
Come, Holy Ghost, in	1092	Olivet	39	Dear Lord and Master	1120	Narenza	45
*Come, Holy Ghost		42	Melancthon	304	Dear Refuge of my	612	Paston	14
Come, Holy Ghost, our	429	{ St. Peter / Lancaster	332 / 281	*Dear Saviour of a	106	Wearmouth	309
				Dear Shepherd of Thy	885	Sudely	461
Come, Holy Spirit, co-	435	Franconia	160	Deathless Principle, a-	724	Cassell	218
Come, Holy Spirit, hea-	430	Tallis	59	Deep in our hearts let	99	Altona	93
Come in, thou blessed	837	Westminster	250	Deep in the dust before	475	Wartburg	145
Come in, ye chosen of	842	Philadelphia	201	Depth of mercy, can	528	Apollos	417
Come, kingdom of our	1220	St. Michael	2	Descend from heaven	699	{ Naples / Styria	234 / 157
*Come, let us anew	310	Mizpah	391				
Come, let us join our ch.	315	Meaux Abbey	153	Descend to thy Jeru-	1033	Ellers	424
Come, let us join our fr.	708	Burmah	323	Did Christ o'er sinners	502	St. Bride	81
Come, let us lift our joy-	395	Exeter	307	Dismiss me not	1159	Jerusalem	294
Come, let us lift our voi-	880	St. George	135	Dismiss us with Thy	794	Rockingham	19
Come, let us to the	1097	Cherwell	367	Do flesh and nature	716	Ravenna	329
Come, Lord, and tarry	928	Boylston	219	Do I believe what Jesus	620	St. James	51
*Come, Lord, and tarry	279	Boylston	219	Do not I love Thee, O	587	Flavian	467
*Come, my soul, thou	289	Canitz	444	Dread Sovereign, let	939	Arnheim	342
Come, my soul, thy	807	Kiel	79	Dying souls, fast bound	514	Arno	148
Come, O come, with	255	Nassau	56				
Come, O Thou all-	522	St. David	97	Each other we have	813	Hawthornden	426
Come on, my partners	631	Hereford	269	Early, my God, with-	82	Bishopsthorpe	255
Come, sound His	140	St. Michael	2	Enthroned on high	426	St. David	97
Come, Thou almighty	783	Albion	326	*Ere another Sabbath's	161	Battishill	299
Come, Thou everlasting	876	Lyons	171	Ere God had built the	306	Lusatia	350
Come, Thou Fount of	666	Corinth	137	Ere I sleep, for every	942	{ Thanet / Altorf	77 / 382
Come, Thou long-ex-	777	{ Minden / Mariners	155 / 293	Ere the blue heavens	305	St. Paul	243
Come, Thou soul-	788	Nazareth	300	Eternal Father	1279	Melita	346
Come to Calvary's holy	510	{ Stepney / Asaph	449 / 260	Eternal God, our won-	693	Bethany	106
				Eternal God, we look	654	French	1
Come to our poor na-	438	Ravensworth	168	Eternal Light, eternal	261	St. Bernard	118
Come unto Me and	1052	Bethsaida	362	Eternal Power, whose	257	Angels' Hymn	85
*Come unto Me, ye	49	Salem	340	Eternal Source of every	956	Eisenach	131
Come, we that love the	693	Newland	58	Eternal Sovereign of	993	London New	95
Come, ye sinners, poor	511	{ Eckington / Regent's Sqre.	5 / 385	Eternal Spirit, by	432	Tallis	59
				Eternal Spirit, we con-	431	Pentecost	186
Come, ye thankful	126	Sharon	373	Eternal Wisdom, Thee	275	Soho	146
Command Thy blessing	784	Nicea	315	Evening and morning	1195	Dresden	190
Communion of my Sa-	672	Berne	409	Ever-blessed Trinity	1194	Cape Town	412
Consider all my sor-	199	Burford	252	Eye hath not seen	1046	Gilead	416
*Creator of the starry	9	Advent Ev. Hy.	35	Exalt the Lord our	150	Hampton	183
Creator Spirit, by whose	433	{ Wycliffe / Carey	73 / 184	Faith is the brightest	603	Colchester	247
Crown Him with many	413	Hampton	183	*Faith of our fathers	312	{ Cana / Melita	475 / 346
				Faith, 'tis a precious	539	Westenhanger	289
Darkly rose the guilty	1036	Sion	33	Far as Thy name is	69	{ Gildas / Silchester	321 / 309
Daughter of Zion	926	St. Magnus	181				
Day by day the manna	591	Milan	117	Far from my heavenly	230	{ Lyte / Wirksworth	342 / 185
Day of judgment, day	419	Lutterworth	214				
Day of wrath	1051	Dies Iræ	647	Far from my thoughts	678	Carmel	267
*Days and moments	282	Sylvester	445	Far from the world, O	679	Paston	14
Dearest of all the	324	Colchester	247	Father, behold with	730	Tallis	59
Dear Jesus, ever at my	905	Furrant	105	Father, here we dedi-	1265	Peniel	413
Dear Lord, accept a	547	St. Ann	54				

INDEX OF TUNES AND HYMNS.

HYMN.	NO.	TUNE.	NO.	HYMN.	NO.	TUNE.	NO.
Father, how wide Thy	299	Salisbury	200	From Greenland's icy	912	Missionary	286
Father, I bless Thy	200	Berne	490	From the cross up-	506	Leipsic	290
Father, I know that	590	Sherwood	134	*From the recesses of	277	Bozrah	395
		Westphalia	312			Clifton	432
Father, I long, I faint	712	Chester	143	From the rich trea-	317	Wareham	22
Father, I sing Thy	98	Byzantium	285	From Thee, my God	711	Sudeley	461
Father in high heaven	1206	Sion	33	From yon delusive	969	St. John	216
*Father, my cup is full	109	Lyte	342	*Full of trembling	60	Elberfeldt	232
Father of all in whom	469	Evan	87				
*Father of all, whose	270	Mainzer	400	*Gently, Lord, O gent-	108	Lux Crucis	495
Father of boundless	822	Holstein	235	Gird on Thy conquer-	62	Silsoe	13
Father of eternal grace	359	Holyrood	237	Give me the faith	887	Rest	477
Father of eternal	915	Kettering	90	Give me the wings of	752	Burmah	323
Father of heaven	447	Incarnation	257	Give thanks to God; He	165	Advent Ev. Hy.	35
Father of life and	930	Whitchurch	149	Give thanks to God in-	163	York	98
Father of lights	1203	Smyrna	313	Give thanks to God mo-	228	Caernarvon	280
Father of love and	997	Hermon	129	Give thanks to God the	226	Glasgow	188
Father of men, Thy	978	Pyrton	221	Give to our God im-	227	Advent Ev. Hy.	35
Father of mercies, bow	892	Winchester	57	Give to the Lord, ye	37	Wartburg	145
Father of mercies, con-	900	Farrant	105	Give to the winds thy	606	Suabia	174
Father of mercies, in thy	891	Advent Ev. Hy.	35	*Give us our daily	181	Zweisimmen	425
*Father of mercies infi-	210	Farrant	105	Glad was my heart to	206	Ramleh	336
Father of peace	1148	Lincoln	62	Glorious things of thee	823	Stuttgart	335
Father, Redeemer	1119	St. Peter	332			Augsburg	282
*Father, that in the	112	Magdala	351	Glory be to Him	1050	Regent's Sqre.	385
Father, Thy gentle	1145	Rest	477	Glory be to Jesus	1039	North Coates	436
Father, throned on	1007	Spire	60			Geneva	170
Father, to thy sinful	535	Cyprus	373	*Glory, glory to God in	243	Seraphim	448
Father, we for our	1227	Arnold	251	Glory to God on high	338	Trinity	11
Father, whate'er of	601	Burmah	323	Glory to the Father	973	Corsica	65
Fierce raged the tem-	1080	St. Aëlred	408	Glory to Thee, my	938	Canon	12
*Fierce was the wild	261	Euroclydon	483	Go labour on	1157	Angelus	442
Firm and unmoved are	208	Swanland	74	Go not far from me	1144	Sherwood	134
Firm as the earth Thy	673	Bedford	163	Go to dark Gethsem-	392	Gethsemane	144
For a season called to	848	Battishill	299			Ajalon	376
For ever blessed be the	238	Dunfermline	9	Go, worship at Im-	319	Smyrna	313
For ever here my rest	875	Durham	414	God bless our native	998	Albion	326
For ever will I bless	46	Jerusalem	294	God in His earthly	124	Rochester	50
For ever with the Lord	1150	Bremen	70	God in His temple let	220	Sherborne	31
For mercies countless	287	Flavian	467	*God of the living, in	341	Rest	477
For the beauty of the	1019	Göttingen	337	*God is in His temple	240	Neander	460
*For the blessings this	212	Altorf	382	God is gone up on high	394	Olney	44
For Thy dear saint	1251	Norland	228	God is love	1023	Sardis	113
For Thy mercy	1266	Sculcoates	455	God is a Spirit, just	774	Paston	14
*Forth from the dark	182	Samaria	450	God is my strong sal-	35	Leven	161
Forth in Thy name, O	934	Neapolis	139	God is our refuge, ever	64	Halle	154
*Forty days and forty	14	Heinlein	349	God is our refuge in	66	Worms	17
Forward be our watch-	1165	Coppet	456	God is our refuge	65	Cherwell	367
Fountain of good	1245	French	1	God is the refuge of	63	Constance	124
Fountain of mercy	950	Glasgow	188	God moves in a mys-	281	Burmah	323
From all evil, all tem-	637	Beverley	278			Exeter	307
From all that dwell	165	Savoy	363	God, my supporter and	108	Gibbons	68
From deep distress and	214	Cannons	287	God of mercy, God of	94	Tiberias	344
From distant corners	866	Melcombe	78			Wells	90
From Egypt's bondage	710	Highbury	238	God of my childhood	103	Southwold	110

INDEX OF TUNES AND HYMNS.

HYMN.	NO.	TUNE.	NO.
God of my life, look...	52	Paston	14
God of my life, through	302	Modena	40
God of my life, to Thee	100	Gibraltar	63
God of my life, whose	665	Angelus	442
*God of our fathers ...	224	Sudeley	461
God of our life, Thy...	957	Evan	87
God of pity, God of ...	533	Dusseldorf	209
God of salvation, we...	300	Advent Ev. Hy.	35
God of the morning,...	930	Ely	48
*God save our gracious	305	Albion	326
God that madest	1207	Upsal	176
God the all-terrible ...	1272	Rephidim	489
God, the Lord	1275	Mount Zion	451
God, who in various...	460	Maccabeus	261
God is the Lord, the...	88	Brunswick	263
Gracious Saviour	1229	Eckington	5
Gracious Spirit	1093	Tiberias	344
Gracious Spirit, Holy	1096	Dusseldorf	209
Grace, 'tis a charming	292	Gildas	321
Grant me, heavenly...	571	Gotha	191
Grant us Thy light	1150	Fulda	127
*Great Creator	154	Leipsic	290
Great Father of each	443	Gloucester	317
Great Father of man-	767	Caernarvon	280
Great Former of this	157	Bohemia	34
Great God, as seasons	952	Ely	48
Great God, attend	119	Ella	94
Great God, how infinite	258	Bedford	163
Great God, I own Thy	729	Windsor	203
Great God, impress our	786	Altona	93
Great God, now con-	858	Westenhanger	289
Great God of heaven...	996	Cannons	287
Great God of wonders	295	{ Salvator / Ephesus }	401 / 306
Great God, permit my	83	Bavaria	249
Great God, the nations	908	Exeter	307
Great God, to what a	668	Eisenach	131
Great God, we sing ...	955	Soldau	175
Great God, what do I	420	Eisleben	102
Great God, where'er...	990	Liverpool	96
Great God, whose uni-	105	{ Melcombe / Hayne }	78 / 217
Great God, with won-	465	Salisbury	200
Great is the Lord, and	225	Northampton	194
Great is the Lord: His	173	Lancaster	281
Great is the Lord, our	69	St. Michael	2
Great King of nations	1269	St. Matthew	167
Great Shepherd of	115	Carmel	267
Great the joy when ...	831	Biberach	339
Great was the day, the	425	Mecklenburg	130
Guide me, O Thou ...	660	Moscow	274
Had I the tongues of	583	Philadelphia	201
Hail! blessed commu-	906	Saxony	67
Hail! morning known	756	Eisenach	131
*Hail the day	32	Arimathea	318
Hail, sacred day	1184	Magdala	351
Hail! Thou God of ...	816	Chichester	182
Hail! Thou once des-	335	{ Salzburg / Crucifer }	128 / 497
Hail to the Lord's	107	{ Lusatia / Bonchurch }	356 / 224
Hail to the Sabbath ...	1183	Gildas	321
Hallelujah! hallelu-	1043	Stuttgart	335
Hallelujah! raise, O	178	Carinthia	199
Hallelujah! song of...	714	Darmstadt	301
Happy soul, thy days	726	Flanders	262
Happy the church	824	Constance	124
Happy the heart where	586	Gloucester	317
Happy the home when	991	Martyrdom	71
Happy the man that...	174	Bishopsthorpe	255
Happy the souls to...	820	Colchester	247
Hark! hark! my soul	1169	Vox Angelica	18
Hark, my soul! it is the	598	{ Dijon / Battishill }	91 / 299
Hark the glad sound...	347	Lincoln	62
Hark! the herald	345	{ Nativity / Praise }	322 / 26
Hark! the song of ...	924	Sharon	373
Hark! the sound	1049	Stuttgart	335
Hark! the voice of love	384	Vesper	270
Hasten, O sinner, to...	492	Babylon	297
Head of the Church...	818	Mecklenburg	130
Head of the Church...	316	St. Andrew	121
Heal us, Immanuel ...	532	Tallis	59
Hear, gracious Sove-	815	Bohemia	34
Hear, my prayer, O ...	945	Sardis	113
Hear what the voice...	731	Southwold	110
Hear Thy children ...	1211	Florence	472
Heavenly Father, all...	1010	Stuttgart	335
Heavenly Father, may	851	Kiel	79
Heavenly Father, to	636	Litany	277
He dies, the Friend of	380	Gregory	83
He filled the cup	1232	Arnheim	343
Help me, my God, to...	1110	Potsdam	192
He reigns, the Lord	144	Modena	40
He that hath made his	132	Patmos	347
*He is gone—a cloud	218	Cassell	218
*He is risen	31	Puran	371
Hence from my soul...	634	Wiltshire	254
Here, O my Lord, I...	1234	{ Dalkeith / Gilead }	239 / 416
He sendeth sun, He...	1141	Samaria	450
High in the heavens...	47	Eisenach	131
High in yonder realms	747	Weimar	66
Ho, every one that	517	Cannons	287
Holy Bible, book	461	Battishill	299
Holy Ghost, dispel our	439	Bethlehem	100
Holy Ghost, with light	1691	Sculcoates	155
Holy, holy, holy Lord	1008	Göttingen	337

INDEX OF TUNES AND HYMNS.

HYMN.	NO.	TUNE.	NO.	HYMN.	NO.	TUNE.	NO.
Holy, holy, holy Lord	454	Cassell	218	*I bless the Christ	263	Narenza	45
Holy, holy, holy Lord	559	Shore	273	I cannot bear Thy	702	Pergamos	319
Holy, holy, holy Lord	455	Heber	123	I do not ask, O Lord	1153	Compton	403
		Monkland	349			Hemingford	404
Holy Lamb, who Thee	572	Sculcoates	455	If God succeed not, all	212	Montgomery	92
Holy Spirit, Lord of	1089	Gotha	191	If human kindness	877	Southwold	110
*Hope of our hearts	143	St. Peter	332	*If Thou but suffer	95	Moravia	147
*Hope of those that	149	Interlachen	443			Puris	427
Hosanna to our con-	408	Emmanuel	465	I give my heart to Thee	1114	Suabia	174
Hosanna to the King	409	Olney	44	*I have no comfort	105	Siloam	352
Hosanna to the living	312	Baden	172	I heard the voice of	1108	Vox Dilecti	489
Hosanna to the Prince	390	Dunfermline	9	*I hunger and I thirst	177	St. Dunstan	292
		St. David	97	I lay my sins on Jesus	1105	Tabor	368
Hosanna with a cheer	936	Masbury	41	I lift my heart to Thee	1116	Southgate	397
*House of our God	297	Bartholomew	302			Budleigh	407
How are Thy servants	106	Lancaster	281	*I'm but a stranger	337	Beulah	396
How beauteous are	400	Ramleh	33	I'm kneeling at the	1176	Tabor	368
*How beauteous were	20	Canonbury	27	I lift my soul to God	29	Southwell	81
How blest the right	727	Holley	409	I love the Lord, He	182	Bedford	163
How bright these	750	Gloucester	317	I love Thy kingdom	828	Hawthornden	426
How can I sink with	589	Chester	143	I need Thee, precious	1104	Tabor	368
How condescending	868	Burmah	323	In grief and fear, to,	1269	Burmah	323
*How dare we pray	46	Thuringia	324	*In heavenly love	130	Aurelia	415
How did my heart	204	Lincoln	62	In the dark and cloudy	1147	Litany	277
How do Thy mercies	592	Canonbury	27	*In the day of thy	114	Linden	462
		Winchester	57			Bethel	320
How firm a foundation	661	Oldenburg	150	*In the hour of my	45	Litany	277
How glorious is our	963	Stukeley	173	In the hour of trial	1113	Labrador	437
How heavy is the night	480	Serbal	381	*In whom shall I	254	Sanctuary	446
How honourable is the	825	Dunfermline	9	I'll praise my Maker	242	Lucerne	210
How honoured, how	121	Houghton	246	I'll speak the honours	60	Salisbury	200
How is our nature	477	Windsor	203	I'm not ashamed to	621	Felix	241
How large the promise	855	Philippi	279	Immortal principles	676	Farrant	105
How oft have sin and	671	Hayne	217	In all my vast concerns	232	Liverpool	96
How pleasant, how	119	Mainzer	400	In all my ways, O God	155	Doncaster	122
How pleased and blest	205	Ascalon	126	In all things like Thy	354	Southwold	110
How precious is the	466	Bethany	166	In anger, Lord, rebuke	8	Abbey	230
How rich are Thy	806	Waldeck	120	In God, most holy, just	77	Burford	252
How sad our state by	478	Manchester	190	In God's own house	251	Soho	146
How shall I follow Him	357	Alsace	275	In Judah, God of old	111	London New	95
How shall I praise the	262	Gloucester	317	In the cross of Christ	372	Sardis	113
How shall the young	192	St. Peter	332			Minden	168
How short and hasty	496	Burford	252	In Thy name, O Lord	765	Eckington	5
How strong Thine arm	310	Solomon	100	In time of tribulation	112	Silesia	142
How sweet and awful	873	Durham	414			Tabor	368
How sweet, how hea-	584	St. James	51	In true and patient	81	Lyte	342
How sweet the name	328	Cherwell	367	Infinite excellence is	309	Meaux Abbey	153
		Westminster	259	Inspirer and Hearer of	937	Welton	53
How sweetly flowed	349	Courland	300	Interval of grateful	943	Cyprus	376
How swift, the torrent	719	Serbal	381	I said, my God, at	1115	Ludwig	101
		Ludlow	179	I send the joys of earth	565	Mamre	223
How vast the treasure	687	Eisenach	131	I sing my Saviour's	381	French	1
How welcome to the	759	Nicea	315	I sing the almighty	274	Masbury	41
How welcome was the	1217	Ramleh	336	I think of Thee, my	1132	Paston	14

INDEX OF TUNES AND HYMNS

HYMN.	NO.	TUNE.	NO.
*I thirst, thou woun-	57	*Alsace*	275
I waited patient for...	54	*Evan*	87
I will extol Thee, Lord	39	*Malaga*	55
I will praise Thee......	776	*Southminster..*	204
I worship Thee, O ...	1136	*Gloucester....*	317
I would commune with	1122	*Belmont*	49
Is there ambition in...	216	*St. Stephen* ...	42
Is this the kind return	524	*Sonning*	3
It came upon the	1273	*Noel*	431
It is not death to die...	1072	*Whitchurch* ...	149
It is the Lord en-	602	*Tallis*.............	50
It is Thy hand, my ...	600	{ *Lyte*	312
		{ *Tirzah*	230
Jehovah reigns exalted	145	*Mecklenburg*...	130
Jehovah reigns, He ...	135	*Rockingham* ...	19
Jehovah reigns, His...	263	*Advent Ev. Hy.*	35
Jerusalem, my happy...	743	{ *Stukeley*	173
		{ *Emmanuel*	465
Jerusalem, the glo- ...	1171	*Munich*	165
*Jerusalem the golden	150	*Salem*	340
Jerusalem the heaven-	1171	*Aurelia*	415
*Jesus,Lord & Saviour	269	*Geneva*	170
Jesus calls us o'er the	1156	*Ellerker*	331
*Jesus cast a look on	76	*Cyprus*	378
Jesus, great Redeemer	1066	*Clarens*	433
*Jesus, if still Thou art	56	*St. Leonard* ...	365
Jesus, I live to Thee .	1069	*Narenza*..........	45
*Jesus, Master of the	178	*Barnabas*	16
Jesus, meek and	1155	*Bemerton*	357
*Jesus, my loving	116	*St. Vincent* ...	20
Jesus, and can it ever	622	*Constance*	124
Jesus, and didst Thou	351	*Culross*	115
Jesus,at Thy command	609	*Burnham*	212
Jesus, exalted far on...	352	*Farrant*	105
Jesus, full of all com-	551	*Elberfeldt*	232
Jesus, I love Thy	326	*Flavian*	467
Jesus, immortal King	920	*St. Magnus* ...	181
Jesus, I my cross have	653	*Crucifer*..........	497
Jesus,in Thee our......	397	*St. Leonard* ...	365
Jesus invitesHis saints	862	*St. Michael* ...	2
Jesus lives, no longer	388	*Thaxted*	136
Jesus, Lord, we look...	830	*Pleyel*	139
Jesus, my all, to heaven	334	*Pascal*	10
Jesus, my strength ...	568	*Westenhanger*	289
Jesus,our best-beloved	829	{ *Courland*	300
		{ *Eisenach*	131
Jesus, our Lord, as- ...	170	*Lincoln*	62
Jesus, refuge of my ...	550	*Hollingside* ...	354
Jesus shall reign	106	*Mecklenburg*...	130
Jesus, still lead on.....	662	*Spire*	60
*Jesus, Sun and Shield	179	*Livonia*	103
*Jesus, Sun of righte-	209	*Battishill*	299
Jesus, the name to.....	327	*Belmont*	49
Jesus, these eyes have	1133	*St. Leonard* ...	365

HYMN.	NO.	TUNE.	NO.
Jesus, Thou art my ...	1054	*Sudeley*	461
Jesus, Thou joy of ...	1239	*Holwy*	409
Jesus, to Thy table ...	1236	*Vevay*.............	460
Jesus,the very thought	329	*French*	1
Jesus, the word of......	808	{ *Solomon*	100
		{ *Emmanuel*......	465
Jesus, Thou everlast-	403	*St. Paul*.......	245
Jesus, Thy boundless	303	{ *Siloam*	352
		{ *Palestrina*......	208
Jesus,Thy church with	927	*Winchester* ...	57
Jesus, Thy robe of......	325	*Eisenach*	131
Jesus, Thy sovereign	836	*Soldau*	175
Jesus, we lift our souls	1228	*Coveney*	355
Jesus, where'er Thy...	883	*Soldau*	175
Jesus, with all Thy ...	337	{ *Emmanuel*	465
		{ *Norwich*..........	328
Join all the glorious...	318	*Iona*	327
Joy is a fruit that will	692	*Harrington* ...	177
Joy to the world, the	147	*Gloucester*......	317
Judge me, Lord, in ...	58	*Cuthbert*	116
Judge me, O Lord......	32	*St. Mary*	141
Just are Thy ways......	14	*Fulda*	127
Just as I am—without	547	{ *St. Thomas* ...	52
		{ *Leeds*	209
Keep silence, all.........	267	*Burford*	252
Kindred in Christ, for	839	*Soldau*	175
*Labouring and heavy	122	*Bethlehem*	106
Laden with guilt, and	467	*Arnheim*..........	343
Lamb of God, whose	869	*Barnabas*	16
Lamp of our feet	463	*Castor*.............	193
Leader of faithful souls	601	{ *Mansfield*	80
		{ *Stella*	441
Lead, kindly light......	1152	{ *Lux Benigna*...	411
		{ *Oriel*	331
*Lead us, heavenly ...	100	*Waltham*	264
Lead us, O Father, in	1149	*Dalkeith*	239
Lead us, O our heaven-	1154	*Waltham*	264
*Let all men know......	188	*Damascus*	388
Let all men praise the	419	*Wittemburg* ...	89
Let all our tongues be	320	*Ludlow*	179
Let all the earth their	143	*Zurich*.............	229
Let all the heathen ...	194	*St. George*......	135
Let all the just to God	43	*St. Stephen* ...	42
Let bitter words no...	585	*Galilee*	295
Let children hear the	113	*Bethany*	166
Let everlasting glories	412	*Rochester*	50
*Let e very heart ex-...	19	*Palestine*	47
Let every mortal ear...	516	*Wearmouth* ...	308
Let God arise, and let	97	*Dettingen*	210
Let God, the mighty .	59	*Suabia*	174
Let me be with Thee .	1173	*Berne*	490
Let me but bear my...	658	*Wartburg*	145

INDEX OF TUNES AND HYMNS.

HYMN.	NO.	TUNE.	NO.	HYMN.	NO.	TUNE.	NO.
Let others boast how...	483	...St. Mary	141	Lord, in the strength	564	...Aynhoe	48
Let party names no ...	819	...St. Michael	2	Lord, in this Thy	1102	{ Witton (2 Tns)	114
Let plenteous grace ...	839	...Martyrdom	71			Lugano	390
Let songs of praise fill	428	...Bezley	211	*Lord, in Thy name ...	230	...Gloucester	317
Let them neglect Thy	301	...Old Winchester	133	Lord, it belongs not to	534	...Furrant	105
Let the whole race of	279	...St. James	51	Lord Jesus, let Thy...	902	...Advent Ev. Hy.	35
Let us, with a glad- ...	229	...Ratisbon	98	*Lord Jesus, when we	88	...Babylon	297
Let Zion and her sons	156	...Exeter	307	Lord, like the publican	531	...St. James	51
Let Zion's watchmen	893	...French	1	Lord, look on all	995	...St. Mary	141
Life is the time to serve	489	...Gregory	83	Lord, my weak thought	1013	...Holley	409
Lift up to God the......	288	...St. Magnus	181	Lord of mercy and of	1199	...Mount Zion	451
Light of life, seraphic	783	...Kiel	79	Lord of mercy and of	332	...Ambrose	69
*Light of light, en- ...	294	...Norminster	464	Lord of our life, and	1217	...Flemming	393
Light of the lonely ...	1218	...Stukeley	173	Lord of the harvest ...	805	...Doncaster	122
*Light of the world ...	92	...Oriel	331	Lord of the living har-	1259	...Aurelia	415
Light of those, whose	323	...Corinth	137	Lord of the lofty and	976	...Eisenach	131
Light up this house ...	882	...Belmont	49	Lord of the Sabbath ...	755	...Soldau	175
Like sheep we went...	379	...Southwell	84	Lord of the vast crea-	770	...Shiloh	222
Lo, God is here, let us	773	...Lubeck	189	Lord of the worlds ...	120	...King's College.	226
Lo, He comes with ...	418	{ Ramah	72	*Lord, speak to me that	307	...Holley	409
		Lutterworth	214	Lord, teach us how to	806	...Southwold	110
Lo, on the inglorious	376	...Holy Cross	15	Lord, Thou hast searc.	233	...Gregory	83
Lo, the storms of life	607	{ Maldon	88	Lord, Thou hast been	1025	...Halle	154
		Boniface	315	*Lord, Thou on earth	204	...St. Margaret	361
Lo, what an entertain-	221	...Solomon	100	*Lord, Thy children...	99	...Tiberias	344
Long as I live I'll bless	239	...Salisbury	200	Lord, Thou wilt hear	4	...Furrant	105
Long have I sat be-...	791	...Abbey	233	Lord, 'tis a pleasant ...	134	...Wareham	22
Look, ye saints, the...	411	...Triumph	29	*Lord, Thy word abi-	262	...Oxford	231
Lord, as a family we...	982	...St. Peter	332	Lord, we adore Thy...	290	...Wartburg	145
Lord, as to Thy dear	353	{ Durham	414	Lord, we are blind, we	260	...Advent Ev.Hy.	35
		Paston	14	Lord, we come before	785	...Pleyel	138
Lord, at Thy feet we...	534	...Arnheim	343	Lord, we confess our	538	...St. Ann	54
Lord, before Thy	207	...Tiberias	344	Lord, when I count...	234	...St. Stephen	42
Lord, behold us few...	833	...Heinlein	349	Lord, when Thou didst	95	...Advent Ev. Hy.	35
Lord, cause Thy face	821	...Thuringia	321	Lord, when we bend...	810	...St. Matthew	167
Lord, dismiss us with	793	...Eckington	5	Lord, while for all......	1000	...St. George	135
Lord, dismiss us with	792	...Dismission	330	Loud hallelujahs to ...	246	...Danube	244
Lord, for ever at Thy	217	...Solicitude	76	Love divine, all love...	364	{ Riston	164
Lord, from my bed ...	931	...Paderborn	43			Lyons	171
Lord, give me light to	1160	...Sudeley	461			Normandy	109
Lord God of my salva-	126	{ Silesia	142	Love me, O Lord	1099	...Durham	414
		Tabor	369	*Loving Shepherd of	87	...Biberach	339
Lord God, the Holy ...	427	...Westenhanger	289	*Low in Thine agony	24	...Redemptor	430
Lord, have mercy when	809	...Refuge	28	Lowly and solemn be	721	...Conway	155
Lord, how delightful...	797	...Bavaria	249	*Lowly kneel, and softly	25	...Cuthbert	110
Lord, how divine Thy	870	...Emmaus	103				
Lord, how secure my	523	...Abridge	156	Man of sorrows and...	373	...Hamburg	196
Lord, I am vile, con-	72	...Pergamos	391	*Master, where abidest	67	...Weimar	86
Lord, I believe a rest	709	...Burmah	323	May the grace of Christ	796	...Alla Trinita.	125
Lord, I have made Thy	195	...Harrington	177	Meet and right it is to	1005	...Barnabas	16
*Lord, I was blind: I	1004	...Nicea	315	Mercy alone can meet	529	...Windsor	203
Lord, I will bless Thee	41	...Constance	124	Met again in Jesus' ...	803	...Shore	273
Lord, if Thou the grace	581	...Armstadt	256	Mighty God, while ...	311	...Chichester	187
Lord, in the morning .	5	...Ballerma	99	Mighty Quickener......	1091	{ Arno	144
						Wareim	68

INDEX OF TUNES AND HYMNS.

NO.	TUNE.	NO.	HYMN.	NO.	TUNE	NO
554	...Gibbons	68	My spirit longs for...	1125	...Ludwig	101
793	...Holley	409	My spirit looks to God	80	...Alsace	275
31	...Swanland	74	My spirit on thy care	39	...Sonning	3
541	...Culross	115	My spirit sinks within	56	...Bohemia	84
1182	...Kettering	90	*My times are in hand	121	...Norland	226
344	...Lincoln	62	My thoughts surmount	700	...Belmont	49
1012	...Sudeley	461	My trust is in the Lord	10	...Burnham	223
718	...Abridge	156				
652	...Sudeley	461	Naked as from the......	597	...Culross	115
358	...Angels' Hymn	85	Nature with open......	370	{ Warrington	236
544	...Olivet	39			{ Neapolis	139
1014	...Burmah	323	Nearer, my God, to...	1127	{ Aspiration	422
236	...Pascal	10			{ Laleham	220
253	...Belmont	49	*Nearer, O God, to...	265	...Aspiration	422
801	...Angelus	442	Never further than......	1061	...Cyprus	378
935	...Ely	48	*No gospel like this...	174	...Newland	58
263	...Tallis	59	No more, my God, I...	543	...Mecklenburg	130
72	...St. Margaret	361	Nor eye hath seen, nor	746	...Tallis	59
1135	...Cherwell	367	Not all the blood of...	546	...Sonning	3
132	...Cherwell	367	Not all the outward...	553	...Tottenham	283
78	...Advent Ev.Hy.	35	Not for a favourite...	834	...Montgomery	92
330	...Carrow	496	Not from the dust......	647	...Windsor	203
101	...Farrant	105	Not the malicious or...	577	...St. Ann	54
560	...Burmah	323	Not Thy garment's...	1067	...Tiberias	344
599	{ Leicester	305	(tying first two notes in v. 2 and 4)			
	{ Sarum	325	Not to condemn the...	497	...Bohemia	84
	{ Troyte	359	Not to ourselves, who	180	...Waldeck	120
103	...Styria	157	Not to the terrors of...	707	...Paston	14
241	{ Magdalen Col.	265	*Not what I am, O Lord	60	{ Gilead	418
	{ Soldau	175			{ Kelso	112
689	...Hawthornden	426	Not what these hands	1107	...Westenhanger	289
688	...Irish	187	Not with our mortal...	696	...Boylston	219
677	{ Carmel	267	Now begin the heaven-	365	...Corsica	65
	{ Gibraltar	63	Now for a tune of lofty	391	...Constance	124
84	...Franconia	160	Now from the altar of	986	...St. Leonard	365
613	...Southwold	110	Now, gracious Lord...	959	...Farrant	105
697	...Wiltshire	254	Now I have found the	611	...Wycliffe	73
50	...Arnold	251	Now is the accepted...	495	...Sonning	3
235	...Hereford	258	Now let our cheerful...	398	...Durham	414
562	...Rochester	50	Now let our mournful	23	...Golgotha	348
1134	...Elim	375	Now let our mourning	736	...Arnheim	343
1137	...Agatha	470	Now let our souls on...	713	...Gibraltar	63
127	...St. Leonard	365	Now let the children...	854	...Westminster	259
237	...Rockingham	19	Now let the feeble all	614	...Wareham	22
61	...St. Michael	2	Now may He who from	795	...Biberach	339
1103	...Willerby	402	Now may the God of	22	...Maccabeus	261
573	...Westenhanger	289	Now may the gospel's	789	...Patmos	317
102	...Exeter	307	Now may the mighty...	919	...Adv. Ev. Hymn	35
24	...St. Peter	332	Now may the Spirit's	787	...Lancaster	231
117	...St. Matthew	167	Now shall my solemn	90	...Cherith	374
198	...Walsal	303	Now thank we all our	1022	...Wittemberg	89
249	...Hanover	100	*Now that the daylight	205	...Palestine	47
159	{ Franconia	160	*Now the day is over	292	{ Geneva	170
	{ Christchurch	159			{ Enon	438
161	...Modena	40	Now to the hands of...	607	...Felix	241

INDEX OF TUNES AND HYMNS.

HYMN.	NO.	TUNE.	NO.	HYMN.	NO.	TUNE.	NO.
Now to the Lord a	304	Melcombe	78	O help us, Lord, each	808	Arnheim	343
Now to the Lord that	415	Eisenach	131	O Holy Ghost, Thou	1090	Paderborn	43
Now to the power of	294	Cannons	287	O holy Saviour	1142	Croyland	37
Now with angels round	451	Leipsic	290	O Holy Spirit, dost	1095	Southwold	110
				O how blest the con-	768	Mannheim	380
O all ye nations, praise	184	Dunfermline	9	O how I love Thy ho y	193	Solomon	100
O be joyful in the Lord	154	Arimathea	318	O Israel, blest beyond	691	Constance	124
O blessed life	1068	Bavaria	249	O Jesus Christ, grow	1065	Flavian	467
O blessed Saviour, is	1085	St. Peter	332	*O Jesus Christ, the	171	Durham	414
O blessed souls are	40	Ludlow	179	O Jesus, ever present	1056	Heidelberg	23
O bless the Lord, my	158	St. Michael	2	O Jesus, in this solemn	846	St. Ann	54
*O blest Creator	206	Nicea	315	O Jesus, King most	405 { St. Peter	332
O bow Thine ear	1256	Winchester	57			Bethany	166
O bread to pilgrims	1238	Lusatia	356	O Jesus, Lord en-	1226	Canonbury	27
O come, O come	1032	Ephratah	372	*O Jesus, Lord of Light	207	Ella	94
O come, Thou Sun of	1197	Mainzer	400	O Jesus, when I think	1074	Farrant	105
*O come to the merci-	48	Hexham	309	O let him whose	1078 { Labrador	437
O breathe upon this	442	Evan	87			Hebron	379
O Christ our hope, our	404	Byzantium	285	O Light of life, O	1207	Palestine	47
*O come and mourn	54	Golgotha	339	O Lord, a wondrous	1231	Lusatia	356
O come, loud anthems	141	Ely	48	O Lord, another day is	984	Farrant	105
O comfort to the dreary	508	Munich	165	O Lord, defend us, as	109	St. Ann	54
O day of rest and	1185	Shiloh	222	O Lord, how happy	593	Kedron	256
O everlasting Light	1079	Doncaster	122	O Lord, how many	3	Alsace	275
O Father, who didst	1214	Fulda	127	O Lord, I would de-	685	Farrant	105
O for a closer walk	644	Southwold	110	O Lord, my best de-	598	French	1
O for a heart to praise	567	Salisbury	200	O Lord my God	1063	Rest	477
O for a shout of sacred	67	Meaux Abbey	153	O Lord of heaven	1246	Hanford	486
O for a thousand	330 { Dunfermline	9	O Lord of hosts	1252	Cana	475
		Byzantium	285	O Lord our God, arise	1221	Aynhoe	46
O for an overcoming	722	Lincoln	62	O Lord our King	8	Durham	414
O give thanks to Him	277 { Brandenburg	353	O Lord, our Lord	7	Gloucester	317
		Leipsic	290	O Lord, Thy heavenly	1118	Oberlin	383
*O God, by whom the	160	French	1	O Lord, Thy work re-	812	Canterbury	271
O God made manifest	1083	Bedford	163	*O Lord, turn not	53	St. Mary	141
O God, my heart is	169	Wareham	22	O Love divine and	1218	Aurelia	415
O God, my Helper	958	Soldau	175	O Love divine, how	362	Innspruck	7
O God, my strength	16	Stukeley	173	*O love that casts out	266	Ludwig	101
O God of Bethel, by	285 { Martyrdom	71	O Love, who formedst	1117	Stella	441
		Tallis	59	*O Master, it is good	247	Danias	475
O God of families, we	979	Palestine	47	O mean may seem	1070	Cherwell	367
O God of life	1011	Damascus	388	O paradise, O para-	1175 { Ledforth	64
O God of love, O	1271	Canonbury	27			Paradise	474
O God of mercy, God	874 { Altona	93	O praise ye the Lord	248	Hanover	103
		Pergamos	301	O risen Lord	1041	Coblentz	418
O God of mercy, hear	74	Bedford	163	O sacred Head, once-	374 { Lutzen	119
O God, Thou art my	85	Sherburne	31			Tabor	368
O God, unseen, yet	1235	Cherith	374	*O Saviour, is Thy	198	Winchester	57
O God, we praise	353	Lincoln	62	O Saviour, may we	1062	St. Margaret	301
O God, who didst Thy	459	Mamre	223	O send Thy light, Thy	771	Melancthon	304
O had I, my Saviour	76	Hexham	309	O show me not	1044	Watford	377
O happy band of	1167	Barton	440	O Spirit of the living	922	Constance	124
O happy day that	563	Winchester	57	*O strength and stay	215 { Willingham	397
O happy man, whose	213	Arnold	251			Itala	423
O happy soul that lives	695	Byzantium	285	'O take away this evil	85	Gregory	89

INDEX OF TUNES AND HYMNS.

Hymn.	No.	Tune.	No.
O that I knew the......	641	...Paston	14
O that the Lord.........	197	...Bedford	163
O the delights, the ...	743	...London New ...	95
O Thou from whom...	619	{ Durham	414
		{ Burford	252
O Thou that hear'st ...	73	...Berlin.............	250
O Thou, the contrite...	399	...Croyland	37
O Thou the true.........	1030	...Altona	93
O Thou, to whom in...	779	{ Wartburg	145
		{ Ernan	459
*O Thou, to whose all	70	...Winchester ...	57
*O Thou, true life of...	213	...Advent Ev.Hy.	35
O Thou who camest ...	570	{ Nicea	315
		{ Maccabeus ...	261
O Thou who didst the	1255	...Mainzer	400
O Thou who didst this	1240	...Croyland	37
O Thou who didst with	1111	...St. Leonard ...	365
O Thou whose cove-	856	...Norwich	323
O Thou whose own ...	1254	...French	1
O Thou whose sacred	1146	...Arnheim.........	343
O Thou who trod the	1280	...Hermon	129
O timely happy, time-	933	{ Pascal	10
		{ Palestine	47
O what amazing words	505	...Chester	143
*O what a lonely	124	...Farrant	105
*O what if we are......	144	...St. Michael ...	2
O what shall I do my	698	...Werburg	311
O where is He	1082	...Petersham ...	482
O where shall rest be	704	...Suabia	174
O who like Thee.........	1086	...Canonbury ...	27
O worship the King...	102	...Houghton	246
O worship the Lord ...	1002	...Hexham	360
O Zion, afflicted with	610	{ Beersheba	398
		{ Hexham	369
Object of my first de-	684	...Benevento ...	248
O'er the gloomy hills	911	...Paran	371
Oft in sorrow, oft in ...	627	...Solicitude	76
Once more, before we	849	...Potsdam	192
Once more, my soul ...	932	...St. Magnus ...	191
One sole baptismal ...	1215	...Pastor Bonus .	494
One sweetly solemn...	1177	...Sonning	3
One there is above......	1075	...Stepney	449
On Jordan's stormy...	741	...Abbey	233
On the dewy breath...	1201	...Crucifer	497
On the first Christian	1040	...Flavian	467
On the Rock of Ages...	1216	...Mannheim	380
Onward let my children	1166	...Maidstone	435
On, towards Zion, on	626	...Broadlands ...	361
*Onward,Christian sol-	328	...Elah	491
Open now thy gates ...	1187	...Paran	371
Oppressed with sin ...	525	...Wirksworth ...	185
Our blest Redeemer...	1087	...Magdala	351
Our Father, God, who	558	...Westminster ...	259
*Our Father, hear......	273	...Cherwell	367

Hymn.	No.	Tune	No.
Our God, how firm ...	670	...Flavian	467
Our God, our help in	130	...St. Mary	141
Our heavenly Father	675	...Potsdam	192
Our helper, God, we...	954	...Seldau	175
Our journey is a	706	...Exeter	307
Our life is hid	1071	...Hawthornden .	426
Our Lord is risen from	28	...Christm.Chorale	66
Our moments fly	131	...Southwell	84
Our spirits join to......	879	...Pentecost	186
Out of the deep I call	1100	...Ludlow	179
Out of the depths I ...	215	...Coburg	176
Peace be to this.........	992	...Corinth	17
Peace, doubting heart	1139	...Melita	346
Pleasant are Thy	1188	...Maidstone	435
Plunged in a gulf of...	360	...Lancaster	281
Pour out Thy Spirit...	689	...Smyrna	313
Praise, everlasting ...	270	...Christm.Chorale	66
Praise God from whom	453	...Savoy	363
Praise, my soul, the ...	1021	...Triumph	29
Praise Jehovah, bow...	149	{ Arnsberg	206
		{ Sion	33
Praise, Lord, for Thee	89	...Adv. Ev. Hymn	35
Praise the God of all	450	...Vienna	111
Praise the Lord, His...	250	...Milan	117
Praise the Lord, ye ...	245	...Frankfort	6
Praise to Thee, Thou	273	...Vienna	111
*Praise to the Holiest	244	...Emmanuel......	465
Praise waits in Zion ...	87	...Lincoln	62
Praise ye Jehovah......	1003	...Sheba	394
Praise ye the Lord, ex-	224	...Nicea	315
Praise ye the Lord; 'tis	243	...Ely	48
Prayer is the soul's...	890	...Durham.........	413
Prostrate, dear Jesus	527	...Windsor.........	203
Questions and doubts	463	...Sherborne	31
Quiet, Lord, my fro-...	589	...Mount Zion ...	451
Raise your triumphant	293	...Doncaster	122
*Reaper I behold the...	187	...Soldau	175
*Rejoice, all ye be-......	37	...Greenland	476
Rejoice, believer in ...	625	...St. Leonard ...	365
Rejoice, the Lord is ...	406	...King's College .	226
Rejoice to-day with ...	1274	...Worms	17
Rejoice, ye righteous...	42	...Lancaster	281
Religion is the chief...	968	...St. Ann	54
Remark, my soul, the	960	...St. Mary	141
*Rest for the toiling...	147	...Sonning	45
Rest from thy labour	735	...Lyte	343
*Rest of the weary ...	336	...Theodora	409
*Resting from His work	26	...Ajalon	376
Return, O wanderer...	520	...Gregory	83
Return, O wanderer, to	521	...Invitation	202
*Revive thy work, O...	197	...Hampton	193

INDEX OF TUNES AND HYMNS.

Hymn.	No.	Tune.	No.
Ride on, ride on in...	1035	Hosanna	471
Rise, my soul, and...	703	Barnabas	16
Rock of Ages, cleft...	549	Cuthbert	116
Round the Lord...	1004	Chichester	182
*Safe across the wa-...	135	Bemerton	357
Safely through another	947	Wells	30
Saints at your heaven-	595	Galilee	295
Salvation is for ever...	122	Smyrna	313
Salvation, O the joyful	500	Emmanuel / Castor	465 / 198
Saviour, abide with us	1212	Hawthornden	426
Saviour, again to Thy	1190	Ellers / Dalkeith	424 / 239
Saviour, blessed Savi-	1045	Goshen / Ramoth	458 / 439
Saviour, breathe an...	985	Bethlehem / Florence	106 / 472
Saviour, let Thy sanc-	988	Ajalon	376
Saviour, sprinkle many	1223	Stuttgart	335
Saviour, when in dust	367	Provence / St. Agnes	284 / 333
Saviour, who Thy...	1230	Alla Trinita / Florence	125 / 472
See how great a flame	817	Weimar	86
See Israel's gentle...	852	St. Peter	332
See what a living stone	189	Franconia	160
Send out Thy light and	1219	Worms	17
Servant of all, to toil	356	Furrant	105
Servants of God, in...	177	Nicea	315
Shall foolish, weak...	259	St. Matthew	167
Shall science distant	904	Northampton	194
Shall we go on to sin	578	Sonning	3
Shepherd divine, our	811	Durham	414
Shepherd of Israel, bend	844	Rockingham	19
Shepherd of Israel, Thou	896	Ely	48
Shepherd of tender...	975	Hermon	129
Shew pity, Lord...	1098	Itala	423
Shine, mighty God, on	92	Meaux Abbey	153
Shine on our souls...	981	Philippi	279
Show p'ty, Lord; O...	71	Gregory	83
Since all the down-...	282	Martyrdom	71
Sinful, sighing to be...	1101	Clarence (change at v. 4)	453
*Sing, hallelujah...	6	Ravenshaw	350
Sing, my tongue, the	878	Irene / Sherbrooke	296 / 410
Sing the great Jeho-	91	Carinthia	199
Sing to the Lord in...	1017	Meaux Abbey	153
Sing to the Lord Je-	129	London New	95
Sing to the Lord of...	1262	Shiloh	222
Sing to the Lord our	116	St. Michael	2
Sing to the Lord, ye...	142	Old Winchester	133
Sinner, O why so...	419	Berlin	250
*Sinners, turn, why...	240	Apollos	471
Sitting around our...	864	Arnheim	313

Hymn.	No.	Tune.	No.
*Sleep thy last sleep	340	Requiem	492
*Sleepers, wake! a...	38	Dumah	32
So did the Hebrew pro-	545	Colchester	247
So let our lips and...	579	Haarlem	197
Soldiers of Christ, a-	624	Gildas	321
*So rest, my Rest...	324	Cheshunt	384
Sometimes a light sur-	686	Waterford	140
Song of God, Thy bles-	659	Sculcoates	455
Son of God, to Thee I	392	Gotha	191
Songs of praise the...	254	Kiel	79
Soon as I heard my	34	Culross	115
Soul, thy week of toil	948	Birkenhead	4
Sovereign of life, be-...	715	Angels' Hymn	85
Sovereign Ruler of the	595	Heinlein	349
*Sowing our seed in	327	Gennesaret	466
Sow in the morn thy	1158	Gildas	321
Spirit Divine, attend...	441	Durham	414
Spirit of everlasting...	814	Galilee	295
Spirit of holiness, de-	813	Emmaus	193
Spirit of life, Thine...	440	Glastonbury	243
Spirit of light and...	901	Ravenna	329
Spirit of power and...	434	St. David	97
Spirit of truth, come...	437	Holstein	235
*Spirit of wisdom...	47	St. Peter	332
*Spread, O spread...	193	Carinthia	199
Stand up and bless...	772	St. Michael	2
Stand up, my soul...	628	Christ. Chorals / Samson	64 / 24
Stand up, stand up...	890	Waterford	140
Stay, Thou insulted...	643	Gregory / Galilee	83 / 295
*Still, still with Thee	86	Willingham	397
Still will we trust tho'	1139	Bozrah	393
*Still with Thee...	271	Hawthornden	426
Straight is the way, the	580	Irish	187
*Summer suns are...	300	Ruth	452
Sun of my soul, Thou	919	Pascal	10
Sweet is the memory	210	St. Ann	54
Sweet is the solemn...	827	Pentecost	186
Sweet is the work, my	133	Ely / Ella	48 / 94
Sweet Saviour, bless...	1102	Siloam / Sutton	352 / 429
Sweet the moments...	871	Birkenhead / Daun	4 / 162
*Sweet was the hour	66	Cherith	374
Sweet the anthem...	999	Carinthia	199
*Take up Thy cross...	104	Canonbury	27
Talk with us, Lord...	680	Evan	87
Teach me, O Lord...	1151	Berne	490
Teach me the measure	53	Abridge	156
Thank and praise Je-	167	Ratisbon	38
That awful day will...	421	Manchester	190
That Thou, O Lord...	110	Hereford	268

INDEX OF TUNES AND HYMNS.

HYMN.	NO.	TUNE.	NO.
*That mystic word ...	85	...Kelso	112
*The Bridegroom......	285	...Advent	485
*The chariot! the	286	...Ophel	447
*The church has wait-	278	...Bremen	70
The church of God ...	125	{ Newland	58
		{ Canterbury ...	271
The dawn of God's ...	1186	...Aurelia	415
The day is past and...	1210	...Anatolius	434
*The day, O Lord, is	221	...Norland	228
The day of resurrec-...	1040	...Lusatia	356
The eternal gates......	1048	...Emmanuel ...	465
The festal morn, my...	757	...Hull	291
*The fish in wave......	7	...Flavian	467
*The Galilean fishers'	138	...Noel	431
*The gloomy night ...	221	...Olmutz	420
The glories of my......	272	...St. George	135
The God Jehovah......	149	...St. Michael ...	2
The God of Abraham	256	...Leoni	132
The God of truth His	825	...Sherborne ...	31
The great redeeming	853	...Bethany	166
The head that once...	410	...Emmanuel	465
The heathen perish ...	914	...Hayne............	217
The heavens declare H	21	...Waterford......	140
The heavens declare Th	17	...Mecklenburg...	130
The hour of my depar-	725	...Berne	490
The hours of evening	949	...Norland	228
The law by Moses ...	475	...Doncaster	122
The law commands ...	471	...Holywell	213
The livelong night ...	818	...Farrant	105
*The Lord be with us	318	...Durham	414
The Lord declares......	476	...Whitchurch ...	149
The Lord, descending	473	...Tallis	59
The Lord—how fear-...	268	...St. George	135
The Lord is King, and	137	...Heidelberg......	23
The Lord is King, lift	407	...Styria............	157
*The Lord is rich and	250	...Noel............	431
The Lord is risen in-	387	...St. Michael ...	2
The Lord Jehovah ...	136	...Hilary	316
The Lord Jehovah ...	266	...Iona	327
The Lord my pasture	27	{ Rest	477
		{ Huntingdon ...	75
The Lord my Shep- ...	25	...Westenhanger	289
The Lord my Shep- ...	24	...Pastor Bonus..	494
The Lord of earth and	961	...Burnham	212
The Lord of glory is...	33	...Bethany	166
The Lord of might ...	416	...Dettingen	240
The Lord of Sabbath .	764	...Dunfermline...	9
The Lord on high pro-	515	...Prague	104
The Lord shall come	417	...Winchester ...	57
The Lord the Judge...	70	...Burmah	323
The Lord will come...	123	...Gloucester......	317
The Lord will happi-	640	...Martyrs.........	8
The mercies of my ...	289	{ Bexley	211
		{ Emmanuel......	465
The night is come	1209	...Holley	409

HYMN.	NO.	TUNE.	No.
The praise of Zion ...	86	...Pentecost	186
The praises of my......	964	...Silchester	309
*The precious seed of	236	...Lutzen	119
The race, that long ...	1031	...Lincoln	62
The radiant morn has	1204	...Hunford.........	496
The roseate hues of ...	1172	...Petersham	482
The Sabbath day has .	1193	...Leeds	269
*The sands of time are	339	...Rutherford ...	473
The Saviour calls: let	518	...York	99
*The shade and gloom	28	...Norwich	328
*The shadows of the...	211	...Arnheim	343
*The sheep renounced	134	...Rest................	477
The Son of God goes...	1161	...Jarrow	488
The spacious firma-...	20	{ Incarnation ...	257
		{ St. Seyf.........	544
The Spirit breathes...	484	{ Salisbury	200
		{ Northampton...	194
The Spirit to our	519	...Whitchurch ...	149
The springtide hour...	1260	...Styria............	157
The strain upraise of...	1016	...Eudoxia	493
The sun is sinking fast	1202	...Horeb	396
*The voice that brea-	233	...Leven	161
*The way is long and	338	...Via Crucis......	406
The year is gone be-...	1264	...Kirkella	389
*The year is swiftly...	301	...Heidelberg	23
Thee, God Almighty...	1009	{ Herrnhutt	428
		{ Dumah	32
Thee we adore, Eter-	484	...St. Mary	141
*Thee will I love	266	...Rest................	477
*There is a blessed ...	146	{ Broadlands	364
		{ Zweisimmen ...	425
There is a book, who...	276	...Durham	414
There is a fold whence	1055	...Durham	414
There is a fountain ...	548	...Southwold	110
There is a house not .	745	{ Bethany	166
		{ Bedford	163
There is a land of pure	742	{ French	1
		{ Emmaus..........	193
*There is an everlast-	63	{ Spandau	419
		{ Magdala	351
There is no sorrow ...	1077	...Southwold	110
Thine arm, O Lord ...	1270	...Kirkella	389
This God is the God...	615	...Saxony	67
This is My body	1233	...Troyte	359
*This is the day of ...	315	...Hawthornden .	426
This is the day the ...	188	...Stukeley.........	173
This is the day when .	754	...Tottenham......	283
This is the word of ...	496	...Constance	124
This night I lift my ...	910	...Croyland	37
This stone to Thee in	881	...Melcombe	78
Thou art gone to the .	733	...Lambeth	258
Thou art gone up on .	1017	...Holstein.........	205
Thou art my portion .	191	...Abbey	233
*Thou art near, yes ...	81	...Sardis............	113
Thou art, O Christ, the	333	...Prague	101
Thou art the ever-......	307	...Lebanon.........	272

INDEX OF TUNES AND HYMNS.

HYMN.	NO.	TUNE.	NO.	HYMN.	NO.	TUNE.	NO.
Thou art the Way	1059	Coventry	355	To our almighty Ma-	146	Soho	146
Thou brightness of	1200	Lincoln	62	To our Redeemer's	331	Old Winchester	133
Thou dear Redeemer	341	Colchester	247	To praise the ever-	951	Masbury	41
*Thou doest all things	127	Westenhanger	289	To realms beyond the	903	St. Basil	36
Thou glorious Sove-	916	Mamre	223	To Thee in ages past	778	Franconia	160
Thou, God, art love	1015	St. Margaret	361	To Thee, O blessed	1128	Salem	340
Thou God of glorious	424	Nuremberg	152	To Thee, O dear, dear	744	Munich	165
*Thou grace divine	80	St. Peter	332	To Thee, O God in,	1223	Franconia	160
Thou gracious God	114	Southwell	84	To Thee, O Lord, I	720	Moravia	147
Thou hidden love of	561	Samaria	450	To Thee, Thou bleed-	552	Rest	477
Thou hidden source of	321	Melancthon	304	To Thy temple I re-	781	Corsica	65
*Thou, Lord, art love	10	St. Margaret	361	To Zion's hill I lift	203	Cherith	374
Thou only Sovereign	646	Gibraltar	63	To-day the Saviour	494	Nain	108
Thou Son of God, and	355	Winchester	57	To-morrow, Lord, is	493	St. Bride	88
Thou sovereign Lord	999	Hayne	217	Tossed upon life's ra-	1277	Crucifer	497
Thou very paschal	336	Christchurch	159	*True bread of life	170	{ Ilala / Kelso	423 / 112
Thou very present aid	655	Holstein	235				
Thou who art en-	763	Cassell	218	*Try us, O God, and	98	Evan	87
Thou who didst stoop	1073	Bethabara	370	'Twas by commission	461	Philadelphia	201
Thou who hast known	1213	Ernan	459	'Twas on that dark	860	Babylon	237
Thou who our faith.	1112	St. Margaret	361				
Thou whose almighty	917	Trinity	11	United prayers ascend	857	Malaga	55
Though sinners take	75	Swanland	74	Unshaken as the sacred	209	Brunswick	263
Though troubles assail	656	Werburg	311	Unveil Thy bosom	732	Babylon	297
*Three in One, and	5	Cape Town	412	*Uplift the banner! let	309	Melanesia	478
Thrice happy souls	983	{ Glasgow / Flavian	188 / 467	Up to the hills I lift	202	Fulda	127
				Up to the Lord that	283	{ Mainzer / Boston	400 / 207
Through all the chang-	45	Tottenham	283				
Through all the trials	1076	Ballerma	99	Vain are the hopes the	542	St. James	51
Through the day Thy	1204	{ Stepney / Sherbrooke	449 / 410	*Victim divine, Thy	169	Melancthon	304
				Wake, awake, for night	1170	Dumah	32
Thus far my God hath	633	Berne	490	Walk in the light, so	632	Colchester	247
Thus far the Lord has	941	Advent Ev. Hy.	35	Walking with Th e my	1129	Beulah	396
Thus saith the high	536	Glastonbury	243	Weary of warfare, striv-	1179	Ellers	424
Thus the eternal Fa-	171	Modena	40	Weary with my load	1106	Cuthbert	116
Thy ceaseless, unex-	296	Old Winchester	133	We bid Thee welcome	845	Angelus	442
Thy favours, Lord, sur-	775	Truro	92	We bless Thee for Thy	1124	St. Peter	332
*Thy home is with	79	Cherwell	367	We bless the Lord, the	96	Waldeck	120
Thy mercies fill the	196	Bexley	211	We bless the Prophet	401	Solomon	100
Thy mercy, my God, is	297	Oldenburg	150	We cannot praise Thee	1001	Aurelia	415
Thy name, almighty	183	Silchester	309	We give immortal	446	Iona	327
Thy way, not mine, O	1143	Broadlands	364	We give Thee but Thine	1244	Hawthornden	426
Time is earnest, pass-	490	Melton	107	We in the lower parts	1212	Ramleh	336
Time! what an empty	485	Chester	143	*We limit not the truth	313	Petersham	482
'Tis by the faith of	604	St. Basil	36	We love Thee, Lord	1024	Petersham	482
'Tis my happiness be-	651	Shore	273	We love the place	1253	Ludwig	101
To bless Thy chosen	93	Aynhoe	46	We love the venerable	1257	Salisbury	200
To Father, Son, and	456	Soho	146	We may not climb the	1057	St. Leonard	365
To God be glory, peace	445	Dunfermline	9	We plough the fertile	1263	Shalford	487
To God on high be	291	Halle	154	*We praise, and bless	73	Coventry	355
To God the Father	457	Wareham	22	We praise, we bless	1006	Islington	405
To God, the great, the	164	Samson	24	We praise, we worship	252	{ Advent Ev. Hy. / Salvator	35 / 401
To God, the only wise	669	Gildas	321				
To heaven I lift my	201	Bethany	166	*We saw Thee not	102	Samaria	450
To Him that chose us	453	Caernarvon	290	We sing His love who	740	Danube	244

INDEX OF TUNES AND HYMNS.

HYMN.	NO.	TUNE.	NO.
We sing the praise	1033	Alsace	275
We sing to Thee, Thou	310	Lincoln	62
*We speak of the	145	Welton	53
We thank Thee, Lord	1018	Cana	475
We've no abiding city	709	Pascal	10
Welcome! brethren	810	Milan	117
Welcome, sacred day	762	Weimar	86
Welcome, sweet day...	761	{ Newland / Whitchurch	58 / 149
Welcome, welcome!	512	Kettering	90
What are these in	751	Leipsic	290
What equal honour	4(2	Mecklenburg	130
What grace, O Lord	1084	Cherwell	367
What means the water	850	Melcombe	79
What shall I render	181	Brunswick	263
What shall the dying	481	Sherborne	31
What sinners value I	13	Modena	40
What various hin-	805	Montgomery	92
When all Thy mercies	290	Dunfermline	9
When any turn from	642	Manchester	190
When blooming youth	971	St. Mary	141
*When from the silent	8	St. Leonard	365
When gathering clouds	369	{ Samaria / Jena	450 / 310
When God is nigh, my	12	Canonbury	27
When God of old came	1083	Flavian	467
When God revealed	211	Castor	198
When, gracious Lord	638	Berne	490
When I can read my	705	{ Southwold / Arnold	110 / 251
When I can trust my	605	St. Vincent	20
When I had wandered	1121	Cherith	374
When I survey the	371	{ Gregory / Babylon	83 / 297
When Israel, freed	179	Mecklenburg	130
*When Jesus come to	36	Baines	500
When morning gilds	1196	Migdol	399
When on Sinai's top I	393	Heinlein	349
When our heads are	648	Capernaum	341
When overwhelmed	79	Lyte	342
*When quiet in my	136	{ Samaria / Siloam	450 / 352
When rising from the	739	Liverpool	96
When sins and fears	635	Fulda	127
When the first parents	361	Northampton	194
When the weary seek-	1181	Intercession	246
When this passing	575	Refuge	28
When Thou, my right-	423	Nuremberg	152
When through the torn	1278	{ Succour / Sarnen	491 / 421
When wounded sore	1033	Arnheim	343
Whence do our mourn-	657	Culross	115
Where high the hea-	400	{ Mecklenburg / Ravenna	130 / 329
Where shall we go to	210	Rockingham	19
Where two or three	304	St. Basil	30
Where'er the man is	30	Aynhoe	40
While all the angel-	452	Westenhanger	299
While Thee I seek	296	Southwold	110
While with ceaseless	962	{ Liguria / St. Agnes	195 / 333
Who can describe the	555	{ Smyrna / Samson	313 / 24
Who in the Lord con-	210	{ Hawthornden / Norland	426 / 228
*Who is this, so weak	323	Scopas	479
Who shall ascend Thy	11	Doversdale	225
Who shall the Lord's	672	Nicea	315
*Who walks the waves	1081	St. Margaret	361
Whom should we love	15	Pastor Bonus	494
Why did the Gentiles	2	Canterbury	271
Why do we mourn de-	730	St. Mary	141
Why is my heart so	639	Martyrs	8
Why should the chil-	414	Harrington	177
Why should this earth	701	Bedford	163
Why should we start	717	Gregory	83
*Winter reigneth o'er	302	Clarence	453
With all my powers of	231	{ Styria / Holywell	157 / 213
With broken heart and	530	Golgotha	338
With glory clad, with	139	Bavaria	249
With grateful hearts	99⁷	{ Lucerne / Coverdale	210 / 288
With heavenly power	897	Winchester	57
With heavenly weapons	629	Exeter	307
With humble heart and	970	Sonning	3
With joy we meditate	368	Sudeley	401
With my whole heart	9	Colchester	247
With reverence let the	128	Exeter	307
With songs and hon-	244	Lincoln	62
*With the sweet word	306	Narenza	45
With Thee, my Lord,	1131	Hawthornden	426
Witness, ye men and	835	Felix	211
Would Jesus have the	503	Siloam	352
Ye dying sons of men	513	Caernarvon	280
Ye hearts, with youth	966	Martyrdom	71
Ye messengers of	899	Prague	101
Ye mourning saints	734	French	1
Ye nations round the	151	Melcombe	79
Ye principalities and	1249	Coveney	355
Ye servants of God	313	Houghton	246
Ye servants of the Al-	176	Savoy	363
Ye servants of tho	619	Franconia	160
Ye sons of men, with	278	{ Samson / Zurich	24 / 229
Ye that delight to	175	Antioch	314
Ye that in these courts	501	Nassau	56
Ye that obey the im-	223	Lancaster	291
Ye virgin souls, arise	422	Burnham	212
Yes, I do feel	1109	Ilala	423
Yes, the Redeemer	346	Caernarvon	280
Yes, we trust the day	1223	Regent Square	384
Your harps, ye tremb-	633	Potsdam	104

4. *Slow.* **Birkenhead.** 8.7.8.7.   Dr. Gauntlett, 1857.

Sweet the moments, rich in bless-ing, Which be-fore the cross I spend;

Life and health and peace pos-sess-ing, From the sin-ner's dy-ing Friend.

5. *Moderate.* **Eckington.** 8.7.8.7.4.7.   Giovanni Martini, *Scuola d'Organo,* 1804.

Come, ye sin-ners, poor and wretched, Weak and wounded, sick and sore;

Je-sus rea-dy stands to save you, Full of pi-ty joined with power.

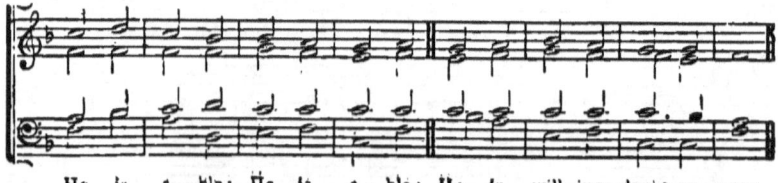

He is a-ble; He is a-ble; He is will-ing: doubt no more.

BARNABAS—continued.

Time shall soon this earth remove : Rise, my soul, and haste away To seats prepared a-bove.

17. *Bold.* **Worms,** or **Fortress.** (CHORAL). 8888, 6666, 8.

LUTHER, 1530.

God is our re-fuge in dis-tress, Our shield of hope thro' ev-ery care,
God is our hope and strength in woe, Thro' earth He maketh wars to cease,

Our Shepherd watching us to bless, And therefore will we not des-pair;
His pow-er break-eth spear and bow, His mer-cy send-eth end-less peace.

Although the mountains shake, And hills their place forsake, And billows o'er them
Then though the earth re-move, And storms rage high above, And seas tem-pestuous

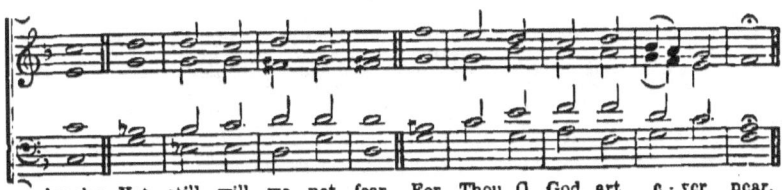

break; Yet still will we not fear, For Thou, O God, art e-ver near.
prove, Yet still will we not fear, The Lord of Hosts is e-ver near.

(7)

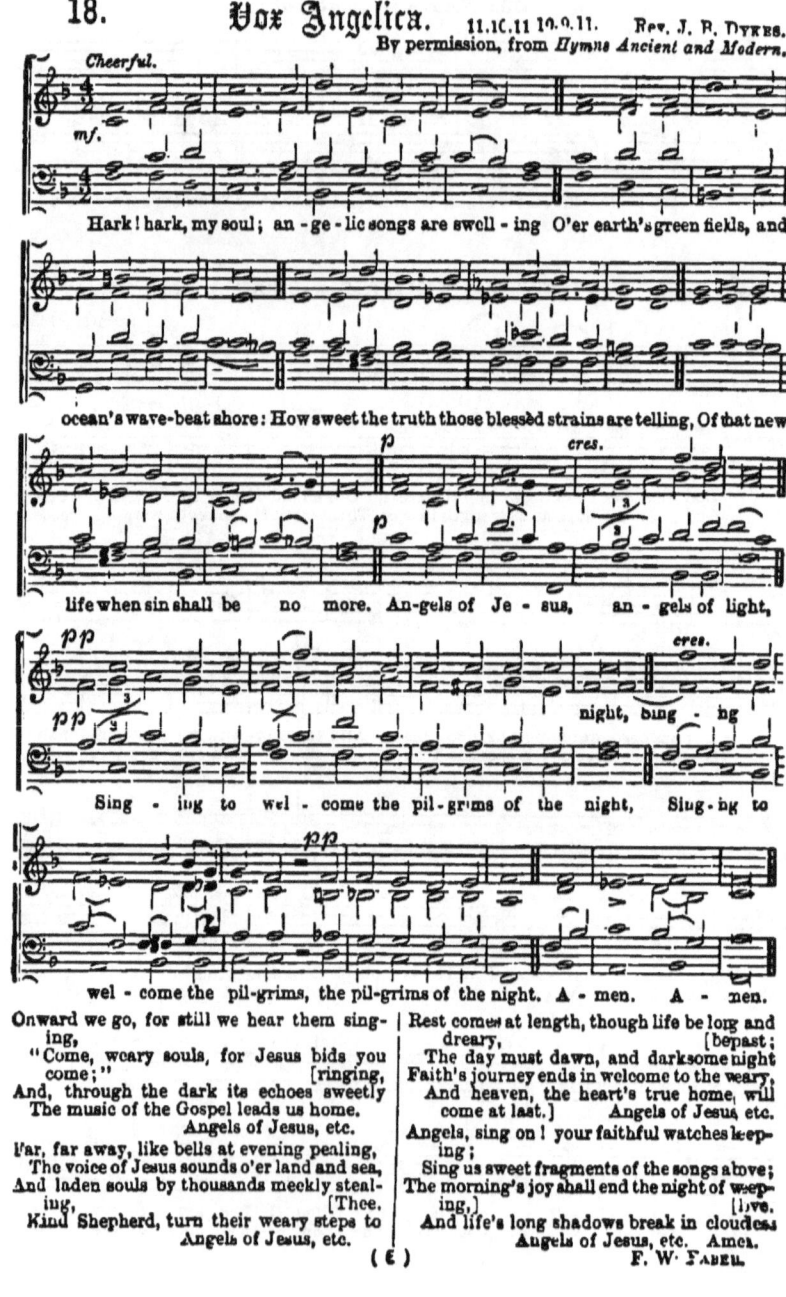

18. Vox Angelica. 11.10.11 10.9.11. Rev. J. B. Dykes.
By permission, from *Hymns Ancient and Modern*.

Onward we go, for still we hear them sing-
ing,
"Come, weary souls, for Jesus bids you
come;" [ringing,
And, through the dark its echoes sweetly
The music of the Gospel leads us home.
Angels of Jesus, etc.
Far, far away, like bells at evening pealing,
The voice of Jesus sounds o'er land and sea,
And laden souls by thousands meekly steal-
ing, [Thee.
Kind Shepherd, turn their weary steps to
Angels of Jesus, etc.

Rest comes at length, though life be long and
dreary, [bepast;
The day must dawn, and darksome night
Faith's journey ends in welcome to the weary,
And heaven, the heart's true home, will
come at last.] Angels of Jesus, etc.
Angels, sing on! your faithful watches keep-
ing,
Sing us sweet fragments of the songs above;
The morning's joy shall end the night of weep-
ing,) [love.
And life's long shadows break in cloudless
Angels of Jesus, etc. Amen.
F. W. Faber.

19. *Moderate.* Rockingham, or Caton. L.M. Dr. Miller, 1797.

Al-migh-ty King, whose wondrous hand Supports the weight of sea and land:

Whose grace is such a bound-less store, No heart in vain shall sigh for more.

20. *Joyful.* St. Vincent. 8 6. 8 6. 8 8. Dr. Gauntlett, 1852.

When I can trust my all with God, In tri-al's fear-ful hour;

Bow, all re-signed, be-neath His rod, And bless His spar-ing power

A joy springs up a-mid dis-tress, A foun-tain in the wil-der-ness.

21. Cyril. 8.5.8.3. A. R. REINAGLE, by permission.

Moderate.

Art thou wea-ry, art thou lan-guid, Art thou sore dis-trest? "Come to me," saith One, "and com-ing, Be at rest."

Hath He marks to lead me to Him,
   If He be my guide?
"In His feet and hands are wound-prints,
       And His side."
Hath He diadem as monarch
   That His brow adorns?
"Yea, a crown, in very surety,
       But of thorns."
If I find Him, if I follow,
   What His guerdon here?
"Many a sorrow, many a labour,
       Many a tear."

If I still hold closely to Him,
   What hath He at last?
"Sorrow vanquished, labour ended,
       Jordan past."
If I ask Him to receive us,
   Will He say me nay?
"Not till earth, and not till heaven
       Pass away."
Finding, following, keeping, struggling,
   Is He sure to bless?
"Angels, martyrs, saints and prophets,
       Answer, Yes!"

22. *Moderate.* Wareham. L.M. W. KNAPP, d. 1768.

Blest be the Fa-ther and His love, To whose ce-les-tial source we owe Ri-vers of end-less joys a-bove, And rills of com-fort here be-low.

23. *Joyful.* Heidelberg. 7.6.7.6. or C.M. M. VULPUIS, 1609.

The Lord is King, and wear - eth A robe of glo - ry bright;

He clothed with strength ap - pear - eth, And girt with powerful might.

24. *Moderate.* Samson. L.M. Arranged from HANDEL.

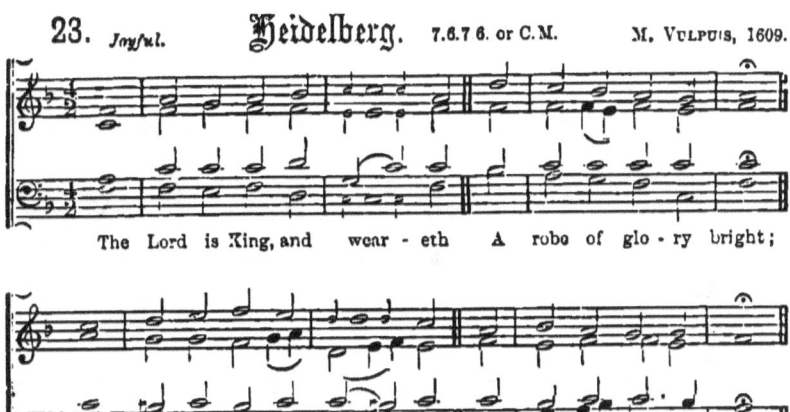

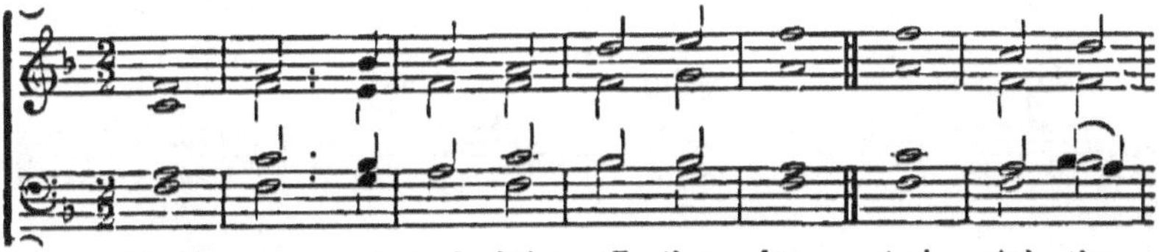

Stand up, my soul, shake off thy fears, And gird the

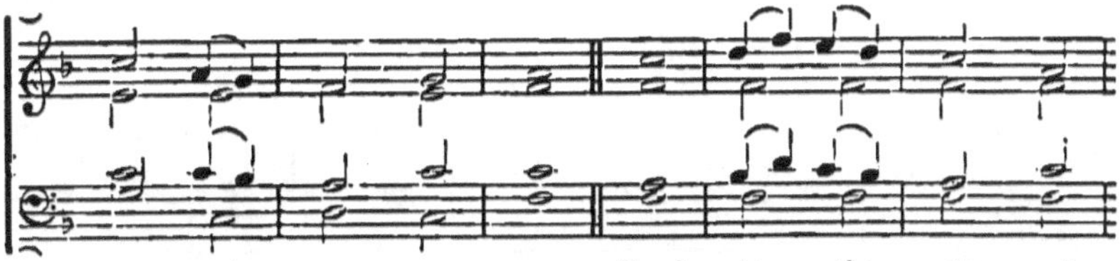

gos - pel ar - mour on: March to the gates of

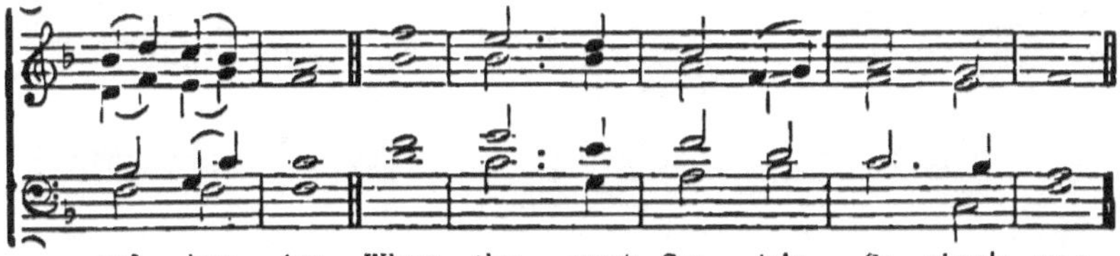

end - less joy, Where thy great Cap - tain - Sa - viour's gone.

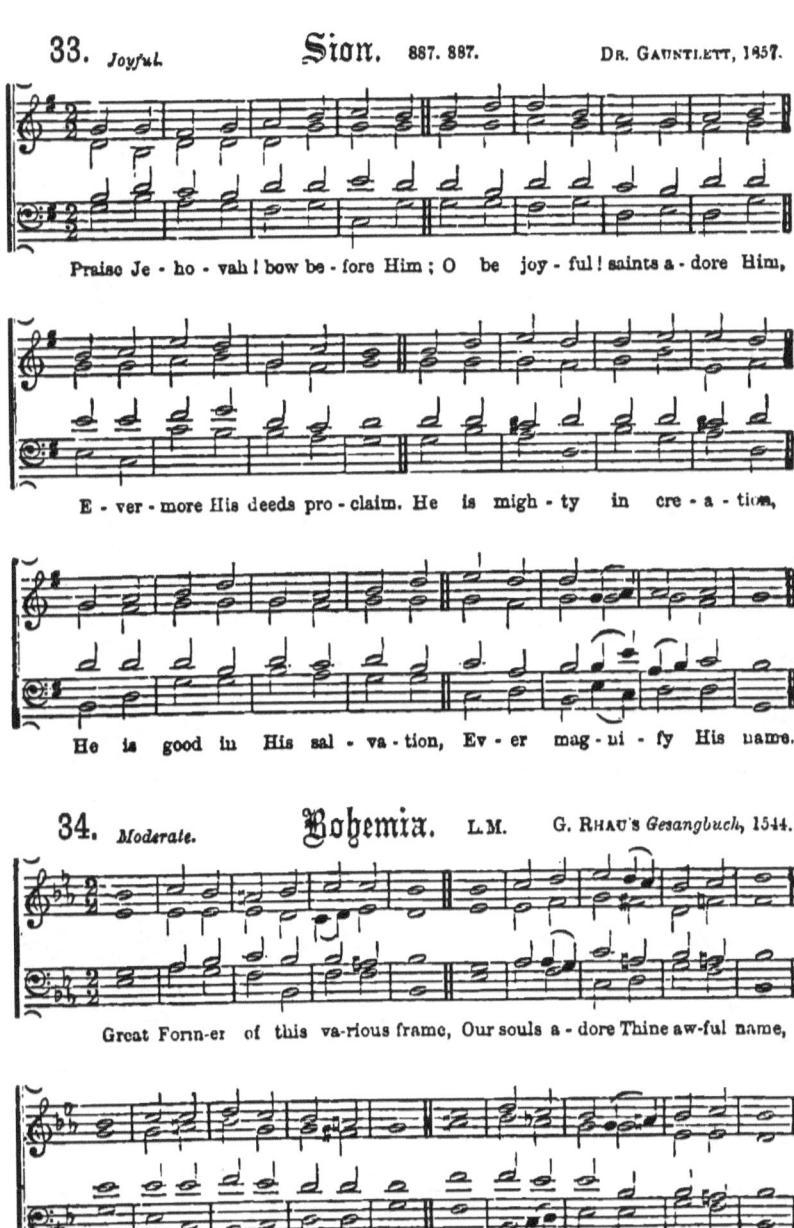

57. *bold.*   **Winchester.** L.M.   *Spiritual Melodies, 1690.*

How do Thy mer - cies close me round! For e - ver be Thy name a-dored;
I blush in all things to a - bound; The ser - vant is a - bove his Lord!

58. *Moderate.*   **Newland.** S.M.   Dr. Gauntlett, 1857.

Come, we that love the Lord, And let our joys be known;
Join in a song with sweet ac - cord, And thus sur-round the throne.

59. *Moderate.*   **Tallis.** C.M.   T. Tallis, 1561.

Come, Ho - ly Spi - rit, heavenly Dove, With all Thy quickening powers;
Kin - dle a flame of sa - cred love In these cold hearts of ours.

60. Spire. 5.5.8.8.5.5. ADAM DRESE, 1650.

Joyful.

Je - sus, still lead on, Till our rest be won; And, al - though the way be cheer - - less, We will fol - low, calm and fear - less: Guide us by Thy hand. To our Fa - ther - land.

61. Ferriby. 6.6.6.4.8.8.4. OLD MELODY.

Grave.

Behold the Lamb of God! O Thou for sinners slain, Let it not be in vain That Thou hast died. Thee for my Saviour let me take, My on-ly refuge let me make Thy piercèd side. A-men.

Behold the Lamb of God!
Into the sacred flood
Of Thy most precious blood
    My soul I cast:
Wash me and make me clean within,
And keep me pure from every sin,
    Till life be past.

Behold the Lamb of God!
All hail, Incarnate Word,
Thou everlasting Lord,
    Saviour most blest:

Fill us with love that never faints,
Grant us with all Thy blessèd saints
    Eternal rest.

Behold the Lamb of God!
Worthy is He alone,
That sitteth on the throne
    Of God above;
One with the Ancient of all days,
One with the Comforter in praise,
    All Light and Love. Amen.

LEDFORTH—continued.

light, All rapture through and through, In God's most holy sight. A - men.

O Paradise, O Paradise,
'Tis weary waiting here;
I long to be where Jesus is,
To feel, to see Him near;
    Where loyal hearts, &c.

O Paradise, O Paradise,
I want to sin no more,
I want to be as pure on earth
As on thy spotless shore;
    Where loyal hearts, &c.

O Paradise, O Paradise,
I greatly long to see
The special place my dearest Lord
In love prepares for me;
    Where loyal hearts, &c.

Lord Jesu, King of Paradise,
O keep me in Thy love,
And guide me to that happy land
Of perfect rest above;
    Where loyal hearts, &c.

65. *Joyful.* **Corsica.** 7.7.7.7. Melody by GLUCK

Now be - gin the heaven-ly theme: Sing a - loud in Je - su's name;
Ye who His sal - va - tion prove, Tri - umph in re - deem-ing love.

66. *Bold and Joyful.* **Christmas Choral.** L.M. M. LUTHER, 1535.

Praise, e - ver - last-ing praise, be paid To Him that earth's foundation laid;
Praise to the God, whose strong decrees Sway the wide realms of earth and seas

69. *Slow and Moderate.* **Ambrose.** 777.5. Dr. Gauntlett.

Lord of mer - cy and of might, Of man - kind the life and light,

Ma - ker, Teach - er, In fi - nite; Je - sus, hear and save.

70. *Moderate.* **Bremen.** S.M.D. I. B. Woodbury.

"For e - ver with the Lord!" Amen; so let it be: Life from the dead is

in that word, 'Tis im - mor - tal - i - ty. Here in the bo - dy pent,

Absent from Him I roam, Yet nightly pitch my moving tent A day's march nearer home.

(31)

73. *Bold.* **Wycliffe.** 8s.8s.8s. Johann Schop, 1641.

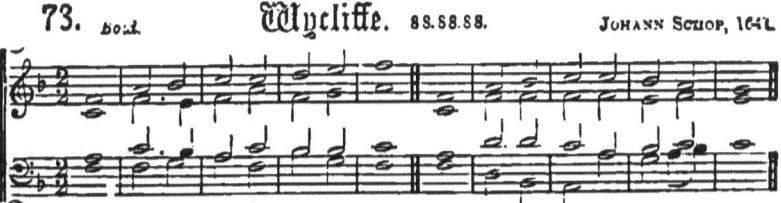

Now I have found the ground wherein Sure my soul's an-chor may re-main:—

The wounds of Je-sus, for my sin Be-fore the world's foun-da-tion slain;

Whose mer-cy shall un-sha-ken stay, When heaven and earth are fled a-way.

74. *Sustained.* **Swanland.** S.M. Dr. Gauntlett, 1857.

Be-hold the a-maz-ing sight, The Sa-viour lift-ed high!
Be-hold the Son, God's chief de-light, Ex-pire in a-go-ny!

75. *Moderate.* **Huntingdon.** 8s.8s.8s.   Dr. G. Untlett, 1857.

The Lord my pas-ture shall pre-pare, And feed me with a Shep-herd's care·

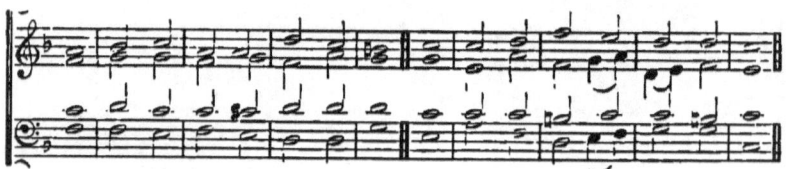

His pre-sence will my wants sup-ply, And guard me with a watch-ful eye:

My noon-day walks He will at-tend, And all our mid-night hours de-fend.

76. *Joyful.* **Solicitude.** 7.7.7.7.   J. Daniell.

Oft in sor-row, oft in woo, On-ward, Christians, on-ward go;

Fight the fight, main-tain the strife, Strengthened with the bread of life.

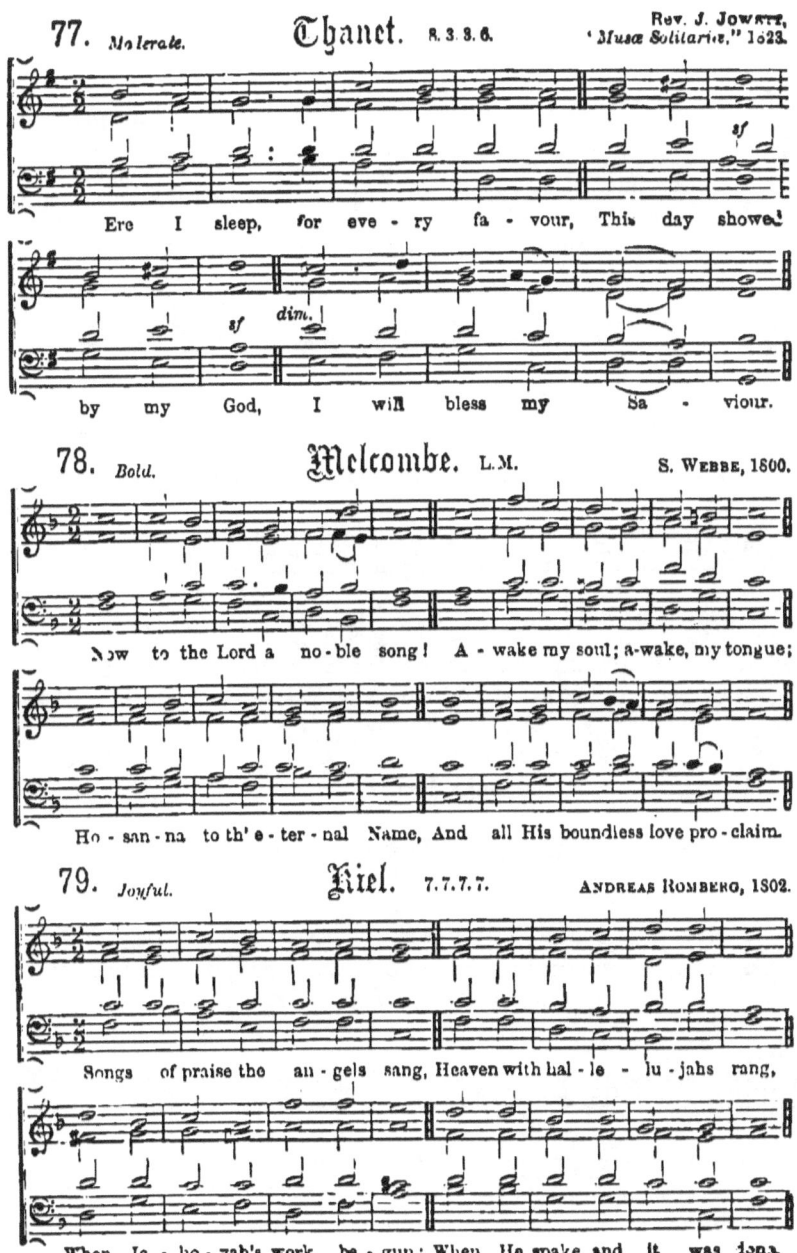

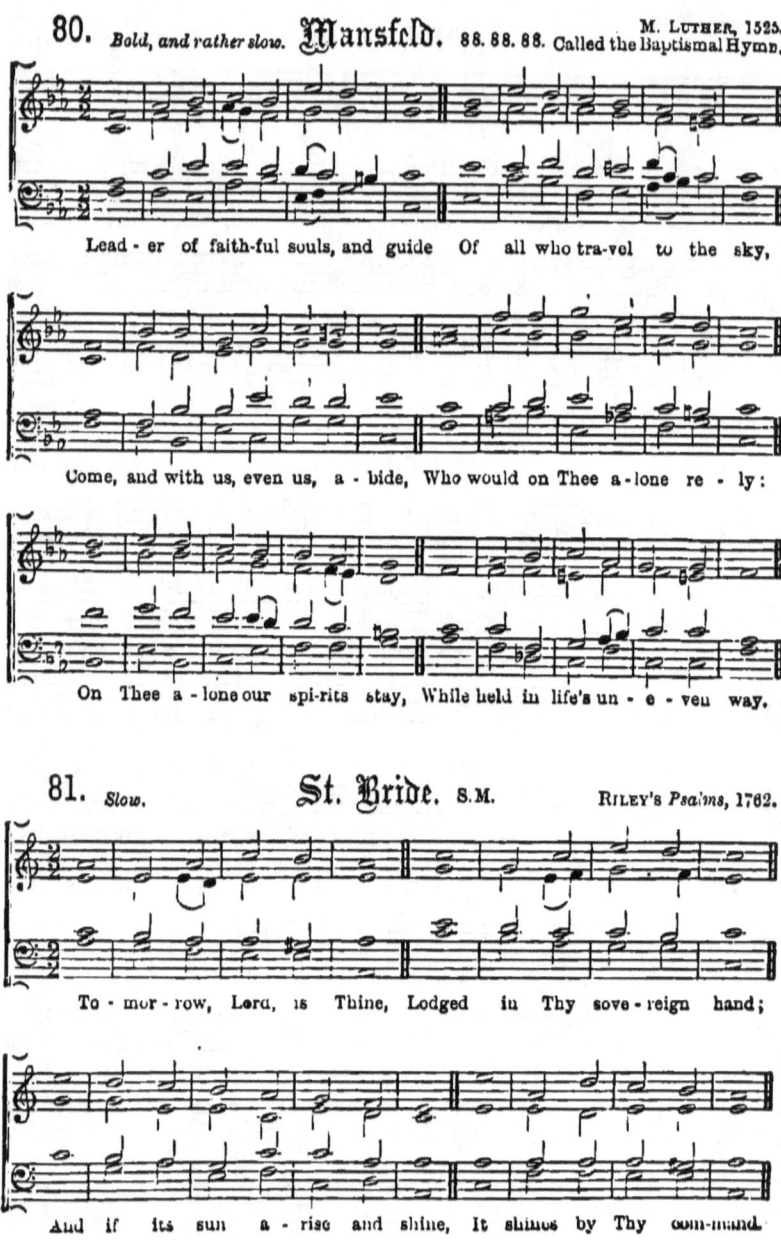

89. Wittemburg.* 6.7.6.7.6.6.6.6.—(CHORAL.)

Joyful.

JOHANN CRÜGER, 1353.

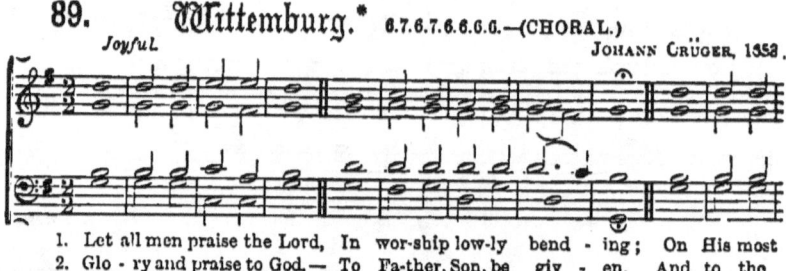

1. Let all men praise the Lord, In wor-ship low-ly bend - ing; On His most
2. Glo - ry and praise to God,— To Fa-ther, Son, be giv - en, And to the

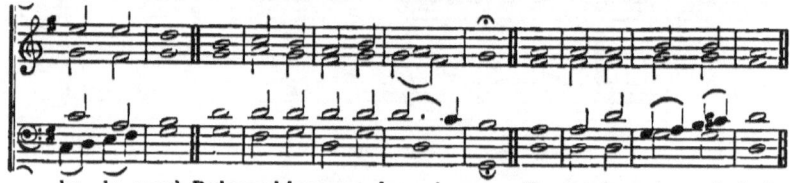

ho - ly word, Redeemed from woe, de-pend - ing. He gra-cious is, and just,
Ho - ly Ghost,— On high enthroned in Hea - ven. Praise to the Tri - une God;

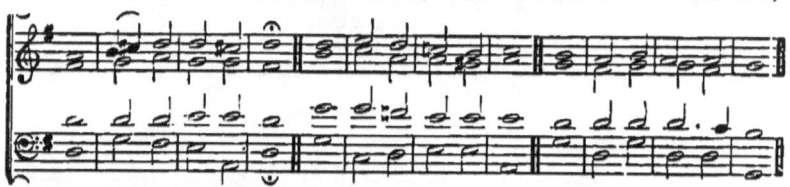

From childhood us doth lead; On Him we place our trust And hope, in time of need.
With powerful arm and strong. He changeth night to day; Praise Him with grateful song.

* The 1st verse may be sung in unison, the 2nd in harmony.

90. Kettering. 7.7.7.7.

Joyful.

DR. BOYCE.

Wel-come, wel-come! sin - ner, hear; Hang not back through shame or fear.

Doubt not, nor dis - trust the call; Mer - cy is pro-claimed to all.

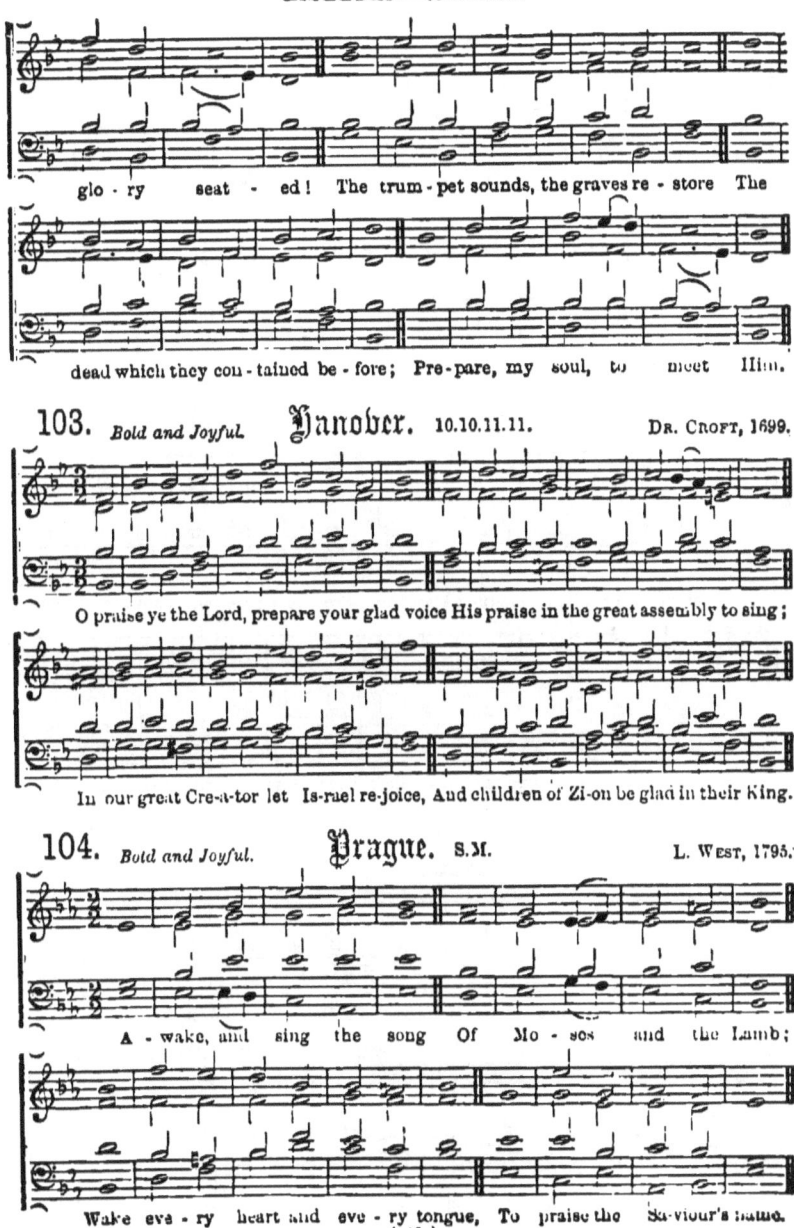

112. *Moderate.*   **Kelso.**   10.10.10.10.   Dr. Gauntlett, 1852.

A - bide with me, fast falls the e - ven - tide: The dark-ness thick - ens: Lord, with me a - bide: When o - ther help - ers fail, and com-forts flee, Help of the help - less, O a - bide with me.

113. *Moderate.*   **Sardis.**   8.7.8.7.   From Beethoven.

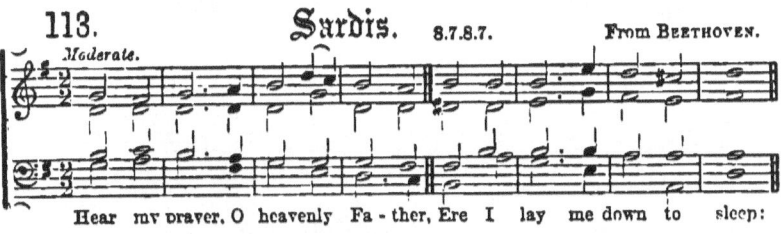

Hear my prayer, O heavenly Fa - ther, Ere I lay me down to sleep:

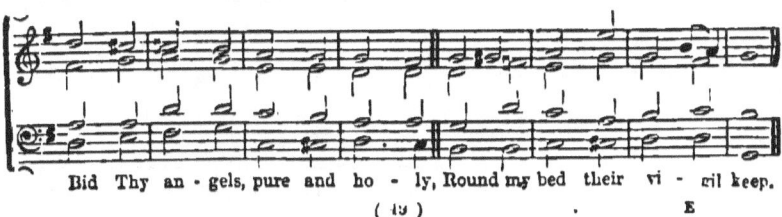

Bid Thy an - gels, pure and ho - ly, Round my bed their vi - gil keep.

116. *Slow.* **Cuthbert.** 7.7 & 7.7.7. Dr. Gauntlett, 1852.

Rock of A - ges, cleft for me, Let me hide my - self in Thee.

Let the wa - ter and the blood, From Thy riv - en side which flowed,

Be of sin the dou - ble cure,—Cleanse me from its guilt and power.

117. *Cheerful.* **Milan.** 7.7.7.7. Stabat Mater.

Day by day the man - na fell; Oh! to learn the les - son well:

Still by con - stant mer - cy fed, Give me, Lord, my dai - ly bread.

LUTZEN—*continued.*

on - ly crown! How pale art Thou with an - guish,

With sore a - buse and scorn! How does that vi - sage

lan - guish, Which once was bright as morn! . . .

120. *Moderate.*   𝔚𝔞𝔩𝔡𝔢𝔠𝔨. L.M.   RINCK.

We bless the Lord, the just, the good, Who fills our hearts with joy and food

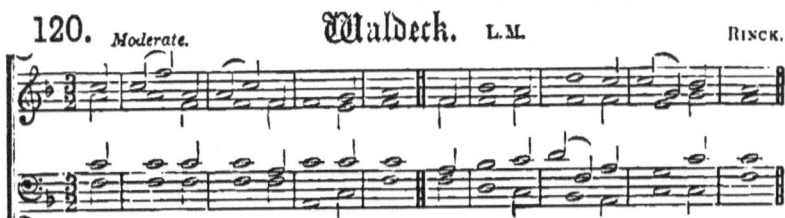

Who pours His blessings from the skies, And loads our days with rich supplies.

(53)

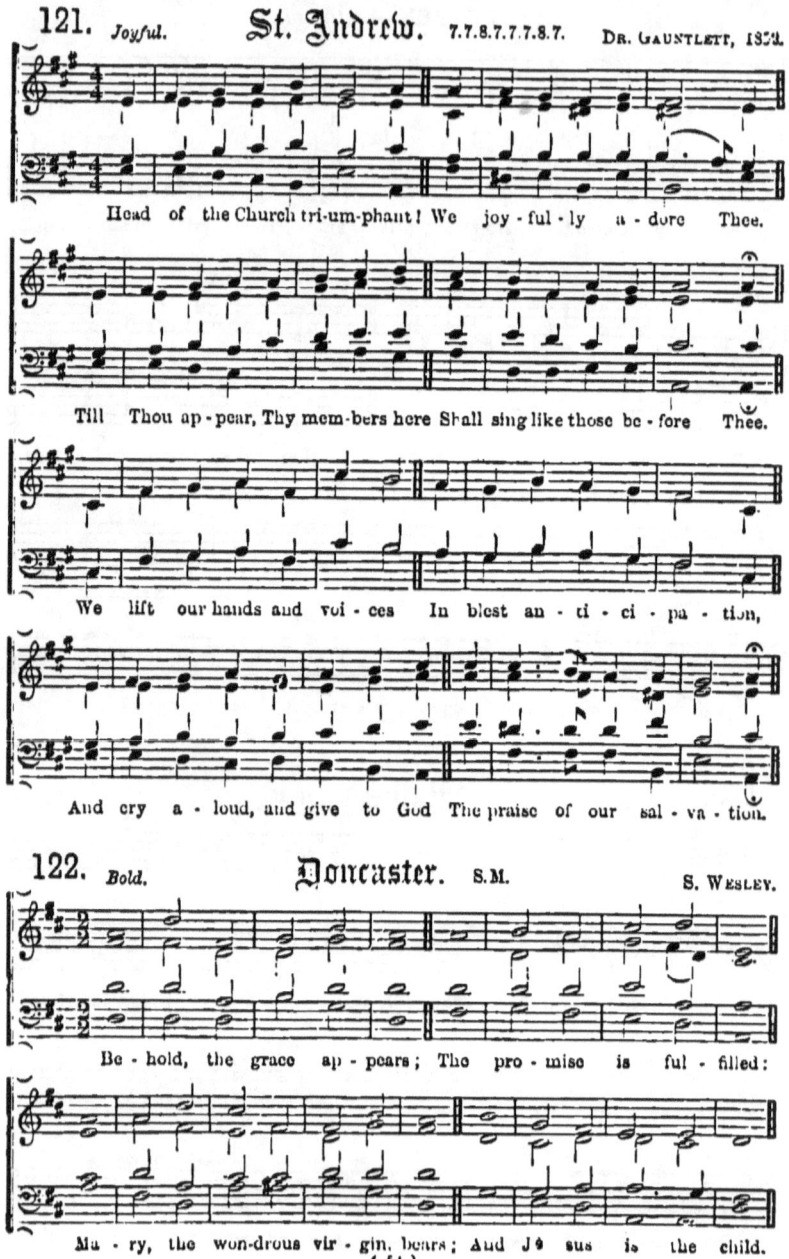

123. *Slowly.* Heber. 11.12.12.10. Dr. Gauntlett, 1858.

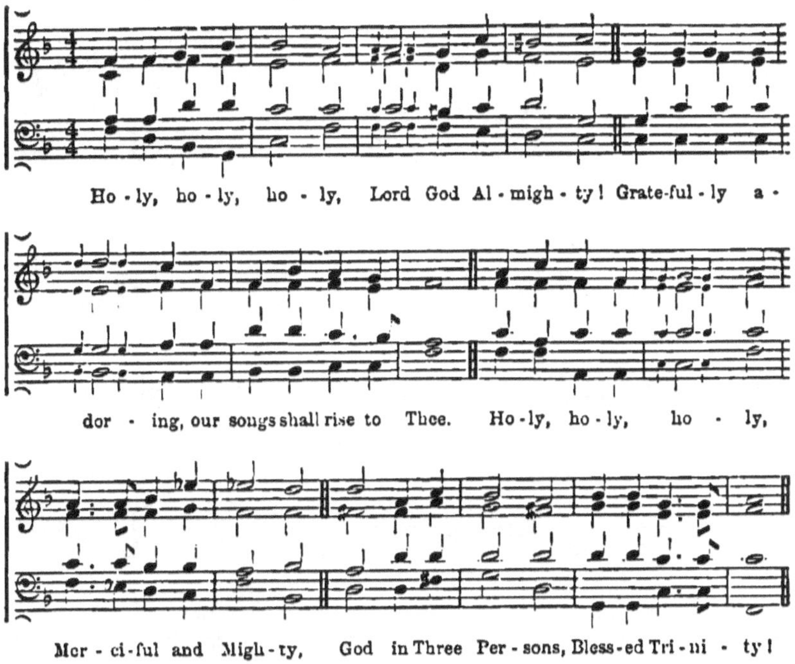

124. *Joyful.* Constance. L.M. Gothaischen Cantional, 1651.

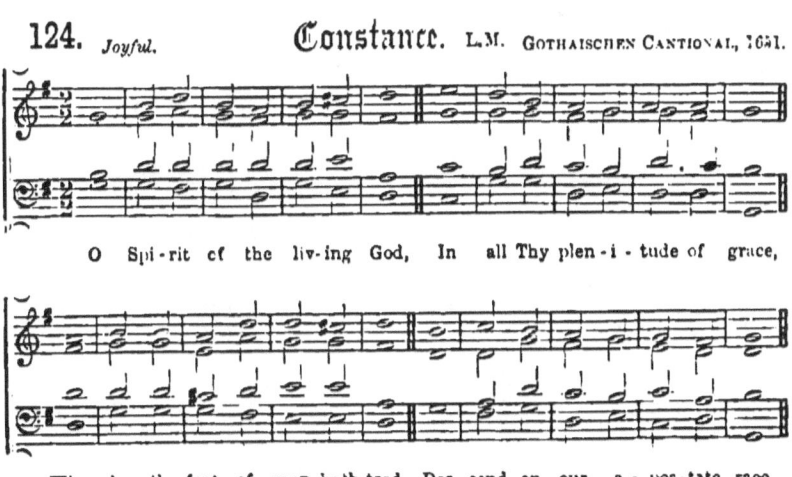

126. *Joyful.*   **Ascalon.** 66s.66s.   CRUSADER'S MELODY.

How pleased and blest was I To hear the peo - ple cry,— Come, let us

seek our God to - day! Yes, with a cheer-ful zeal We haste to

Zi - on's hill, And there our vows and ho - nours pay.

127. *Moderate.*   **Fulda.** L.M.   BEETHOVEN.

Just are Thy ways, and true Thy word, Great Rock of my se - cure a - bode;

Who is a God be-side the Lord? Or where's a re - fuge like our God?

HERMON—*continued.*

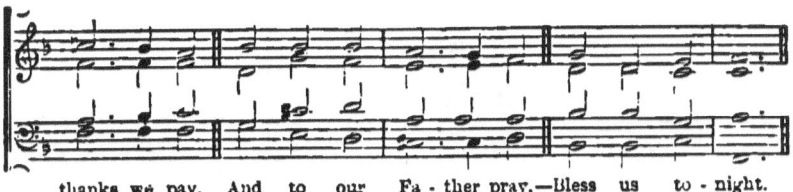

thanks we pay, And to our Fa-ther pray,—Bless us to-night.

130. *Bold.* Mecklenburg. L.M. J. S. BACH, 1736.

Je-sus shall reign wher-e'er the sun Doth his suc-ces-sive jour-neys run;

His kingdom stretch from shore to shore, Till moons shall wax and wane no more.

131. *Bold.* Eisenach. L.M. JOHANN HERMANN SCHEIN, 1628.

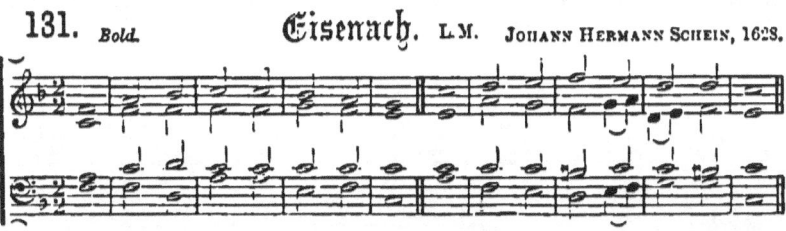

Je-sus, Thy robe of right-cous-ness My beau-ty is, my glo-rious dress;

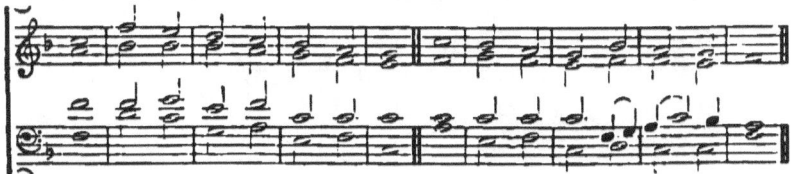

'Midst flam-ing worlds, in this ar-rayed, With joy shall I lift up my head.

134. *Moderate.*   **Sherwood.**   8s.6s.8s.6.   Dr. Gauntlett, 1856.

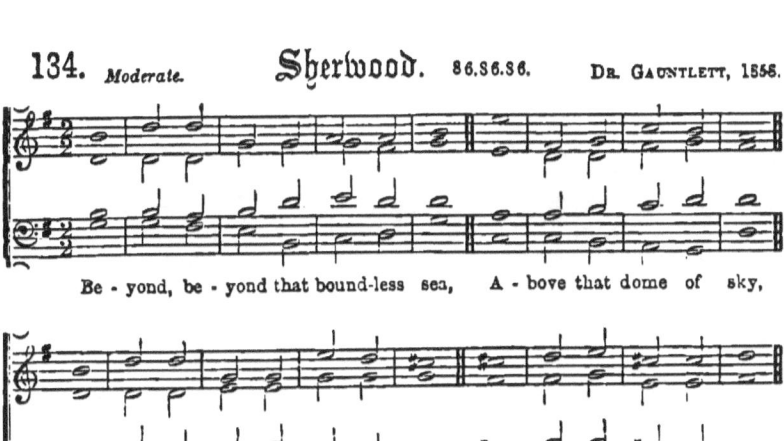

Be-yond, be-yond that bound-less sea, A-bove that dome of sky,

Far-ther than thought it-self can flee, Thy dwell-ing is on high;

Yet dear the aw-ful thought to me, That Thou, my God, art nigh.

135. *Bold.*   **St. George.**   C.M.   Nicolaus Hermann, 1560.

How con-de-scend-ing and how kind Was God's e-ter-nal Son!

Our mis-er-y reached His heavenly mind, And pi-ty brought him down.

144. **Gethsemane** 7.7.7 7.7.7.   OLD LATIN MELODY.

Plaintive.   (May also be sung in Common time.)

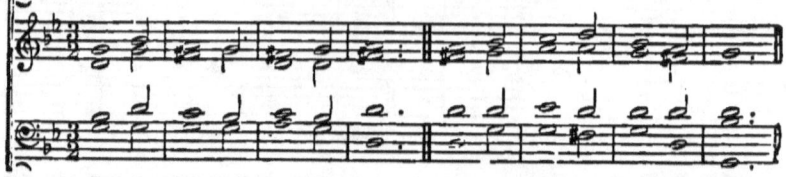

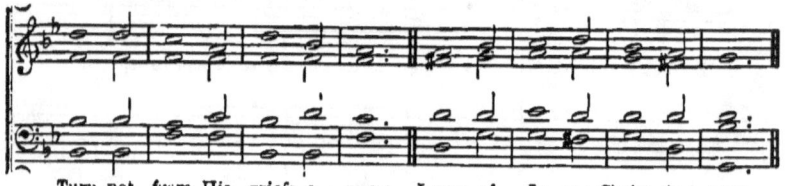

145. *Bold and fervent.*   **Wartburg.** L.M.   MARTIN LUTHER, 1543.

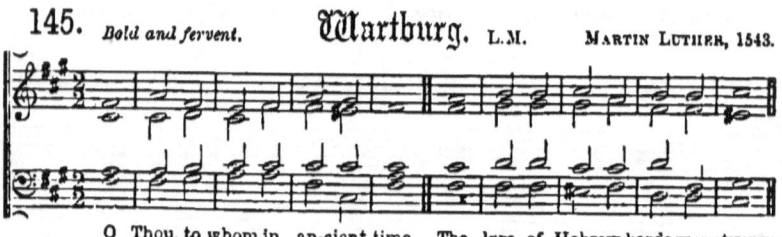
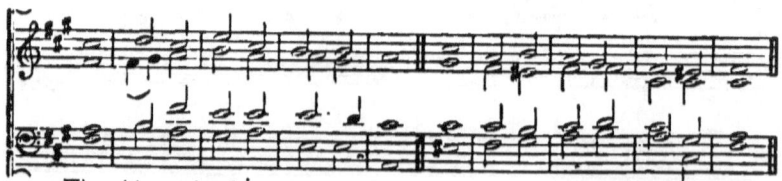

146. *Joyful.*   **Soho.** C.M.   OLD CHANT.

In God's own house pro-nounce His praise, His grace He there re - veals;

To heaven your joy and won - der raise, For there His glo - ry dwells.

147. *Slowly.*   **Moravia.** 9.8.9.8.8.8.—(CHORAL.)   CH. NEUMARK, 1657.
Or L.M. six lines, by omitting the last note in the 1st and 3rd lines.

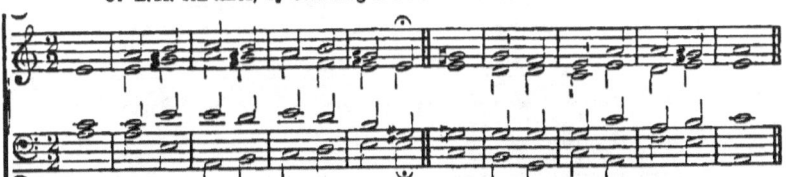

To Thee, O Lord, I yield my spi - rit, Who break'st in love this mor-tal chain;

My life I but for Thee in - he - rit, And death be-comes my chief - e-t gain.

In Thee I live, In Thee I die, Con - tent, for Thou art o - ver nigh

152. *Grave.* **Nuremberg.** 886.886. Hans Sach, 1552.

When Thou, my righteous Judge, shalt come, To fetch Thy ransomed peo - ple home,

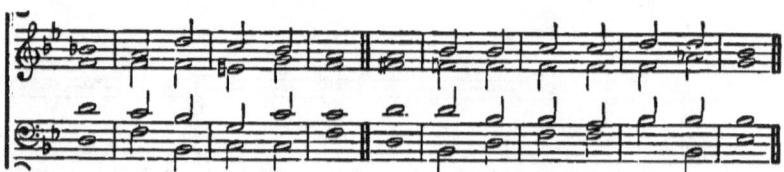

Shall I a - mong them stand? Shall such a worth-less worm as I,

Who some-times am a - fraid to die, Be found at Thy right hand?

153. *Cheerful.* **Meaux Abbey.** C.M. Johann Cruger, 1658.

Come, let us join our cheer-ful songs With an - gels round the throne;

Ten thou-sand thou-sand are their tongues, But all their joys are one.

RISTON—*continued.*

Je-sus, Thou art all com-pas-sion; Pure, un-bound-ed love Thou art:

Vi-sit us with Thy sal-va-tion: En-ter eve-ry long-ing heart.

165. *Cheerful.* 𝕸𝖚𝖓𝖎𝖈𝖍. 7.6.7.6.7.6.7.6. GOTHAISCHEN CANTIONAL, 1715

To thee, O dear, dear coun-try, Mine eyes their vi-gils keep;

For ve-ry love, be-hold-ing Thy hap-py name, they weep.

The men-tion of thy glo-ry Is unc-tion to the breast,

And me-di-cine in sick-ness, And love and life and rest.

(75)

179. *Plaintive.* **Ludlow.** S.M. Ravenscroft's *Whole Booke of Psalms*, 1621.

How swift the tor - rent rolls That bears us to the sea,
The tide that bears our death-less souls To vast e - ter - ni - ty!

180. *Moderate.* **Dresden.** (CHORAL.) 5.5.5.5.10.11.11.10. J. G Ebeling, 1666. Words from Mercer's Psalter.

Evening and morn-ing, Sun - set and dawn-ing, Wealth, peace, and glad - ness,
Com - fort in sad - ness, These are Thy works; all the glo - ry be Thine.
Times without num - ber, A - wake or in slum - ber, Thine eye ob - serves us, From
dan - ger pre - serves us, Caus - ing Thy mer - cy up - on us to shine.

Father, O hear me! Pardon and spare me!
Quench all my terrors, Blot out my errors,
That by Thine eyes they may no more be scanned.
Order my goings, direct all my doings,
As it may please Thee, retain or release me,
All I commit to Thy Fatherly hand

Griefs of God's sending, All have an ending;
Clouds may be pouring, Wind and wave roaring,
Sunshine will come when the tempest has passed.
Joys still increasing, and peace never ceasing,
Faith lost in vision, and hope in fruition;
These are the joys which I look for at last.

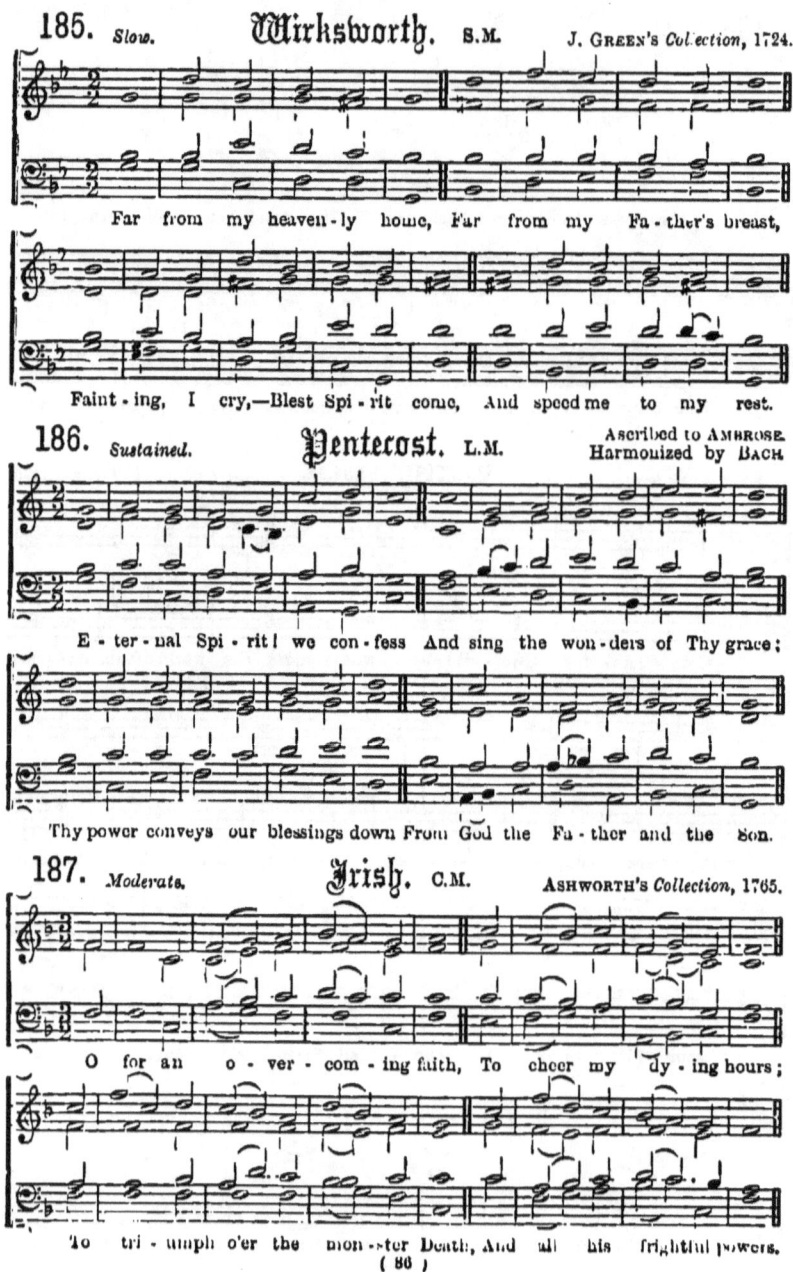

188. Joyful. Glasgow. C.M. — ANDRO HART'S PSALTER, 1615.

Thrice hap-py souls, who born from heaven, While yet they so-journ here,

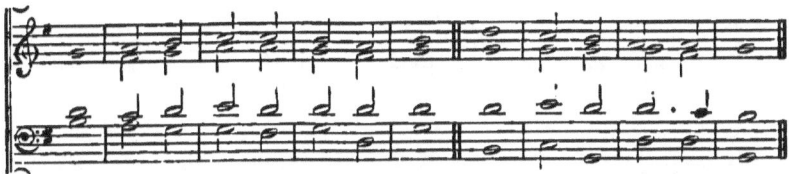

Thus all their days with God be-gin, And spend them in His fear.

189. Moderate. Lubeck. 8.8.8.8.8.8. — LUTHER, 1537. Harmonized by MENDELSSOHN.

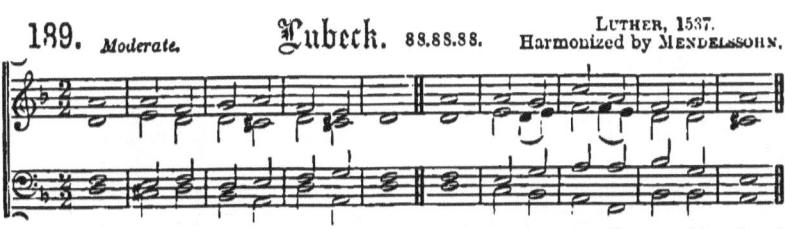

Lo! God is here; let us a-dore, And own how dreadful is this place!

Let all with-in us feel His power, And si-lent, bow be-fore His face;

Who know His power, His grace who prove, Serve Him with awe, with reverence love.

190. *Moderate.* **Manchester.** C.M.   Dr. Wainwright, d. 1782.

How sad our state by na-ture is Our sin, how deep it stains!
And sa-tan binds our cap-tive souls Fast in his slav-ish chains.

191. *Calm and slow.* **Gotha.** 7.7.7.7.7.7.   German Choral.

Son of God, to Thee I cry; By the ho-ly mys-te-ry
Of Thy dwell-ing here on earth, By Thy pure and ho-ly birth,
Lord, Thy pre-sence let me see. Man-i-fest Thy-self to me.

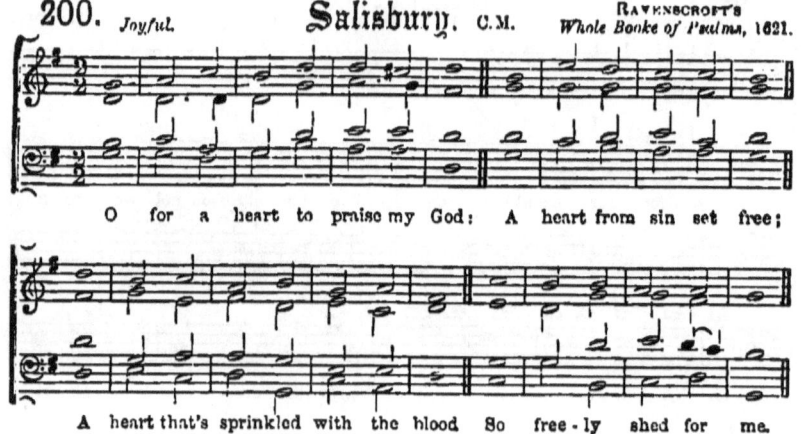

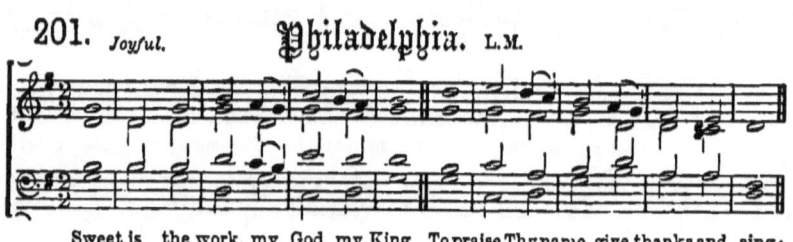

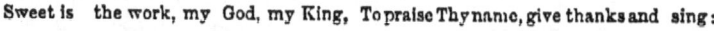

207. Moderate. **Boston.** L.M. Italian Melody, adapted by Dr. Lowell Mason.

Up to the Lord, that reigns on high, And views the nations from a - far.

Let e-ver-last-ing prais-es fly, And tell how large His boun-ties are.

208. Moderate. **Palestrina.** 8S.8S.8S. PALESTRINA.

Je-sus, Thy boundless love to me No thought can reach, no tongue de-clare;

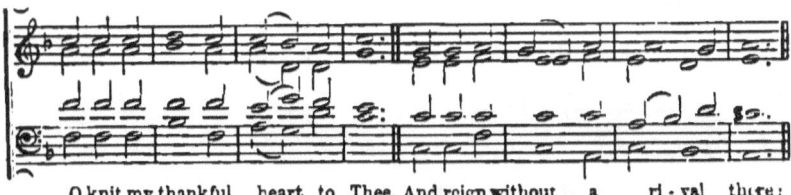

O knit my thankful heart to Thee, And reign without a ri-val there:

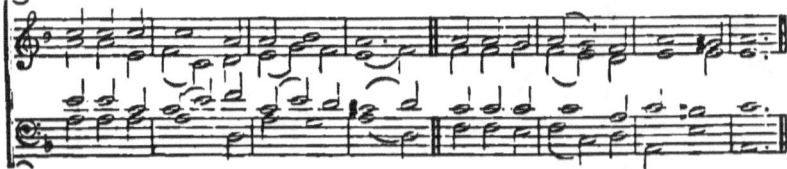

Thine wholly, Thine a - lone, I am: Lord, with Thy love my heart in - flame.

209. *Moderate*   **Dusseldorf.** 7.7.7.5.   JOHANN CRÜGER, 1656.

God of pi-ty, God of grace, When we hum-bly seek Thy face,

Bend from heaven, Thy dwell-ing place: Hear, for-give, and save.

210. *Joyful*   **Lucerne.** 888.888.   *Strasburg Gesangbuch,* 1525.

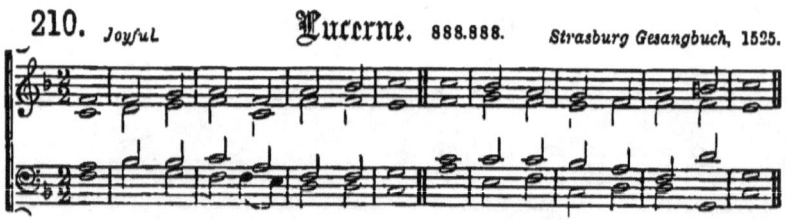

I'll praise my Ma-ker with my breath, And when my voice is lost in death,

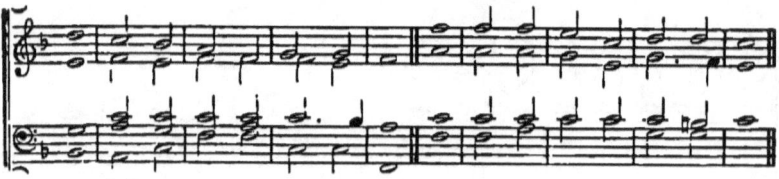

Praise shall em-ploy my no-bler powers: My days of praise shall ne'er be past,

While life and thought and be-ing last, Or im-mor-tal-i-ty en-dures.

211. *Moderate.*   **Bexley.** C.M.   From *Sacred Harmony*, 1760.

The mer-cies of my God and King My tongue shall still pur-sue;

O hap-py they who, while they sing Those mer-cies, share them too.

212. *Moderate.*   **Burnham.** 6.6.6.6.8.8.   Dr. Croft, d. 1727.

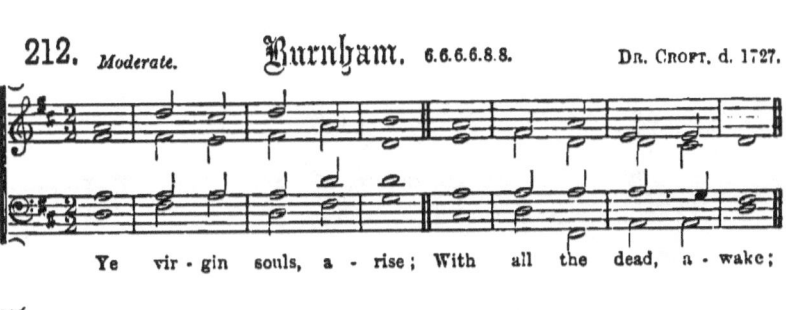

Ye vir-gin souls, a-rise; With all the dead, a-wake;

Un-to sal-va-tion wise, Oil in your ves-sels take:

Up-start-ing at the midnight cry, Be-hold the heavenly Bridegroom nigh.

213. *Bold.* **Holywell.** L.M.   GLUCK.

With all my powers of heart and tongue, I'll praise my Ma-ker in my song;

An-gels shall hear the notes I raise, Ap-prove the song, and join the praise.

214. *Grave.* **Lutterworth.** 8.7.8.7.4.7.   ANCIENT MELODY. (*Stabat Mater,* or *Dies Iræ.*)

Lo! He comes with clouds de-scend-ing, Once for favoured sin-ners slain;

Thousand thousand saints at-tend-ing, Swell the tri-umph of His train:

Hal-le-lu-jah! Hal-le-lu-jah! Je-sus comes, and comes to reign.

221. *Bold.* **Pyrton.** L.M.

Away from eve-ry mor-tal care, Away from earth our souls re-treat;
We leave this worthless world a-far, And wait and wor-ship near Thy seat.

222. *Moderate.* **Shiloh.** 7.6.7.6.7.6.7.6. S. SALVATORI.

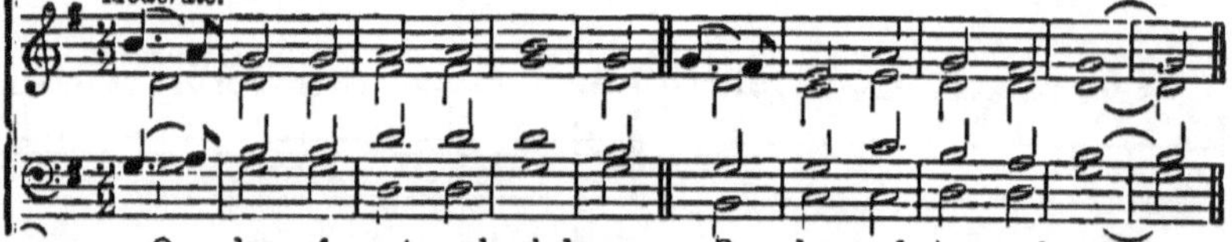

O day of rest and glad-ness, O day of joy and light,
O balm of care and sad-ness, Most beau-ti-ful, most bright! 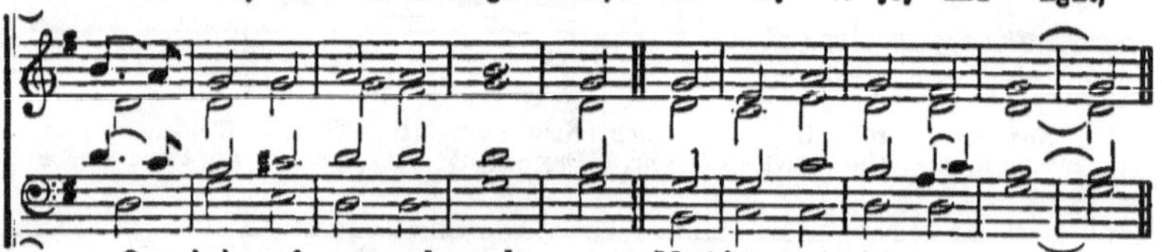
Thou art a cool-ing foun-tain In life's dry, drea-ry sand; 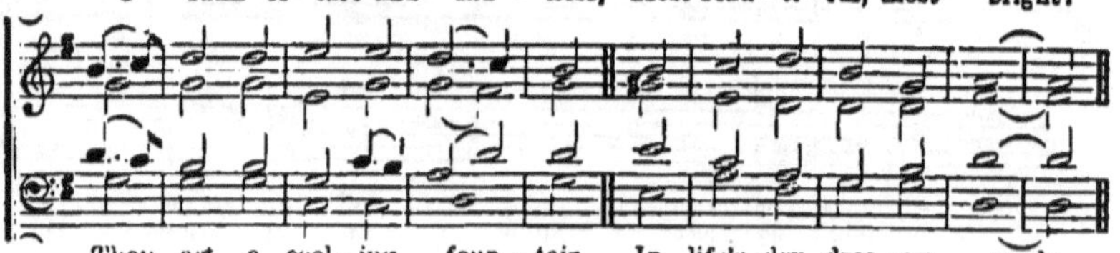
From thee, like Pis-gah's moun-tain, We view our pro-mised land. 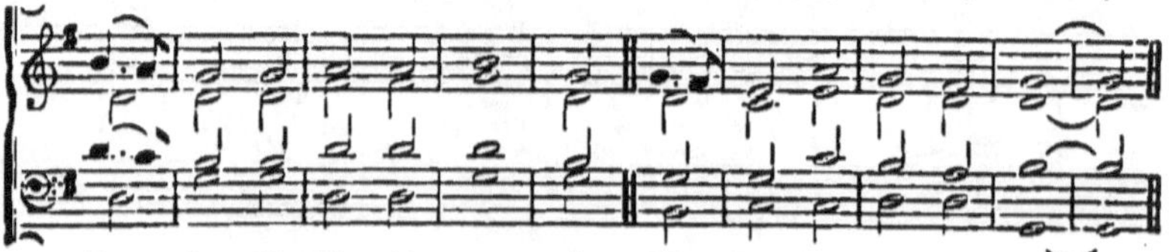

(102)

MULHAUSEN—continued.

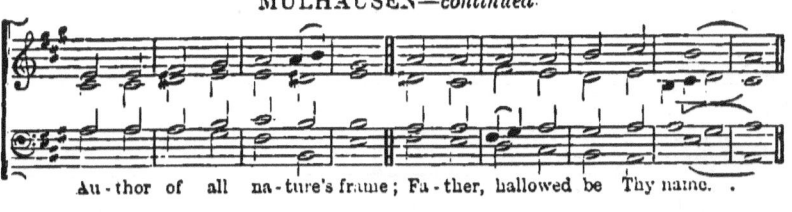

Au-thor of all na-ture's frame; Fa-ther, hallowed be Thy name.

228. *Moderate.* Norland. S.M.

Who in the Lord con-fide, And feel His sprin-kled blood,

In storms and hur-ri-canes a-bide Firm as the mount of God.

229. *Moderate.* Zurich. 888.888. SWISS MELODY.

Let all the earth their voi-ces raise, To sing the choi-cest psalm of praise,

To sing and bless Je-ho-vah's name: His glo-ry let the hea-then know,

His won-ders to the na-tions show, And all His sav-ing works proclaim.

230. *Slow.*   **Tirzah.** S.M.   HENRI PURCELL.

It is Thy hand, my God, My sor-row comes from Thee:

I bow be-neath Thy chasten-ing rod, 'Tis love that bruis-es me

231 *Moderate.*   **Oxford.** 6.6.6.6. (Trochaic.)   J. B. KÖNIG, 1738.

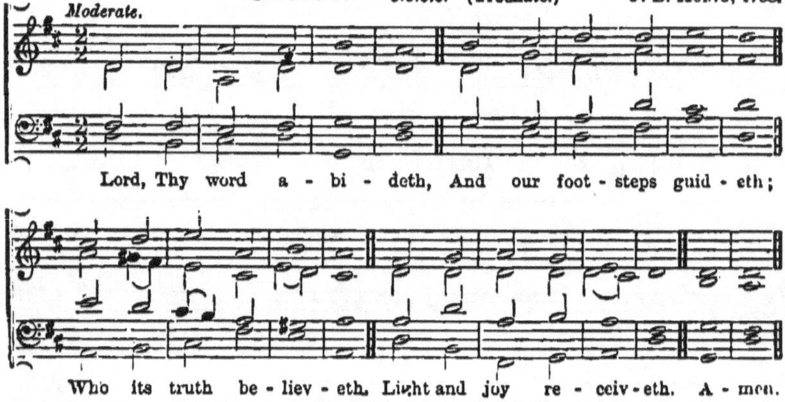

Lord, Thy word a-bi-deth, And our foot-steps guid-eth;

Who its truth be-liev-eth, Light and joy re-ceiv-eth. A-men.

232. *Moderate.*   **Elberfeldt.** 8.7.8.7.8.7.8.7.   JOHANN CRÜGER, 1649.
(An adaptation of this melody will be found in No. 178.)

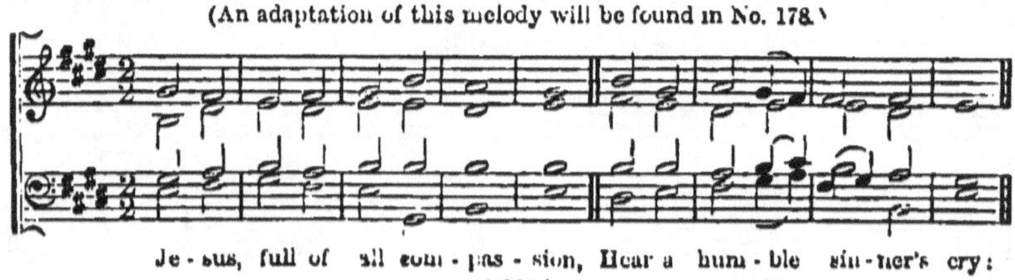

Je-sus, full of all com-pas-sion, Hear a hum-ble sin-ner's cry;

ELBERFELDT—*continued.*

Let me see Thy great sal-va-tion, Or in dark de-spair I die.

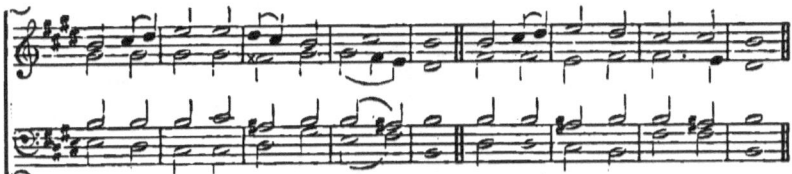
Guil-ty, but with heart re-lent-ing, O-ver-whelmed with helpless grief;

Pros-trate at Thy feet re-pent-ing, Send, O send me quick re-lief.

233. *Joyful.* Abbey. C.M. ANDRO HART'S PSALTER, 1615.

Spi-rit Di-vine, at-tend our prayers, And make this house Thy home;

De-scend with all Thy gra-cious powers, O come, great Spi-rit, come!

(107)

HOLSTEIN—continued.

'Mid raging storms exults to find An everlasting rest.

236. *Joyful.* Warrington. L.M. Rev. R. Harrison, d. 1810.

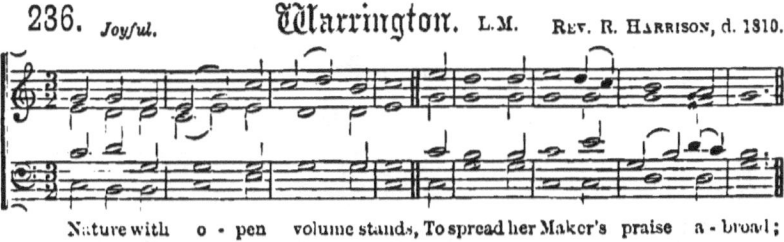

Nature with open volume stands, To spread her Maker's praise abroad;

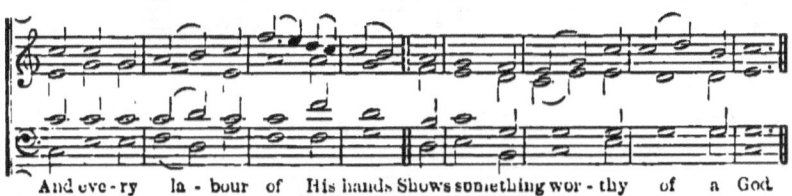

And every labour of His hands Shows something worthy of a God.

237. *Slow.* Holyrood. 7.7.7.7. Romberg.

Father of eternal grace, Glorify Thyself in me;

Meekly beaming in my face May the world Thine image see.

244. *Bold.* **Danube.** 88.88.88. MENDELSSOHN.

We sing His love, who once was slain, Who soon o'er death re-vived a-gain,

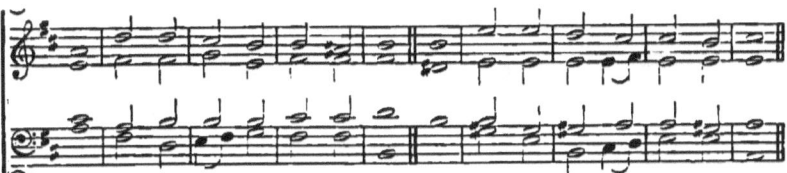

That all His saints through Him might have E-ter-nal con-quest o'er the grave.

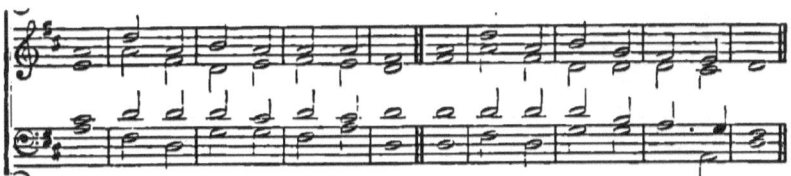

Soon shall the trum-pet sound, and we Shall rise to im-mor-tal-i-ty.

245. *Bold.* **St. Paul.** L.M. C. F. LAMPE, c. 1745.

Je-sus, Thou e-ver-last-ing King, Ac-cept the tri-bute which we bring;

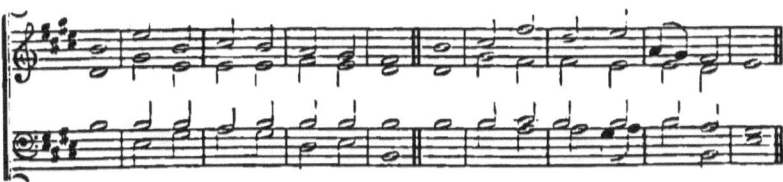

Ac-cept the well-deserved re-nown, And wear our prais-es as Thy crown

246. *Moderate.* **Houghton.** 10.10.11.11. DR. GAUNTLETT, 1860.

247. *Cheerful.* **Colchester.** C.M. PLAYFORD.

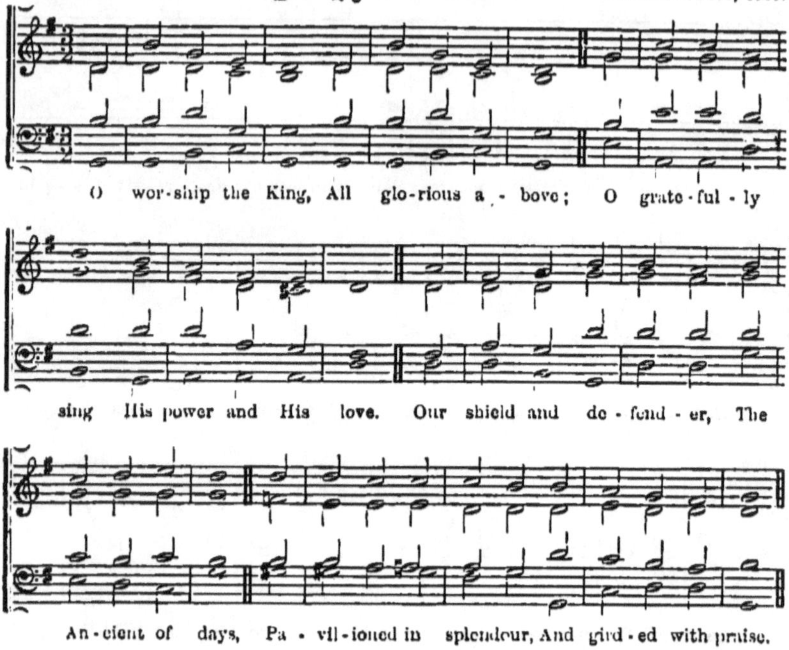

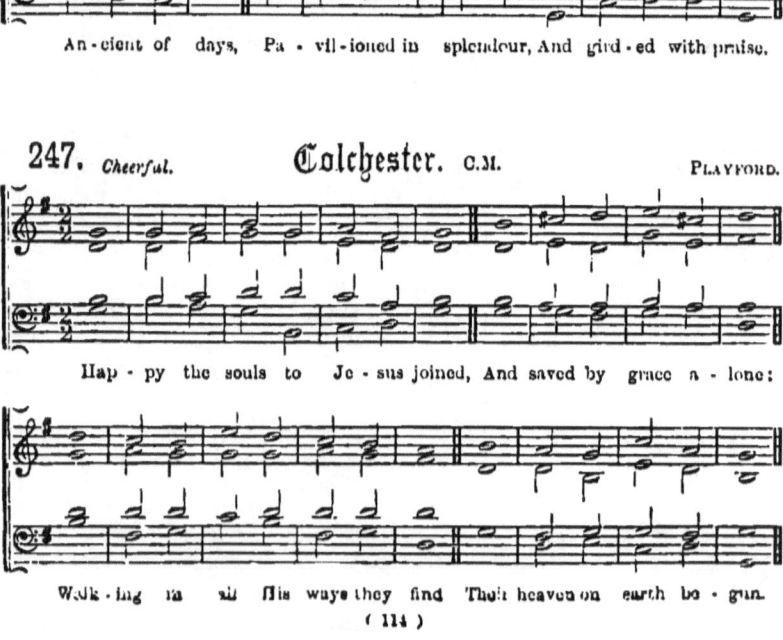

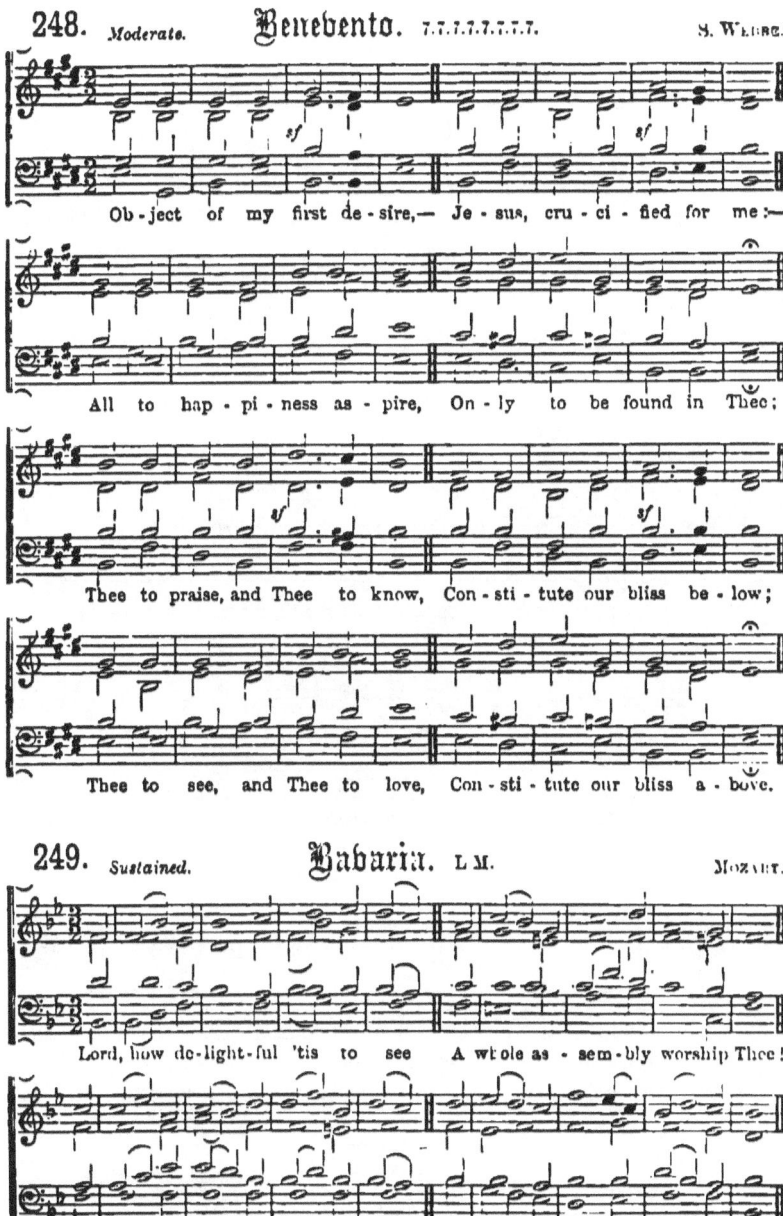

253. *Cheerful* Ghent. 66.66.88.

A-wake, ye saints, a-wake! And hail this sa-cred day:
In loft-iest songs of praise Your joy-ful ho-mage pay:
Come, bless the day that God hath blest, The type of heaven's e-ter-nal rest.

254. *Moderate.* Wiltshire. C.M.   Sir George Smart, d. 1867.

My God, the spring of all my joys, The life of my de-lights,
The glo-ry of my bright-est days, And com-fort of my nights.

(117)

INCARNATION—continued.

Al - migh-ty Son! In - car - nate Word! Our Pro-phet, Priest, Re -
deem - er, Lord, Be - fore Thy throne we sin - ners bend; To
us Thy sa - ving grace ex - tend, To us Thy sa - ving grace ex - tend.

258. *Moderate.* Lambeth. 13.11.13.12. (Irregular.) Dr. Gauntlett, 1860.

Thou art gone to the grave! but we will not de-plore thee, Though sorrows and
darkness en - com - pass the tomb; The Saviour has passed through its por-tal be-
fore thee, And the lamp of His love is thy guide through the gloom.

259. *Moderate.* Westminster. C.M. Dr. Nares, d. 1783.

How sweet the name of Je - sus sounds In a be - liev - er's ear!

It soothes his sor - rows, heals his wounds, And drives a - way his fear.

260. *Moderate.* Asaph. 8.7.8.7.7.7., or 8.7.4. Henry Purcell.

Come to Cal-vary's ho - ly mountain, Sin - ners, ru - ined by the fall;

Here a pure and heal-ing foun-tain Flows to you, to me, to all,

In a full, per - pet - ual tide. Open - ed when our Sa - viour died.

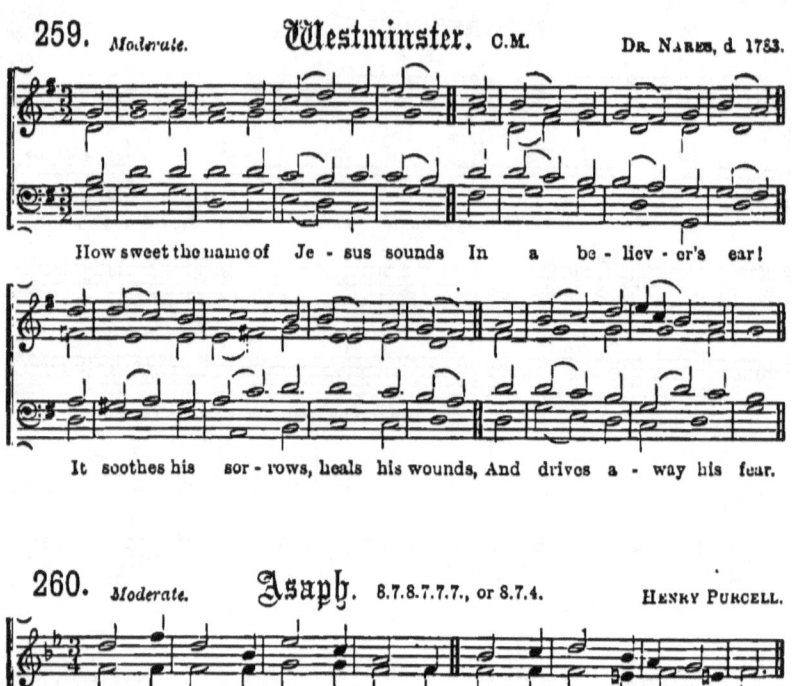

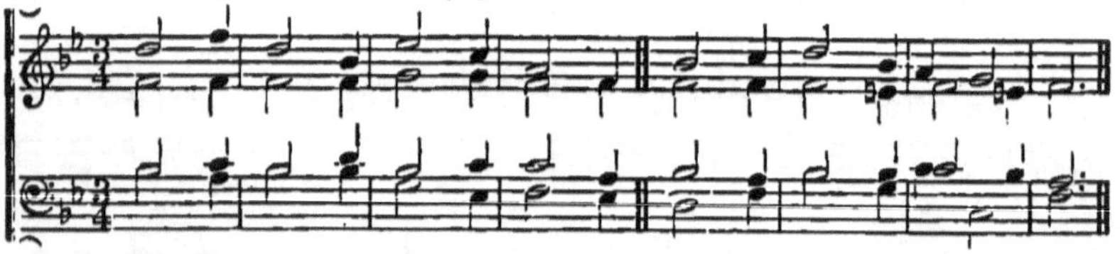

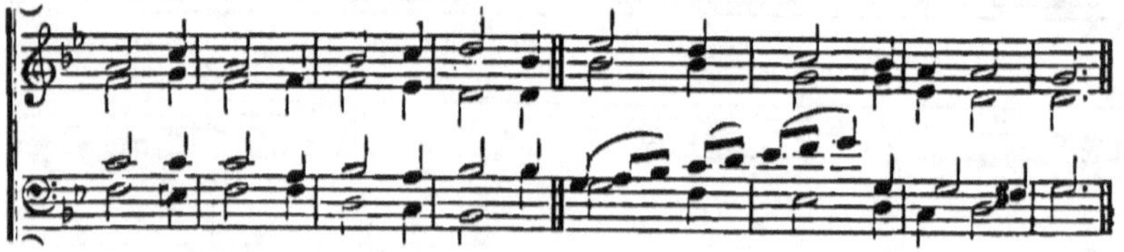

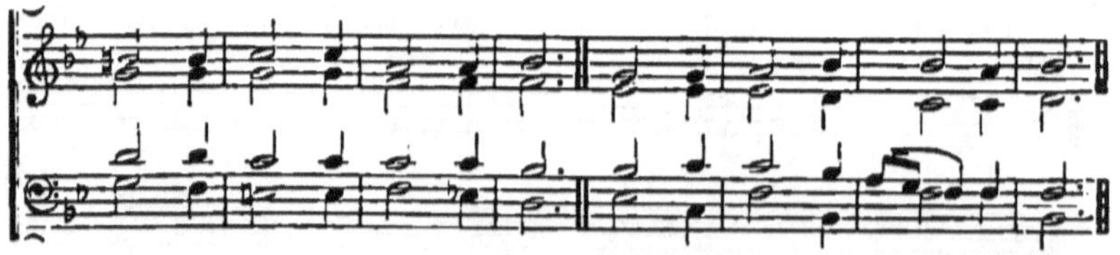

263. *Moderate.* **Brunswick.** C.M.   From HANDEL.

What shall I ren-der to my God For all His kind-ness shown?

My feet shall vi-sit Thine a-bode, My songs ad-dress Thy throne.

264. **Waltham,** or **Braylesford.** 8.7.8.7.8.7.   Dr. GAUNTLETT.
Moderate.

Lead us, Heavenly Fa-ther, lead us O'er the world's tempestuous sea; Guard us,

guide us, keep us, feed us, For we have no help but Thee; Yet pos-

-sess-ing ev-'ry bless-ing, If our God our Fa-ther be. A-men.

265. *Cheerful.* Magdalen College. L.M.
DR. BENJ. ROGERS, 1695.
(His original parts.)

My God, my King, Thy va - rious praise Shall fill the remnant of my days;

Thy grace employ my hum - ble tongue Till death and glo - ry raise the song.

266. *Moderate.* Kedron. 886.886.
HANDEL, c. 1742.

O Lord, how hap-py should we be, If we could cast our care on Thee,

If we from self could rest; And feel at heart that One a - bove,

In per - fect wis - dom, per - fect love, Is work - ing for the best.

267. *Bold.*   **Carmel.**   L.M.   J. Bishop, 1700. (His original parts.)

My God, per-mit me not to be A stran-ger to my-self and Thee

A-midst a thou-sand thoughts I rove, For-get-ful of my high-est love.

268. *Joyful.*   **Hereford.**   886.886.   Dr. W. Boyce, 1745.

Come on, my part-ners in dis-tress, Ye pilgrims through the wil-der-ness

Who still your sor-rows feel; A-while for-get your griefs and fears,

And look be-yond this vale of tears, To that ce-les-tial hill.

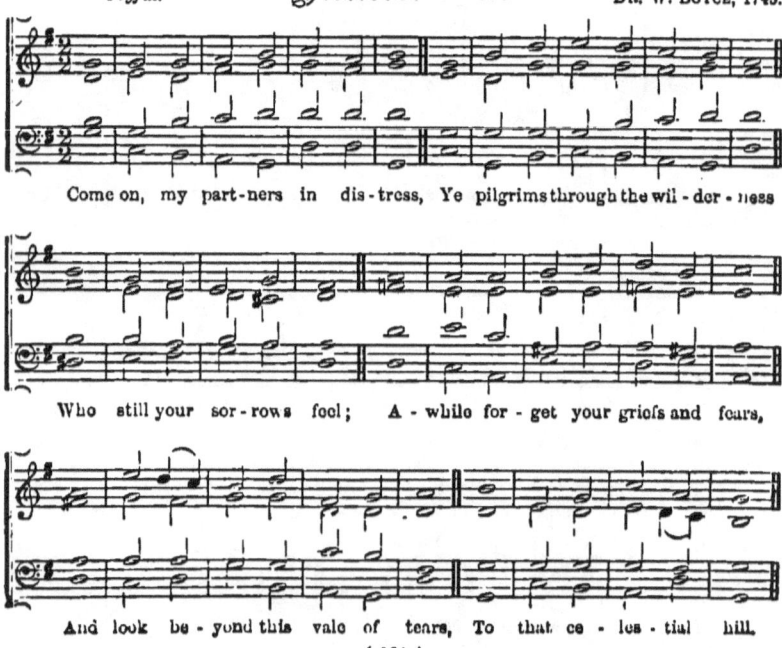

269. *Calmly.* **Leeds.** 888.6. Dr. Lowell Mason.

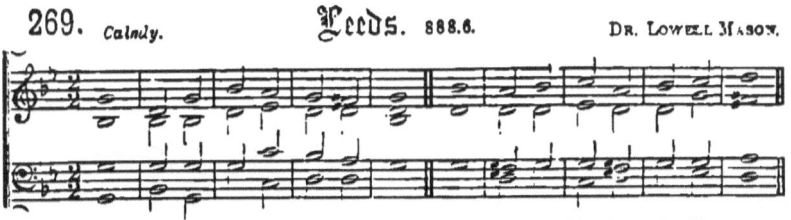

Just as I am—without one plea, But that Thy blood was shed for me,

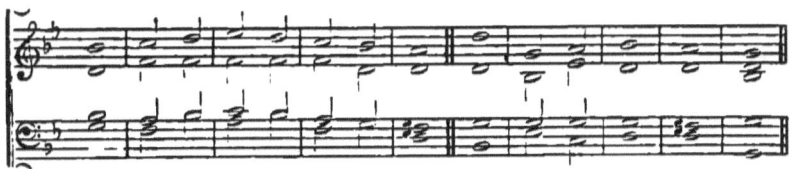

And that Thou bidst me come to Thee, O Lamb of God, I come.

270. *Slowly.* **Vesper.** S.7.8:7.4 7. Sir J. Stevenson.

Hark! the voice of love and mer-cy Sounds a-loud from Cal-va-ry;

See, it rends the rocks a-sun-der, Shakes the earth and veils the sky:

It is finished! It is fin-ished! Hear the dy-ing Sa-viour cry.

271. *Moderate.* Canterbury. S.M. From Ravenscroft, 1621.

272. *Moderate.* Lebanon. 86.86.88. Dr. Louis Spohr.

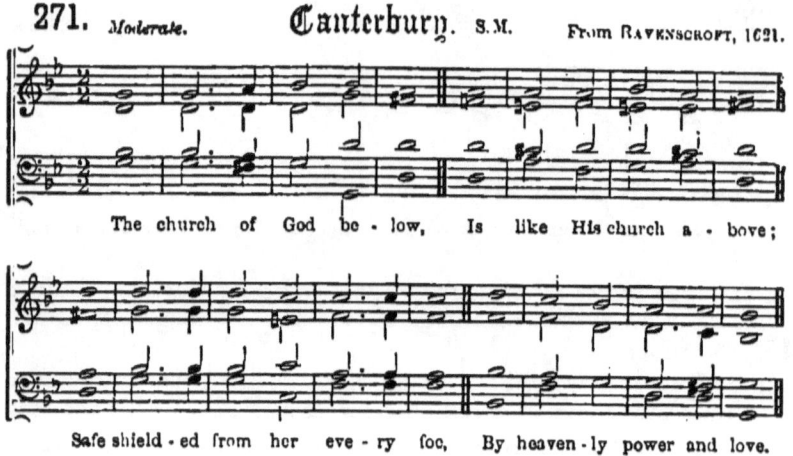

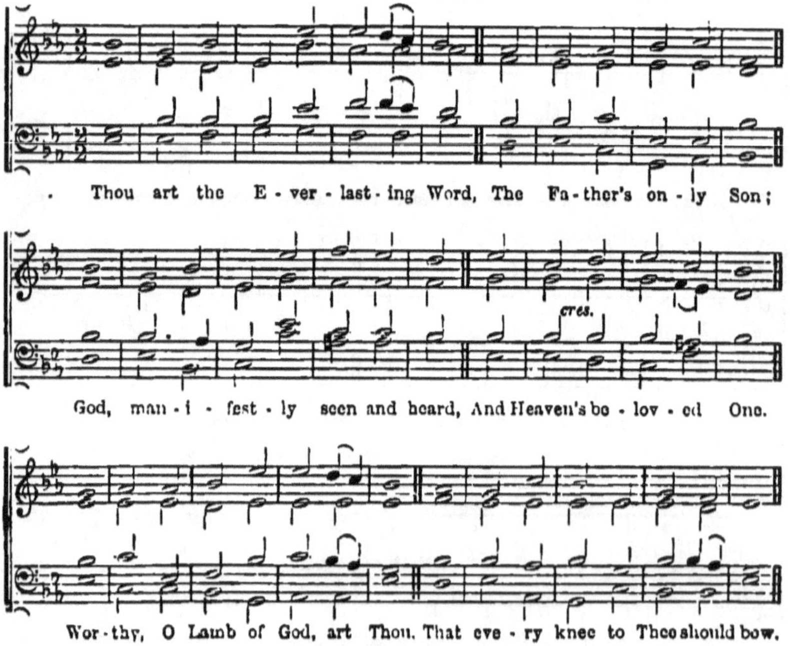

275. *Sustained.*   **Alsace.** L.M.   BEETHOVEN.

How shall I fol - low Him I serve? How shall I co - py Him I love?
Nor from those blessed foot-steps swerve, Which lead me to His seat a - bove?

276. *Slow.*   **Morrah.** 5.5.11.5.5.11.   DR. GAUNTLETT, 1860.

All ye that pass by, To Je - sus draw nigh; To you is it
nothing your Sa - viour should die? Your ran - som and peace, Your 
sure - ty He is? Come, see if there e - ver was sor - row like His.

277. *Moderate.* Litany. 777.6., or 7.7.7.7. John Hatton.

278. *Slow.* Beverley. 87.87.88. From Pergolesi's *Stabat Mater.*

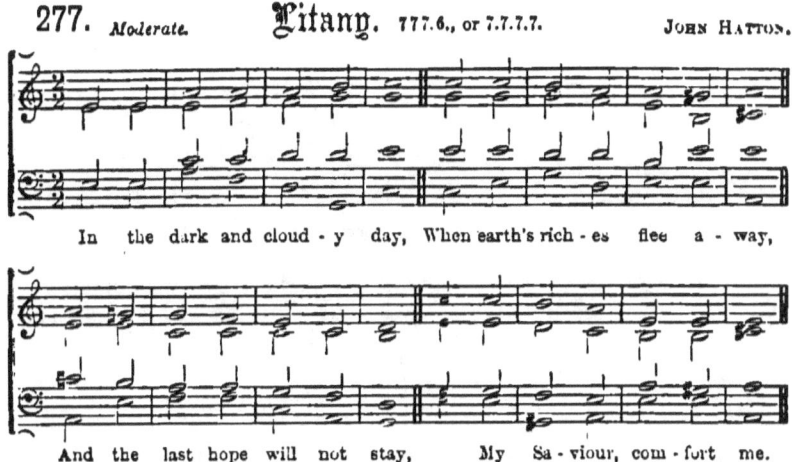

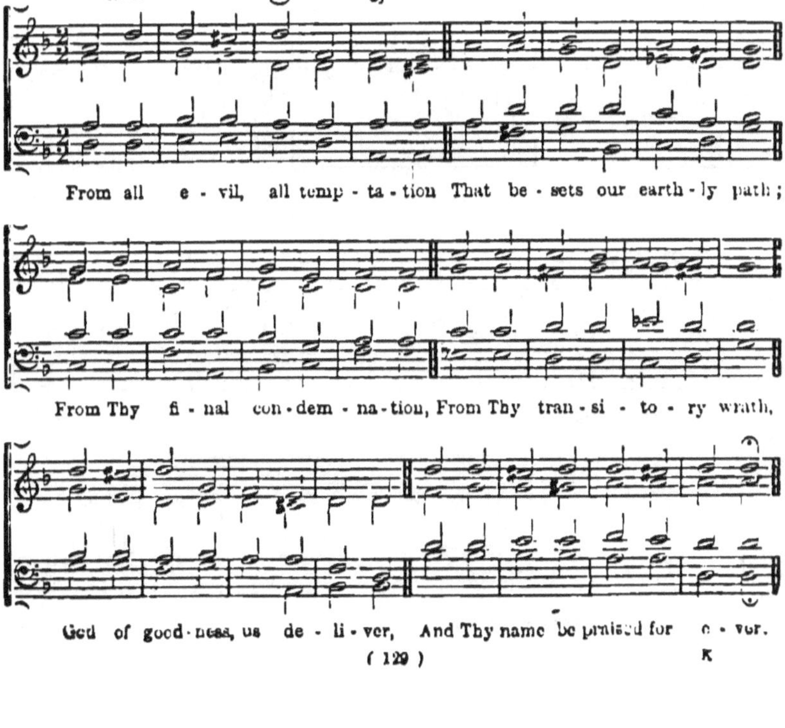

 K

279. Moderate. **Philippi.** C.M. (By permission, from the *Psalmist.*) S. WESLEY.

A - wake, my soul, stretch eve - ry nerve, And press with vi - gour on:

A heaven - ly race de - mands thy zeal, And an im - mor - tal crown.

280. Joyful. **Caernarvon.** 66.66.88. HANDEL, c. 1742.

Give thanks to God most high, The u - ni - ver - sal Lord,

The sove - reign King of kings; And be His grace a - dored.

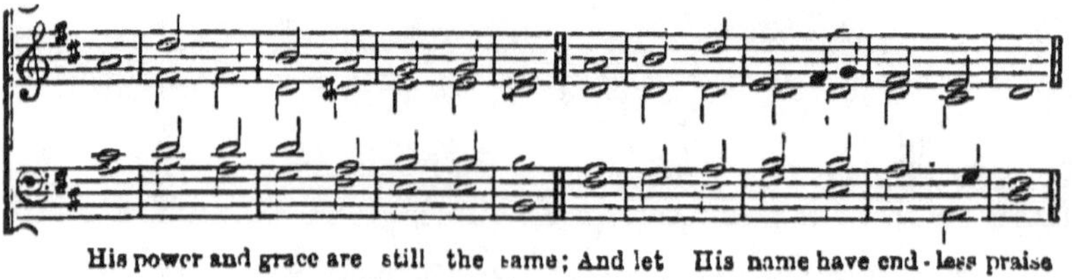

His power and grace are still the same; And let His name have end - less praise

287. *Moderate.* **Cannons.** L.M. HANDEL, c. 1742.

Ho! eve - ry one that thirsts, draw nigh; Thus God in - vites the fall - en race;

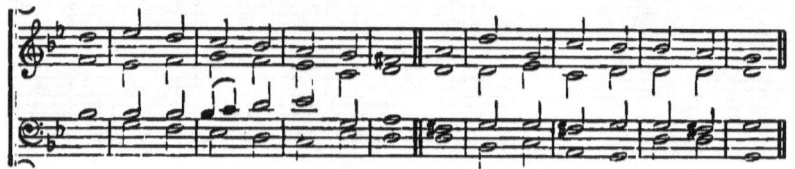

Mer - cy and free sal - va - tion buy,—Buy wine and milk and Gos - pel grace.

288. *Moderate.* **Coverdale.** 888.888. JOHANN WALTER'S *Gesangbuch*, 1525.

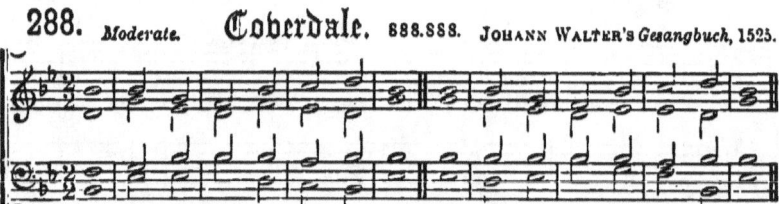

With grate - ful hearts, with joy - ful tongues, To God we raise u - ni - ted songs;

His power and mer - cy we proclaim. Through eve - ry age may Bri - tons own,

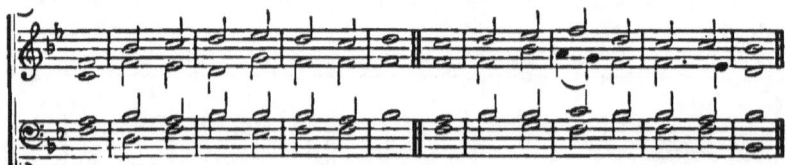

Je - ho - vah here has fixed His throne, And tri - umph in His migh - ty name.

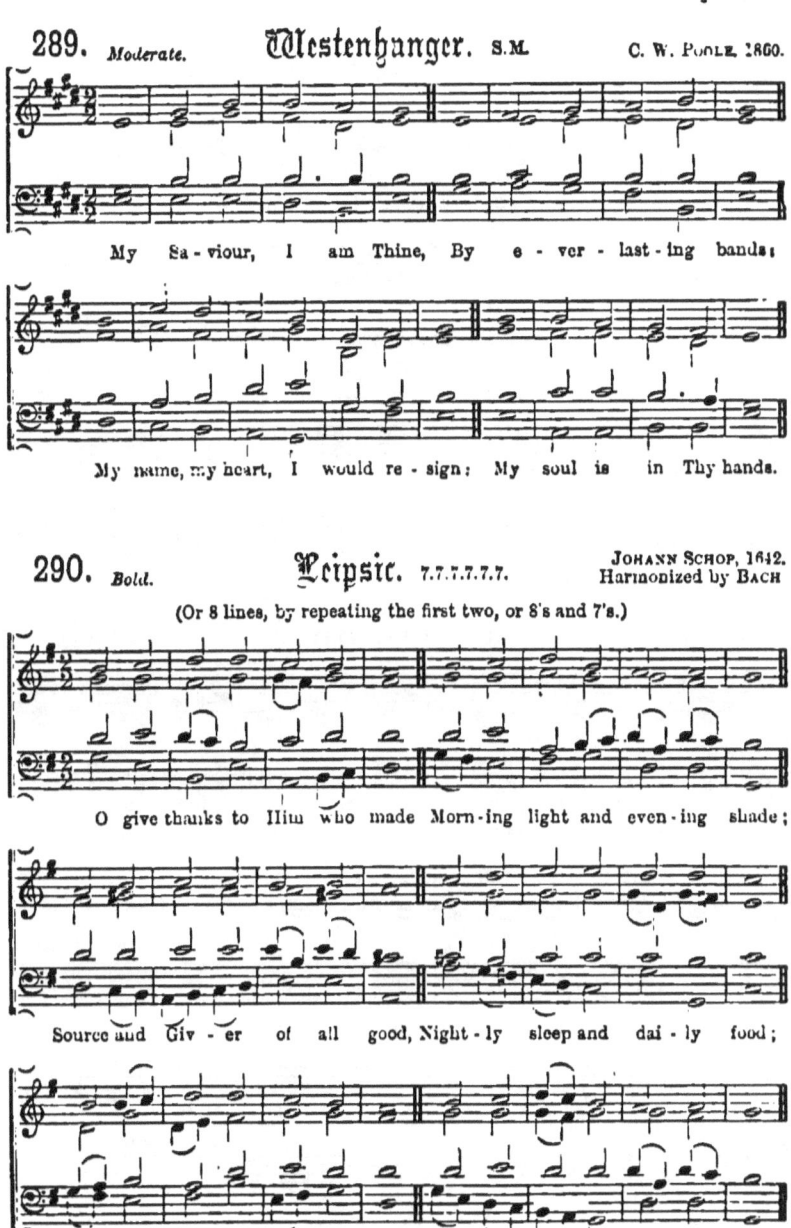

PORTUGUESE—*continued.*

breast, And hide all my cares in Thy shel-ter-ing breast!

293. *Joyful.* **Mariners.** 8.7.8.7. SICILIAN MELODY.

Come, Thou long-ex-pect-ed Je-sus, Born to set Thy peo-ple free;

From our fears and sins re-lease us: Let us find our rest in Thee.

294. *Moderate.* **Jerusalem.** 86.86.86. JOHANN CRÜGER, 1653.

For ev-er will I bless the Lord, Nor cease His praise to speak:

My song His good-ness shall re-cord, That the oppressed and weak

May trust in Him who will re-ward The hum-ble and the meek.

295. *Moderate.* **Galilee.** L.M.   Old Latin. *Crudelis Herodes.*

Stay, Thou in-sult-ed Spi-rit, stay, Though I have done Thee such de-spite;

Nor cast the sin-ner quite a-way, Nor take Thine e-ver-last-ing flight.

296. *Slow.* **Irene.** 87.87.87., or 87.87.47.   Dr. Louis Spohr.

Sing, my tongue, the Saviour's glo-ry, Of His cross the mys-tery sing;

Lift on high the wondrous tro-phy, Tell the tri-umph of the King:

He, the world's Re-deem-er, conquers Death, through death now vanquishing.

297. Grave. Babylon. L.M.
Dr. T. Campion, 1606.

When I sur-vey the wondrous cross On which the Prince of glo-ry died,

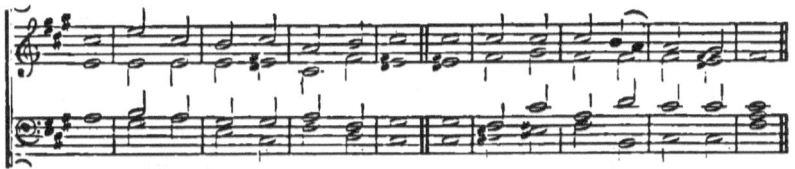

My rich-est gain I count but loss, And pour contempt on all my pride.

298. Cheerful. Strasburg. 11.10.11.10.
John Rudolph Ahle, d. 1673.

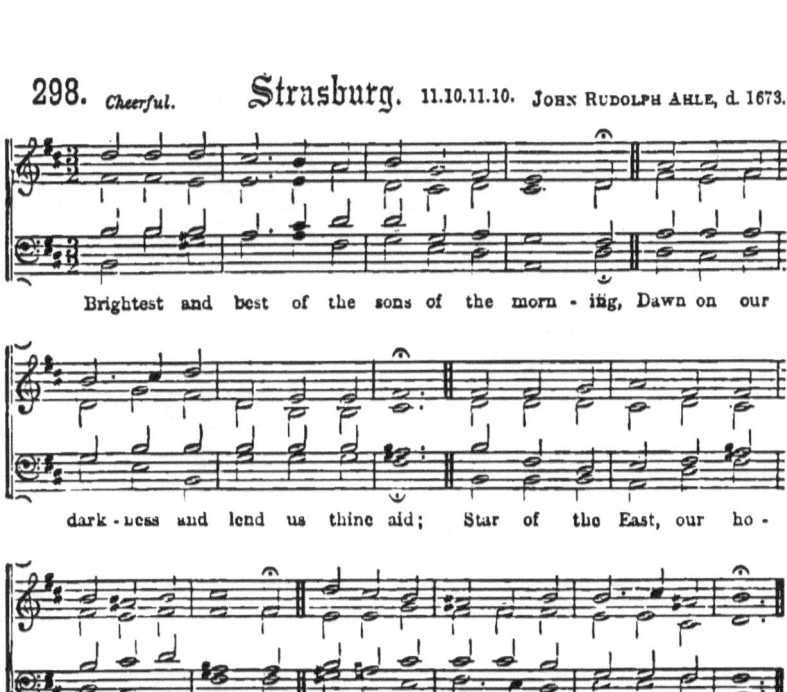

Brightest and best of the sons of the morn-ing, Dawn on our

dark-ness and lend us thine aid; Star of the East, our ho-

ri-son a-dorn-ing, Guide where our in-fant Re-deem-er is laid.

306. *Moderate and bold.* **Ephesus.** 8s.8s.8s.   Luther, *Erfurt Enchiridion,* 1524.

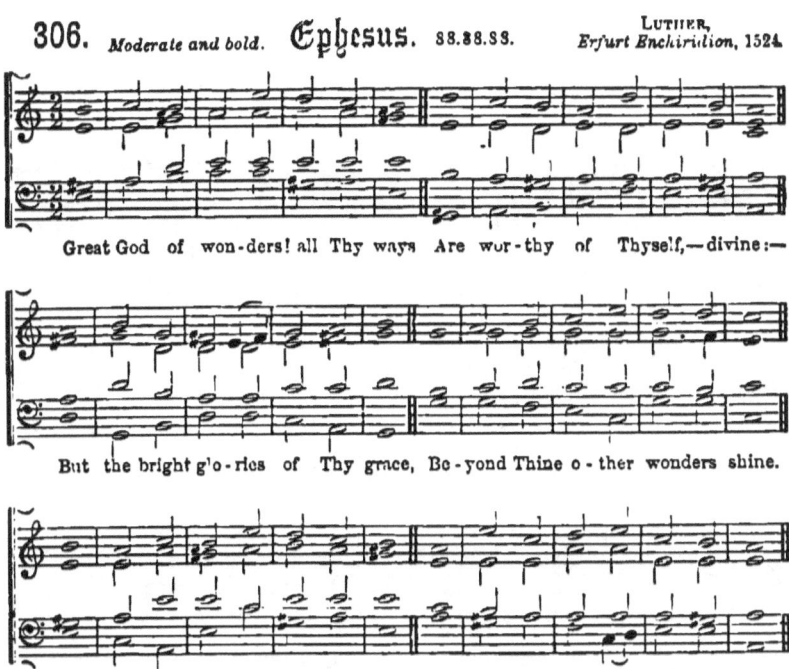

Great God of won-ders! all Thy ways Are wor-thy of Thyself,—divine:—

But the bright glo-ries of Thy grace, Be-yond Thine o-ther wonders shine.

Who is a pardoning God like Thee? Or who has grace so rich and free?

307. *Bold.*   **Exeter.** C.M.   Ravenscroft.

God moves in a mys-te-rious way His won-ders to per-form:

He plants His footsteps in the sea, And rides up-on the storm.

310. *Slow.* **Jena.** 8.8.8.8.8.8. OLD LATIN, adapted by LUTHER. WALTHER'S *Gesangbuch*, 1525.

When gath-er-ing clouds a-round I view, And days are dark and friends are few,
On Him I lean, who not in vain Ex-pe-rienced eve-ry hu-man pain.
He sees my wants, al-lays my fears, And counts and trea-sures up my tears.

311. *Joyful.* **Werburg.** 10.10.11.11. RAVENSCROFT'S *Whole Booke of Psalms*, 1621.

Be-gone, un-be-lief; My Sa-viour is near, And for my re-
lief Will sure-ly ap-pear. By prayer let me wres-tle, And
He will per-form; With Christ in the ves-sel, I smile at the storm.

(145)
L

312. *Moderate.* 𝔚𝔢𝔰𝔱𝔭𝔥𝔞𝔩𝔦𝔞. 86.86.86. Walther's *Gesangbuch*, 1525. Luther.

(Or 8 lines, by repeating the first two.)

Fa-ther, I know that all my life Is por-tioned out for me,

The chang-es that will sure-ly come I do not fear to see;

I ask Thee for a pre-sent mind In-tent on pleas-ing Thee.

313. *Moderate.* 𝔖𝔪𝔶𝔯𝔫𝔞. L.M. "Jesu Redemptor omnium." Old Latin.

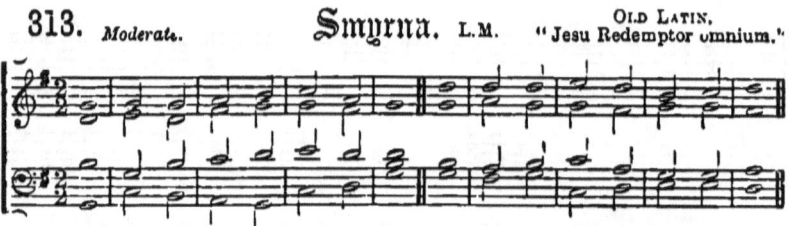

Who can de-scribe the joys that rise Through all the courts of Par-a-dise,

To see a prod-i-gal re-turn, To see an heir of glo-ry born!

(146)

314. *Moderate.* **Antioch.** 888.888.

OLD LATIN. "Veni Sancte Spiritus."
Adapted by LUTHER in his *Eight Spiritual Songs*, 1524.

Ye that de-light to serve the Lord, The ho-nours of His name re-cord,

His sa-cred name for ev-er bless: Where-e'er the cir-cling sun dis-plays

His ris-ing beams, or set-ting rays, Let lands and seas His power con-fess.

315. *Moderate.* **Nicea.** L.M.

OLD LATIN. "Lucis Creator."
7th or 8th Century.

Com-mand Thy bless-ing from a-bove, O God, on all as-sem-bled here:
Be-hold us with a Fa-ther's love, While we look up with fil-ial fear.

316. *Bold.*   **Hilary.**   668.668.   Marot and Beza's *Psalms*, 1561.

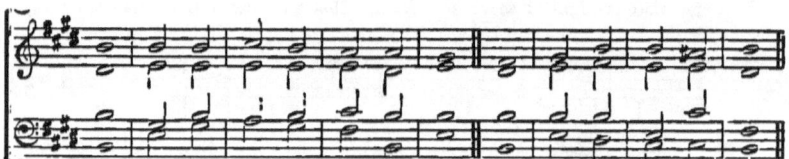

The Lord Je - ho - vah reigns, And roy - al state main - tains,

His head with aw - ful glo - ries crowned; Ar - rayed in robes of light,

Be - girt with sove-reign might, And rays of ma - jes - ty a - round.

317. *Joyful.*   **Gloucester.** C.M.   Ravenscroft's *Whole Booke of Psalms*, 1621.

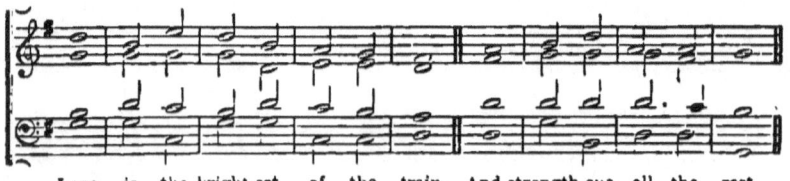

Hap - py the heart where gra - ces reign, Where love in - spires the breast:

Love is the bright-est of the train, And strength-ens all the rest.

(148)

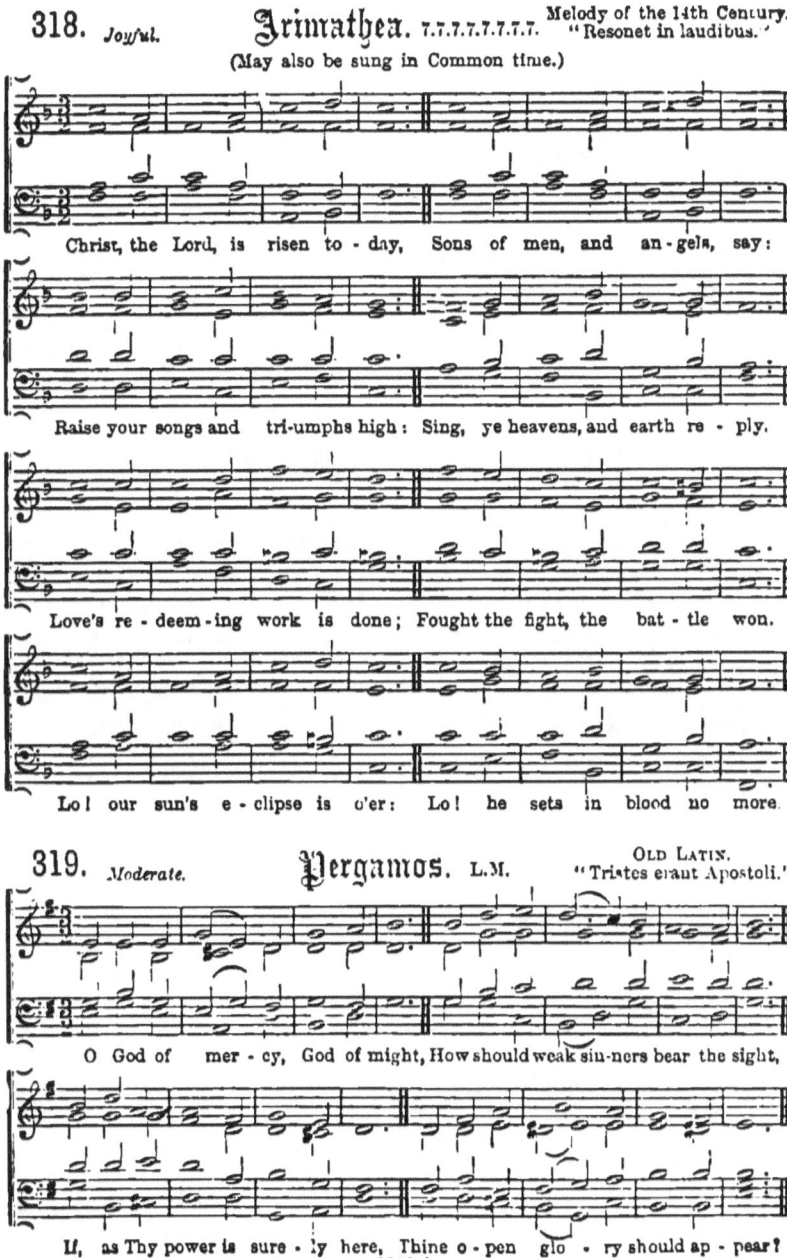

320. *Slow and earnestly.* **Bethel.** 7.6.7.6.7.7. H. A. WEDD. 1859.

In the day of thy dis-tress, May Je-ho-vah hear thee;
In the hour when dan-gers press, Ja-cob's God be near thee;
Send thee, from His ho-ly place, Time-ly aid or strength'ning grace.

May thy prayers and offerings rise,
 By thy God recorded;
Thine oblations reach the skies,
 Graciously rewarded;
Granted be thy heart's request;
All thy purposes be blest!

Thy success our heart shall cheer;
 We, with exultation,
In Jehovah's name will rear
 Trophies of salvation.

Go beneath His guardian care,
And the Lord fulfil thy prayer.

Vain the despot's haughty boasts,
 Fleets or martial forces;
Be our trust the God of hosts,
 Heavenly our resources:
Theirs shall be defeat and shame;
We shall triumph in Thy name.
                       J. CONDER.

321. *Joyous.* **Gildas.** S.M. Attributed to PETER ABELARD, A.D. 1120. "Mittet ad Virginem."

Sol-diers of Christ, a-rise, And put your ar-mour on,
Strong in the strength which God sup-plies Through His e-ter-nal Son.

322. *Joyful.* **Natibity.** 7.7.7.7.7.7.7.7. OLD LATIN. 15th Century.
"In dulci jubilo"
(May also be sung in Common time.)

Hark! the he-rald an-gels sing,— Glo-ry to the new-born King;

Peace on earth, and mer-cy mild; God and sin-ners re-con-ciled.

Joy-ful all ye na-tions rise; Join the tri-umph of the skies:

With th'an-gel-ic host pro-claim,—Christ was born in Beth-le-hem.

323. *Moderate.* **Burmah.** C.M.

Give me the wings of faith to rise With-in the veil, and see

The saints a-bove, how great their joys! How bright their glo-ries be!

330. *Moderate.* **Dismission.** 8.7.8.7.8.7.8.7.

Lord, dis-miss us with Thy bless-ing, Bid us all de-part in peace;
Still, on gos-pel man-na feed-ing, Pure se-ra-phic joys in-crease:
Fill our hearts with con-so-la-tion, Un-to Thee our voi-ces raise;
When we reach that bliss-ful sta-tion We will give Thee no-bler praise.

331. *Moderate.* **Oriel.** 10.4.10.4.10.10.   Wm. Birtwhistle.
Words by Dr. J. H. Newman.

1. Lead, kindly Light, amid the encircling gloom, Lead Thou me on. The night is dark, and I am far from home

Lead Thou me on. Keep Thou my feet; I do not ask to see The distant scene,—one step enough for me.

2 I was not ever thus, nor pray'd that Thou
   Should'st lead me on.
I loved to choose and see my path; but now
   Lead thou me on.
I loved the garish day, and, spite of fears,
Pride ruled my will, remember not past years.

3. So long Thy power hath blest me, sure it still
   Will lead me on,
O'er moor and fen, o'er crag and torrent, till,
   The night is gone,
And with the morn those angel faces smile
Which I have loved long since and lost awhile.

334. *Moderate.*   **Ellerker.** 8.7.8.7.   J. B. König, 1738. Harmonized by Ludwig Erk.

Sweet the moments, rich in bless-ing, Which be-fore the cross I spend;

Life and health and peace pos-sess-ing, From the sin-ner's dy-ing Friend.

335. *Bold.*   **Stuttgart.** 87.87.87.87. (or six lines).   J. Rosenmüller, 1650. Harmonized by Bach.

Glorious things of thee are spo-ken, Zi-on, ci-ty of our God!
He whose word can-not be bro-ken, Formed thee for His own a-bode.

On the Rock of a-ges found-ed, What can shake thy sure re-pose?

With sal-va-tion's walls sur-round-ed, Thou may'st smile at all thy foes.

336. *Joyful.*   **Ramleh.** S.M.   Dr. GAUNTLETT, 1852.

How beauteous are their feet Who stand on Zi-on's hill!

Who bring sal-va-tion on their tongues, And words of peace re-veal.

337. *Cheerful.*   **Göttingen.** 7.7.7.7.7.7.,   MICHAEL WEISS, 1531. Harmonized by Dr. FILITZ.
(Or 8 lines, by repeating the first two lines.)

Bless-ed are the sons of God; They are bought with Christ's own blood;

They are ransomed from the grave; Life e-ter-nal they shall have

With them numbered may we be, Now and through e-ter-ni-ty.

338. *Gravely.* **Golgotha.** L.M. Rev. J. B. Dykes. By permission, from *Hymns Ancient and Modern*.

O come and mourn with me a-while; O come ye to the Saviour's side; O come, together let us mourn; Jesus, our Lord, is crucified.

Have we no tears to shed for Him,
 While soldiers scoff and Jews deride?
Ah! look how patiently He hangs;
 Jesus, our Lord, is crucified.
How fast His hands and feet are nailed;
 His throat with parching thirst is dried;
His failing eyes are dimmed with woe;
 Jesus, our Lord, is crucified.
Seven times He spake, seven words of love;
 And all three hours His silence cried

For mercy on the souls of men;
 Jesus, our Lord, is crucified.
Come, let us stand beneath the Cross;
 The fountain opened in His side,
Shall purge our deepest stains away;
 Jesus, our Lord, is crucified.
A broken heart, a fount of tears,
 Ask, and they will not be denied;
The broken heart He heals and saves;
 For us our Lord was crucified.
    F. W. FABER, D.D.

339. *Joyful.* **Biberach.** 7.7.7.7. J. H. KNECHT, 1797. From the *Würtemberg Choralbuch.*

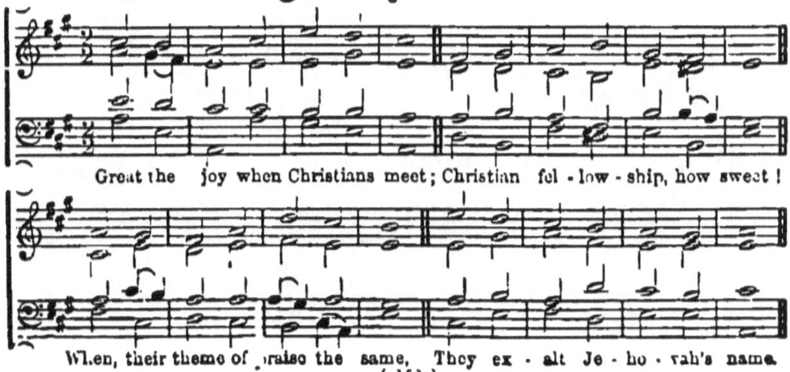

Great the joy when Christians meet; Christian fellowship, how sweet! When their theme of praise the same, They exalt Jehovah's name.

340. *Cheerful.* **Salem.** 7.6.7.6.7.6.7.6. A. EWING, Bishop of Argyll.
Inserted by his permission.

Je-ru-sa-lem, the gol-den, With milk and honey blest; Beneath thy contem-pla-tion Sink heart and voice oppressed. The home of fade-less splen-dour, Of flowers that have no thorn; Where they shall dwell as children, Who here as exiles mourn.

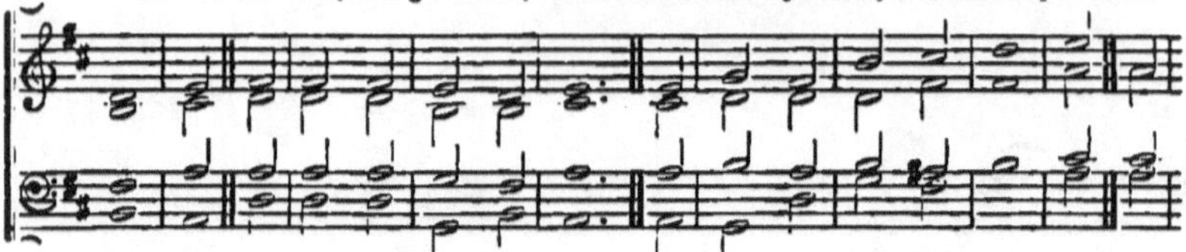

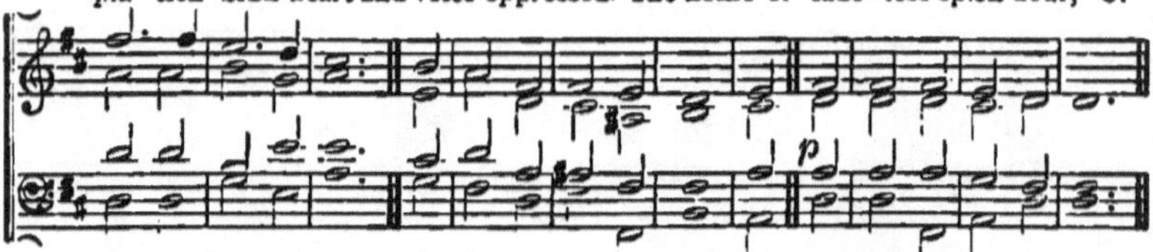

Jerusalem, the only,
  That look'st from heaven below;
In thee is all my glory;
  In me is all my woe.
I strive to win that glory;
  I toil to gain that light;
Send hope before to grasp it,
  Till hope is lost to sight.

Jerusalem! exulting,
  On that securest shore;
I hope thee, wish thee, sing thee,
  And love thee evermore.
O happy, holy city,
  The portion of the blest;
True vision of true beauty,
  Sweet balm of all distrest.

Thou hast no shore, fair ocean!
  Thou hast no time, bright day!
Dear fountain of refreshment
  To pilgrims far away!

Upon the Rock of Ages,
  They raise thy holy tower;
Thine is the victor's laurel,
  And thine the golden dower.
The Lamb is all thy splendour,
  The Crucified thy praise;
His laud and benediction,
  Thy ransomed people raise.

And He whom now we trust in,
  Shall then be seen and known;
And they that know and see Him
  Shall have Him for their own.
O sweet and blessed country,
  When shall I see thy face?
O sweet and blessed country,
  When shall I win thy grace?
Exult, O dust and ashes!
  The Lord shall be thy part;
His only, His for ever,
  Thou shalt be, and thou art.
Cento from the Rhythm of ST. BERNARD.

341. *Grave.* **Capernaum.** 7.7.7.7. R. REDHEAD. Inserted by purchased permission.

When our heads are bowed with woe, When our bit-ter tears o'er-flow,

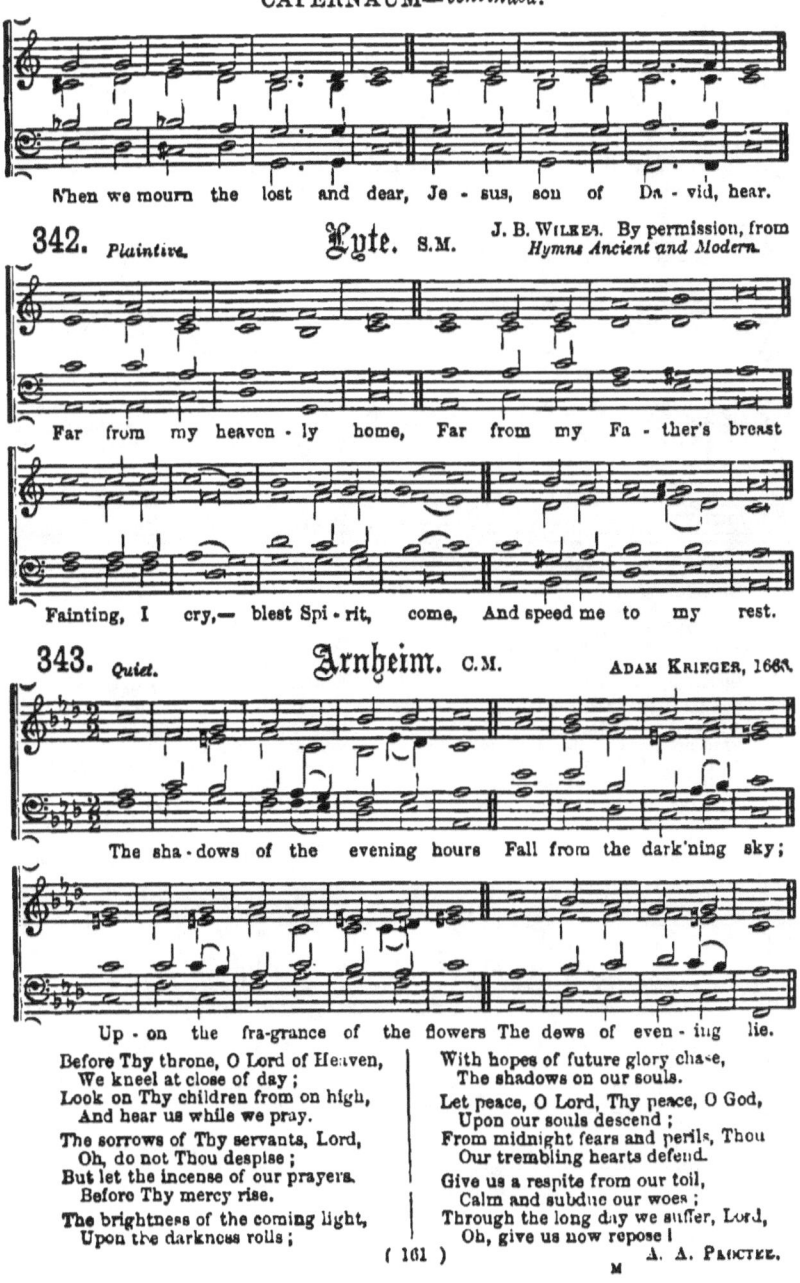

Before Thy throne, O Lord of Heaven,
  We kneel at close of day ;
Look on Thy children from on high,
  And hear us while we pray.
The sorrows of Thy servants, Lord,
  Oh, do not Thou despise ;
But let the incense of our prayers
  Before Thy mercy rise.
The brightness of the coming light,
  Upon the darkness rolls ;

With hopes of future glory chase,
  The shadows on our souls.
Let peace, O Lord, Thy peace, O God,
  Upon our souls descend ;
From midnight fears and perils, Thou
  Our trembling hearts defend.
Give us a respite from our toil,
  Calm and subdue our woes ;
Through the long day we suffer, Lord,
  Oh, give us now repose !
  A. A. PROCTER.

344. *Moderate*   **Tiberias.** 77.77.77.   CONRAD KOCHER. From his *Zionsharfe*, 1855.

Gra-cious Spi-rit, dwell with me, I my-self would gra-cious be;
And with words that help and heal, Would Thy life in mine re-veal;
And with ac-tions bold and meek, Would for Christ, my Sa-viour, speak.

Truthful Spirit, dwell with me,
I myself would truthful be;
And with wisdom kind and clear,
Let Thy life in mine appear;
And with actions brotherly,
Speak my Lord's sincerity.

Tender Spirit, dwell with me,
I myself would tender be;
Shut my heart up like a flower,
In temptation's darksome hour;
Open it when shines the sun,
And His love by fragrance own.

Mighty Spirit, dwell with me,
I myself would mighty be;
Mighty so as to prevail,
Where, unaided, man must fail;
Ever, by a mighty hope,
Pressing on and bearing up.

Holy Spirit, dwell with me,
I myself would holy be;
Separate from sin, I would
Choose and cherish all things good;
And whatever I can be,
Give to Him, who gave me Thee.

                                            T. T. LYNCH.

345. *Moderate.*   **Boniface.** 8.8.8.6.   *Darmstadt Gesangbuch*, 1698.

Lo! the storms of life are breaking, Faithless fears our hearts are shaking;
For our suc-cour un-der ta-king, Lord and Saviour, help us.

(162)

346. Melita. 8s.8s.8s. Rev. J. B. Dykes. By permission, from *Hymns Ancient and Modern*.

E - ter - nal Fa - ther, strong to save, Whose arm hath bound the restless wave,

Who bid'st the mighty o - cean deep Its own ap - point - ed lim - its keep;

O hear us when we cry to Thee For those in pe - ril on the sea. A-men.

O Christ, whose voice the waters heard,
And hushed their raging at Thy word,
Who walkedst on the foaming deep,
And calm amidst its rage did'st sleep;
 O hear us when we cry to Thee
 For those in peril on the sea.

Most Holy Spirit, who did'st brood
Upon the chaos dark and rude,
And bid its angry tumult cease,
And give, for wild confusion, peace;
 O hear us when we cry to Thee
 For those in peril on the sea.

O Trinity of love and power,
Our brethren shield in danger's hour;
From rock and tempest, fire and foe,
Protect them wheresoe'er they go;
 Thus evermore shall rise to Thee
 Glad hymns of praise from land and sea.
   WHITING.

347. *Moderate.* Patmos. L.M. Latin Melody of the 7th Century.

A - way from every mor - tal care, A - way from earth our soul's re - treat;

We leave this worthless world a - far, And wait and wor - ship near Thy seat.

RAVENSHAW—continued.

Ex-alt our God with loud ac-cord, And in His name re-joice;
Ne'er cease to sing, thou ransomed host, Praise Fa-ther, Son, and Ho-ly Ghost,
Un-til in realms of end-less light, Your prais-es shall u-nite.

There, we to all eternity,
Shall join th' angelic lays,
And sing, in perfect harmony,
To God the Saviour's praise:

"He hath redeemed us by His blood;
Hath made us kings and priests to God:
For us the heavenly Lamb was slain;
Praise ye the Lord. Amen." SWEETNER

351. Moderate. Magdala. 86.84. Rev. J. B Dykes. By permission, from *Hymns Ancient and Modern*.

Our blest Re-deem-er, ere He breathed His ten-der last fare - well,
A Guide, a Com-fort-er, bequeathed With us to dwell. A-men.

He came sweet influence to impart,
A gracious willing Guest,
While He can find one humble heart,
Wherein to rest.

And His that gentle voice we hear,
Soft as the breath of even,
That checks each thought, that calms each fear,
And speaks of heaven.

And every virtue we possess,
And every conquest won,

And every thought of holiness,
Are His alone.

Spirit of purity and grace,
Our weakness, pitying, see:
O make our hearts Thy dwelling place
And worthier Thee.

O praise the Father; praise the Son;
Blest Spirit, praise to Thee;
All praise to God, the Three in One.
The One in Three. H. AUBER.

352. *Moderate.* **Siloam.** 88.88.88. W. H. MONK. By permission, from *Hymns Ancient and Modern.*

Sweet Saviour, bless us ere we go; Thy word into our minds instill;
And make our lukewarm hearts to glow With lowly love and fervent will.
Thro' life's long day and death's dark night, O gentle Jesus, be our Light. A-men.

The day is gone, its hours have run,
And Thou hast taken count of all,
The scanty triumphs grace hath won,
The broken vow, the frequent fall.
Through life's long day and death's dark night,
O gentle Jesus, be our Light.

Grant us, dear Lord, from evil ways
True absolution and release ;
And bless us, more than in past days,
With purity and inward peace.
Through life's long day and death's dark night,
O gentle Jesus, be our Light.

Do more than pardon ; give us joy,
Sweet fear, and sober liberty,
And simple hearts without alloy,

That only long to be like Thee.
Through life's long day and death's dark night,
O gentle Jesus, be our Light.

Labour is sweet, for Thou hast toiled ;
And care is light, for Thou hast cared ;
Ah ! never let our works be soiled
With strife, or by deceit ensnared.
Through life's long day and death's dark night,
O gentle Jesus, be our Light.

For all we love, the poor, the sad,
The sinful, unto Thee we call ;
O let Thy mercy make us glad ;
Thou art our Jesus, and our all.
Through life's long day and death's dark night,
O gentle Jesus, be our Light. F. W. FABER, D.D.

353. *Joyful.* **Brandenburg.** 77.77.77., or 78.78.77. JOHANN CRÜGER, 1653.

O give thanks to Him who made Morning light and evening shade ; Source and Giver of all good,
Nightly sleep and daily food; Quickener of our wearied powers ; Guard of our unconscious hours.

(166)

354. *Moderate.* **Hollingside.** 77.77.77.77. Rev. J. B. Dykes. By permis., from *Hymns Ancient and Modern.*

Je-su, re-fuge of my soul, Let me to Thy bo-som fly, While the near-er

wa-ters roll, While the tempest still is high: Hide me, O my Saviour, hide, Till the

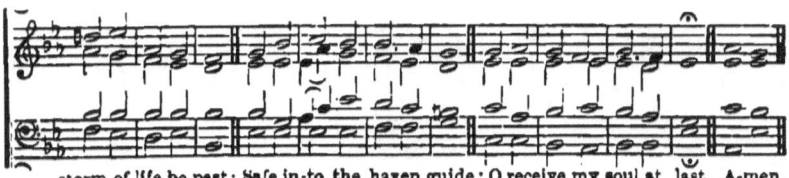

storm of life be past: Safe in-to the haven guide: O receive my soul at last. A-men.

355. *Moderate.* **Coveney.** C.M. T. M. Wood, 1866.
Harmonized by J. Banister. Inserted by permission.

Christ and His cross is all our theme; The mysteries that we speak

Are scan-dal in the Jews' es-teem, And fol-ly to the Greek.

BEMERTON—continued.

Pity-ing, lov-ing Saviour, Hear Thy children's cry.

Pardon our offences,
  Loose our captive chains,
Break down every idol
  Which our soul detains.

Give us holy freedom,
  Fill our hearts with love;
Draw us, holy Jesus,
  To the realms above.

Lead us on our journey,
  Be Thyself the Way
Through terrestrial darkness,
  To celestial day.

Jesu, meek and gentle,
  Son of God most high,
Pitying, loving Saviour,
  Hear Thy children's cry.—PRYNNE.

358. **Ebentide.** 10.10.10.10. W. H. MONK. By permission, from *Hymns Ancient and Modern.*

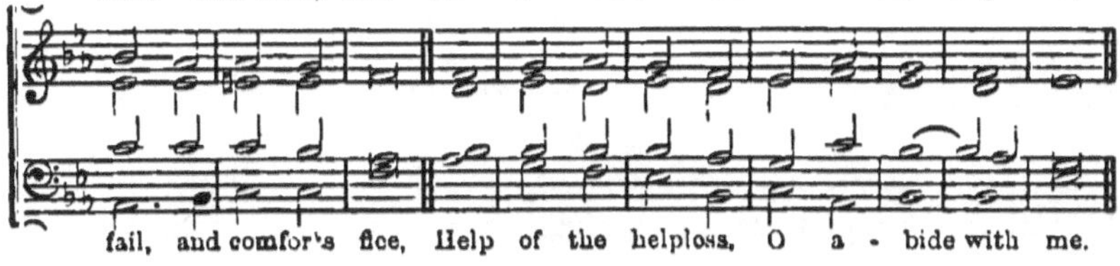

A-bide with me, fast falls the e-ven-tide: The darkness thickens; Lord, with me a-bide. When o-ther helpers fail, and comfor's flee, Help of the helpless, O a-bide with me.

[OR THIS CHANT.]

359. **Troyte.** A. H. D. TROYTE, d. 1859. Inserted by permission.

A-men.

362. *Moderate.* **Bethsaida.** 6.10.6.10. Dr. Gauntlett, 1801.

Birds have their qui - et nest, Fox - es their holes, and man his peace - ful bed; All crea - tures have their rest: But Je - sus had not where to lay His head.

Ana yet He came to give
The weary and the heavy laden rest,
   To bid the sinner live,   [breast.
And soothe my griefs to slumber on His

I— who once made Him grieve,
I—who once bade His gentle spirit mourn ;
   Whose hand essayed to weave
For His meek brow the cruel crown of thorn.

O, why should I have peace ?
Why ? but for that unchanged, undying love
   Which would not, could not cease
Until it made me heir of joys above ?

Yes, but for pardoning grace,
I feel I never should in glory see
   The brightness of that face,
That once was pale and agonized for me.

Let the birds seek their nest,
Foxes their holes, and man his peaceful bed ;
   Come, Saviour ! in my breast
Deign to repose Thine oft-rejected head.

On earth Thou lovest best
To dwell in humble souls that mourn for sin·
   O come and take Thy rest,
This broken, bleeding, contrite heart within.

J. B. Monsell, LL.D.

363. *Moderate.* **Savoy,** or **Old Hundredth.** Guil. Franc, 1545. (Original form.)

All peo - ple that on earth do dwell, Sing to the Lord with cheerful voice: Him serve with mirth, His praise forth tell; Come ye be-fore Him and re - joice.

364. *Moderate.* Broadlands. 66.66.66.66. Arranged by Dr. Rimbault.
French Collection for the *Churches of the Augsburg Confession*, 1846.

Thy way, not mine, O Lord, How-e-ver dark it be! Lend me by Thine own hand, Choose out the path for me. Smooth let it be or rough, It will be still the best, Winding or straight, it leads Right onward to Thy rest.

I dare not choose my lot;
I would not if I might:
Choose Thou for me, my God,
So shall I walk aright.
The kingdom that I seek
Is Thine; so let the way
That leads to it be Thine,
Else I must surely stray.

Take Thou my cup, and it
With joy or sorrow fill,
As best to Thee may seem;
Choose Thou my good and ill.
Not mine, not mine the choice,
In things or great or small;
Be Thou my guide, my strength,
My wisdom, and my all.

H. Bonar, D.D.

365. *Moderate.* St. Leonard. C.M. Henry Smart.
By permission, from *Psalms and Hymns for Divine Worship.*

All that I was, my sin, my guilt, My death, was all mine own;
All that I am I owe to Thee, My gra-cious God, a - lone.

366. *Moderate.* **Intercession.** 75.75.75.75.88.
W. H. Calcott, 1866,
partly from Mendelssohn.
By permission, from *Psalms and Hymns for Divine Worship.*

When the weary, seeking rest, To Thy goodness flee; When the heavy la-den cast All their load on Thee; When the troubled, seeking peace, On Thy name shall call; When the sin-ner, seeking life, At Thy feet shall fall: Hear, then in love, O Lord, the cry, In heaven, Thy dwelling-place on high.

When the worldling, sick at heart,
　Lifts his soul above;
When the prodigal looks back
　To his Father's love ;
When the proud man from his pride,
　Stoops to seek Thy face ;
When the burdened brings his guilt
　To Thy throne of grace :
Hear then, in love, O Lord, the cry,
In heaven, Thy dwelling-place on high.

When the stranger asks a home,
　All his toils to end ;
When the hungry craveth food,
　And the poor a friend ;
When the sailor on the wave
　Bows the fervent knee ;
When the soldier on the field
　Lifts his heart to Thee ;
Hear then, in love, O Lord, the cry,
In heaven, Thy dwelling-place on high.

When the man of toil and care
　In the city crowd ;
When the shepherd on the moor
　Names the name of God ;
When the learned and the high,

Tired of earthly fame,
　Upon higher joys intent,
Name the blessed Name :
Hear then, in love, O Lord, the cry,
In heaven, Thy dwelling-place on high.

When the child, with grave fresh lip,
　Youth, or maiden fair ;
When the aged, weak and grey,
　Seek Thy face in prayer ;
When the widow weeps to Thee,
　Sad and lone and low ;
When the orphan brings to Thee
　All his orphan woe ;
Hear then, in love, O Lord, the cry,
In heaven, Thy dwelling-place on high.

When creation, in her pangs,
　Heaves her heavy groan ;
When Thy Salem's exiled sons
　Breathe their bitter moan :
When Thy waiting, weeping church,
　Looking for a home,
Sendeth up her silent sigh,
　Come, Lord Jesus, come !
Hear then, in love, O Lord, the cry,
In heaven, Thy dwelling-place on high.

H. Bonar, D.D.

(173)

367. *Moderate.* **Cherwell.** C.M. J. TURLE.
Inserted by permission.

God is our refuge, tried and proved Amid a stormy world;
We will not fear though earth be moved, And hills in ocean hurled.

368. *Moderate.* **Tabor.** 7.6.7.6.7.6.7.6. H. KUGELMANN, 1540.
(May also be sung in Common time.)

I lay my sins on Jesus, The spotless Lamb of God; He bears them all and frees us From the accursed load. I bring my guilt to Jesus, To wash my crimson stains White in His blood most precious, Till not a spot remains.

I lay my wants on Jesus;
  All fulness dwells in Him;
He heals all my diseases,
  He doth my soul redeem.
I lay my griefs on Jesus,
  My burdens and my cares;
He from them all releases,
  He all my sorrows shares.

I rest my soul on Jesus;
  This weary soul of mine;
His right hand me embraces,
  I on His breast recline.

I love the name of Jesus,
  Immanuel, Christ, the Lord;
Like fragrance on the breezes,
  His name abroad is poured.

I long to be like Jesus,
  Meek, loving, lowly, mild;
I long to be like Jesus,
  The Father's only child.
I long to be with Jesus,
  Amid the heavenly throng,
To sing with saints His praises,
  To learn the angels' song.

H. BONAR, D.D.

369. Hexham. 11.11.11.11.
Moderate. — Mendelssohn, d. 1847.

O had I, my Saviour, the wings of a dove, How soon would I soar to Thy presence above! How soon would I fly where the weary have rest, And hide all my cares in Thy sheltering breast!

370. Bethabara. 6.6.10.6.6.10.
Slowly. — Dr. Gauntlett, 1866.

Thou who didst stoop be-low To drain the cup of woe, And wear the form of frail mor-tal-i-ty. Thy bless-ed la-bours done, Thy crown of victory won, Hast passed from earth,—passed to Thy home on high.

It was no path of flowers,
Through this dark world of ours,
Beloved of the Father, Thou didst tread;
And shall we in dismay,
Shrink from the narrow way, [spread?
When clouds and darkness are around it

O Thou, who art our life,
Be with us through the strife; [bowed.
Thine own meek head by rudest storms was

Raise Thou our eyes above,
To see a Father's love,
Beam like a bow of promise thro' the cloud.
'Een through the awful gloom,
Which hovers o'er the tomb,
That light of love our guiding-star shall be
Our spirits shall not dread
The shadowy path to tread, [to Thee.
Friend, Guardian, Saviour, which doth lead

Sibella E. Miles, 1840.

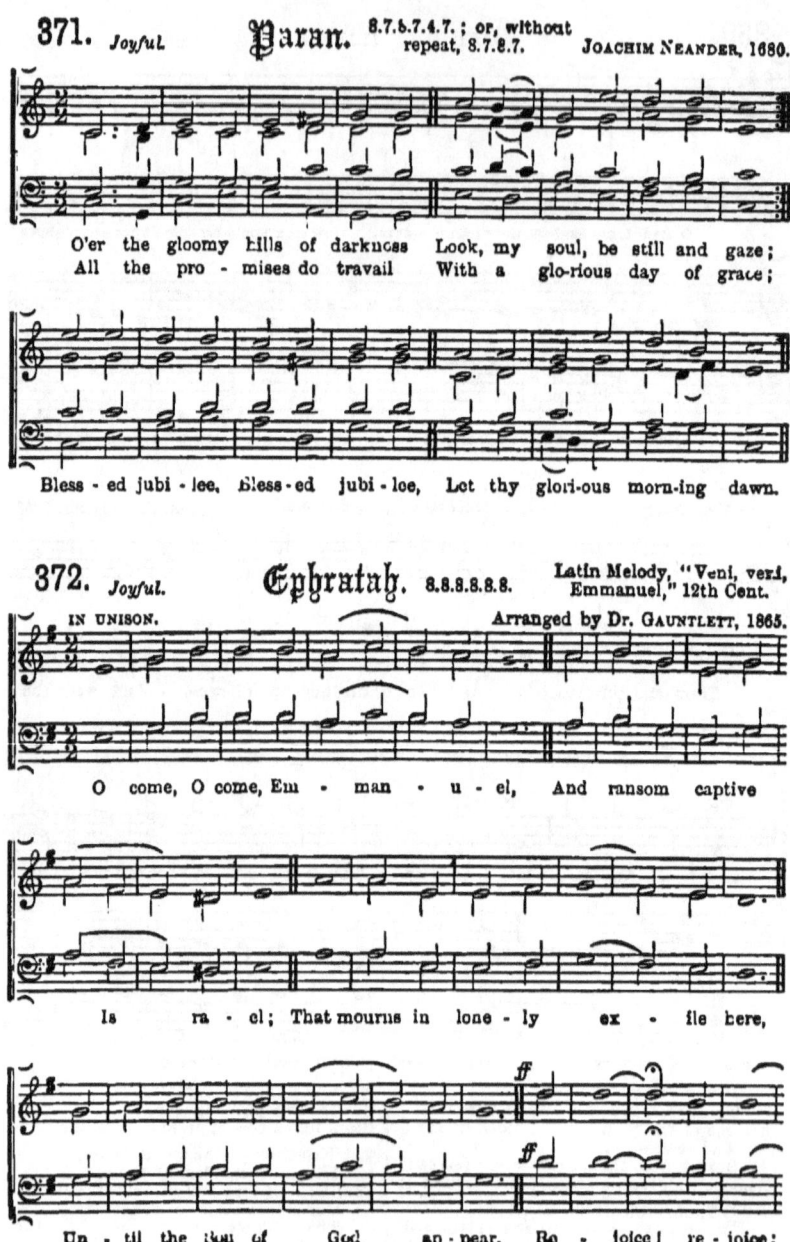

EPHRATAH—continued.

joice! Em - man - u - el Shall come to Thee, O Is - ra - el!

O come, thou rod of Jesse, free
Thine own from Satan's tyranny;
From depths of hell Thy people save,
And give them victory o'er the grave.
Rejoice! rejoice! Emmanuel
Shall come to thee, O Israel!

O come, Thou Day-spring, come and cheer
Our spirits by Thine Advent here;
Disperse the gloomy clouds of night.
And death's dark shadows put to flight.
Rejoice! rejoice! Emmanuel
Shall come to thee, O Israel!

O come, Thou Key of David, come,
And open wide our heavenly home;
Make safe the way that leads on high,
And close the path to misery.
Rejoice! rejoice! Emmanuel
Shall come to thee, O Israel!

O come, O come, Thou Lord of might!
Who to Thy tribes, on Sinai's height,
In ancient times didst give the law,
In cloud, and majesty, and awe.
Rejoice! rejoice! Emmanuel
Shall come to thee, O Israel!

J. M. NEALE, D.D.

373. *Joyful.* **Sharon.** 7.7.7.7.7.7.7.7. G. J. Elvey, Mus. Doc. Inserted by his permission.

Come, ye thank-ful peo-ple, come, Raise the song of Har-vest-Home!
All is safe-ly gath-ered in, Ere the win-ter storms be-gin;
God, our Ma-ker, doth pro-vide For our wants to be sup-plied:—
Come to God's own tem-ple, come; Raise the song of Har-vest Home!

All this world is God's own field,
Fruit unto His praise to yield;
Wheat and tares together sown,
Unto joy or sorrow grown:
First the blade, and then the ear,
Then the full corn shall appear:
Lord of Harvest, grant that we
Wholesome grain and pure may be.

For the Lord our God shall come,
And shall take His Harvest home;
From His field shall in that day
All offences purge away;

Give His angels charge at last,
In the fire the tares to cast;
But the fruitful ears to store
In His garner evermore.

Even so, Lord, quickly come
To Thy final Harvest-Home!
Gather Thou Thy people in,
Free from sorrow, free from sin;
There, for ever purified,
In Thy presence to abide;
Come, with all Thine angels, come,
Raise the glorious Harvest-Home!

Dean Alford (revised for this work.)

374. *Moderate.* **Cherith.** C.M. Dr. Louis Spohr, d. 1859.

O God un-seen, yet e-ver near, Thy pre-sence may we feel:

(173)

CHERITH—continued.

And thus in-spired with ho-ly fear, Be-fore thine al-tar kneel.

Here may Thy faithful people know
The blessings of Thy love;
The streams that through the desert flow,
The manna from above.

We come, obedient to Thy word,
To feast on heavenly food.

Our meat, the body of the Lord;
Our drink, His precious blood.

Thus may we all Thy words obey,
For we, O God, are Thine;
And go rejoicing on our way,
Renewed with strength Divine.—E. OSLER.

375. *Moderate.* **Elim.** C.M.D. (irreg.)   W. H. CALCOTT. By permission, from *Psalms and Hymns for Divine Worship.*

My heart is rest-ing, O my God,— I will give thanks and sing;

My heart is at the se-cret source Of eve-ry pre-cious thing.

Now the frail ves-sel Thou hast made No hand but Thine shall fill.

For the wa-ters of the earth have failed, And I am thirs-ty still.

I thirst for springs of heavenly life,
And here all day they rise;
I seek the treasure of Thy love,
And close at hand it lies.
And a new song is in my mouth
To long-loved music set;
Glory to Thee for all the grace
I have not tasted yet.

Glory to Thee for strength withheld,
For want and weakness known;
And the fear that sends me to Thyself
For what is most my own.

I have a heritage of joy
That yet I must not see;
But the hand that bled to make it mine
Is keeping it for me.

My heart is resting, O my God,
My heart is in Thy care;
I hear the voice of joy and health
Resounding everywhere.
"Thou art my portion," saith my soul,
Ten thousand voices say,
And the music of their glad Amen
Will never die away.   A. L. WARING.

WATFORD—*continued.*

For He has left the dead. Then bid me not that form sus-pend - ed For my Re - deem - er own, Who, to the high - est heavens as - cend - ed, In glo - ry fills the throne.

Weep not for Him on Calvary dy.ng;
  Weep only for thy sins.
Come see the place where he was lying;
  'Tis there our hope begins.
Yet stay not there, thy sorrows feeding,
  Amid the scenes He trod :
Look up and see Him interceding
  At the right hand of God.

Still in the shameful cross I glory,
  Where His dear blood was spilt ;
His shameful cross, set forth before me,
  Hath cancelled all my guilt.

Yet what 'mid conflict and temptation,
  Shall strength and succour give?—
He lives, the Captain of Salvation ;
  Therefore His servants live.

By death, He death's dark king defeated,
  And overcame the grave :
Rising, the triumph He completed ;
  He lives, He reigns to save.

Heaven's happy myriads bow before Him :
  He comes, the Judge of Men ;
These eyes shall see Him and adore Him :
  Lord Jesus! own me then.   CONDER.

378. *Moderate.*   Cyprus. 7.7.7.7.   MENDELSSOHN, d. 1847

In - ter - val of grate - ful shade, Wel-come to my wea - ry head;
Wel-come slum-ber to mine eyes, Tired with glar - ing van - i - ties.

379. *Moderate.* **Hebron.** 6.5.6.5.6.5.6.5. Melody of the 15th Century.

O, let him whose sor - row No re - lief can find, Trust in God and bor - row Ease for heart and mind. When the mourner weep - ing, Sheds the se - cret tear, God His watch is keep - ing, Though none else is near.

God will never leave thee,
All thy wants He knows,
Feels the pains that grieve thee
Sees thy cares and woes.
Raise thine eyes to heaven
When thy spirits quail.
When by tempests driven.
Heart and courage fail.

When in grief we languish,
He will dry the tear,
Who His children's anguish
Soothes with succour near.

All our woe and sadness
In this world below,
Balance not the gladness
We in heaven shall know.
On Thy truth relying,
In the mortal strife,
Lord, receive us dying
To eternal life.

Jesus, gracious Saviour,
In the realms above,
Crown us with Thy favour;
Fill us with Thy love.

HEINRICH S. OSWALD.

380. *Bold.* **Mannheim.** 8.7.8.7.8.7., or 8.7.8.7.4.7. German Chorale, arranged by DR. LOWELL MASON.

O how blest the con - gre - ga - tion, Who the gos - pel know and prize! Joy - ful ti - dings of sal - va - tion Brought by Je - sus from the skies.

383 Oberlin. 8.8.8.8.6.
Moderato.   *Magdeburg Choral Book,* 1540.

O Lord, Thy heaven-ly grace im-part, And fix my frail, in-con-stant heart; Hence-forth my chief de-sire shall be, To de-di-cate my-self to Thee. To Thee, my God, to Thee.

Whate'er pursuits my time employ,
One thought shall fill my soul with joy:
That silent, secret thought shall be,
That all my hopes are fixed on Thee.
On Thee, my God, on Thee.

Thy glorious eye pervades all space;
Thou'rt present, Lord, in every place:
And wheresoe'er my lot may be,
Still shall my spirit cleave to Thee.
To Thee, my God, to Thee.

384 Cheshunt. 4.4.7.7.7.6.
Grave.   CHRISTOPH PETER.

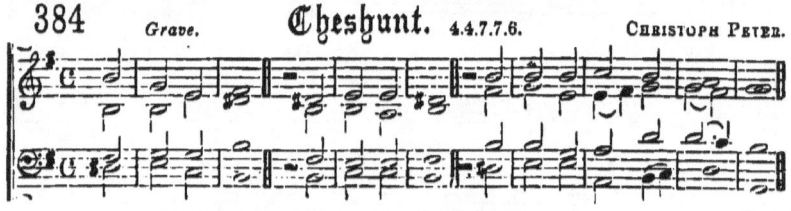

So rest, my Rest! Thou e - ver blest, Thy grave with sin - ners mak - ing; By Thy power of life through death My dead soul a - wak - ing. A men.

* *Small notes for vv.* 2, 3, 5.

385. Regent's Square. 8.7.8.7.4.7. HENRY SMART.

Bold and joyous. By permission, from *Psalms and Hymns for Divine Worship.*

Come, ye sinners, poor and wretched, Weak and wounded, sick and sore;

Jesus ready stands to save you, Full of pity join'd with power.

He is able; He is able: He is willing, doubt no more. Amen.

386. Horeb. 6.4.6.6. HENRY SMART.

Tenderly. By permission, from *The Hymnary.*

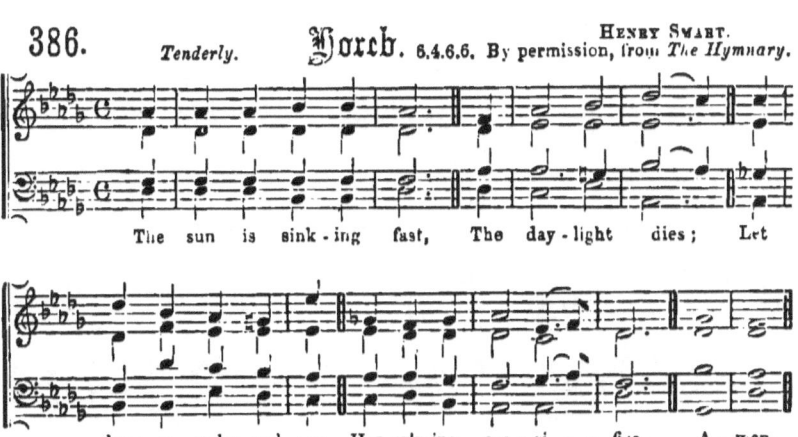

The sun is sinking fast, The daylight dies; Let love awake, and pay Her ev'ning sacrifice. Amen.

387 *Moderate.* Southgate. 6.4.6.4.10.10. FRED. B. BENEYEN

388 *Moderate.* Damascus. 8.8.8.

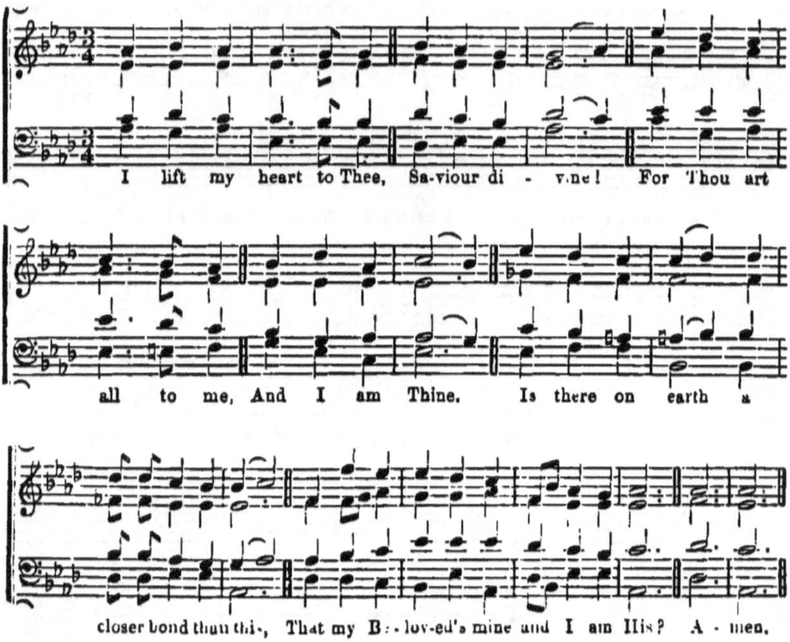

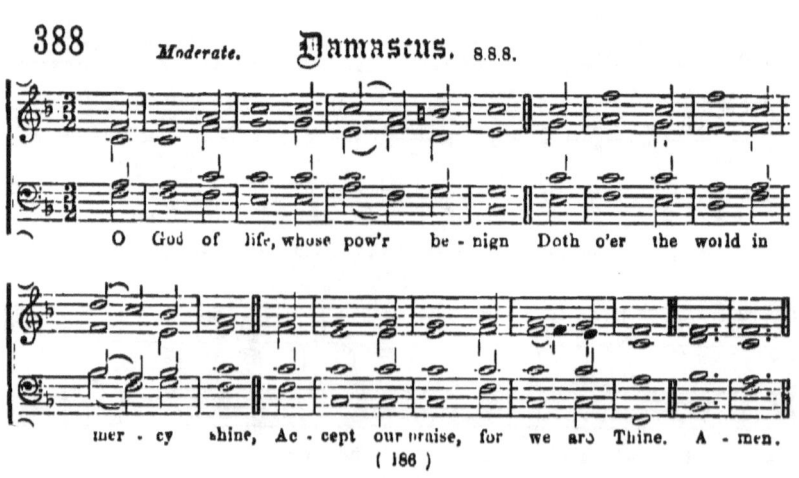

399 *Bold and joyous.* **Migdol.** 6.6.6.6.6.6. D. Theme from HAYDN. By per. from *Crown of Jesus.*

When morn-ing gilds the skies, My heart a-wak-ing cries, May Je-sus Christ be praised! A-like in work and prayer, To Je-sus I re-pair; May Je-sus Christ be praised! To Thee, O God a-bove, I cry with glowing love, May Jesus Christ be praised! This song of sa-cred joy, It nev-er seems to cloy: May Jesus Christ be praised! A-men, A-men.

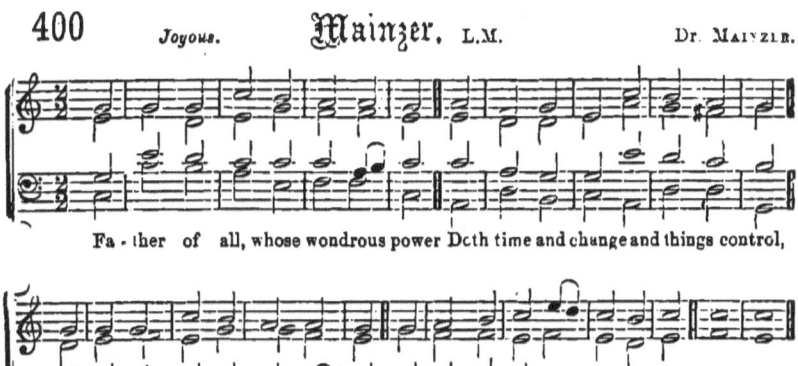

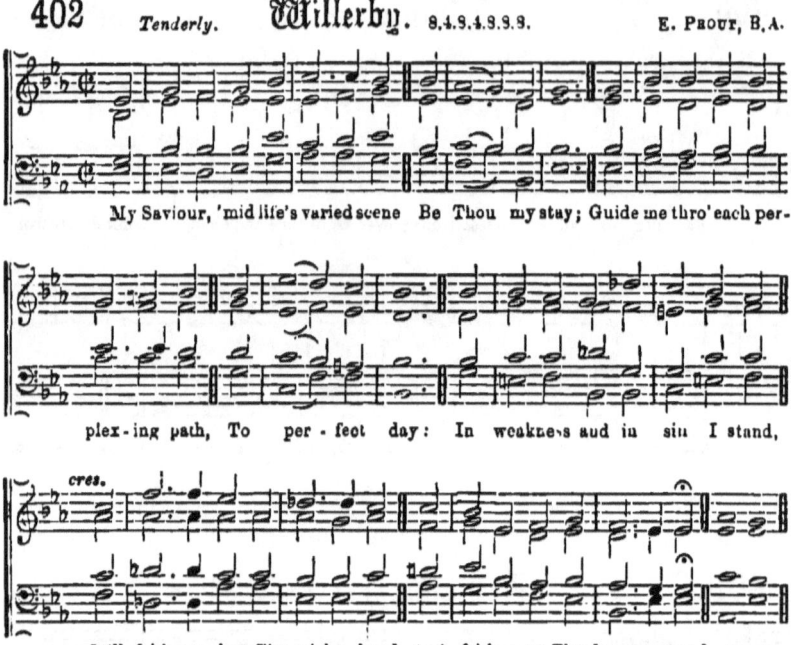

Or this Chant—

404 **Hemingford.** 10.4.10.4. (METRICAL CHANT.)

A-men.

405 *Moderate.* **Islington.** 5.5.7.5.5.7.10.10. RICHARD PAYNE.

We praise, we bless Thee, Lord, we con-fess Thee, Un-cre-a-ted

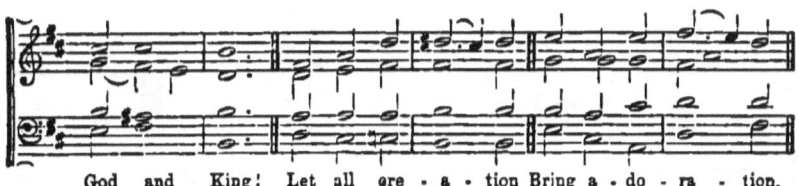

God and King! Let all cre-a-tion Bring a-do-ra-tion,

Earth and heav'n Thy prais-es sing. Father e-ter-nal, all shall a-dore Thee!

Lord God Al-migh-ty, all shall im-plore Thee! plore Thee! A- men.

406 Via Crucis.

7.6, Irregular.   Rev. J. B. Dykes, M.A. Mus. D.

The way is long and drea - ry, The path is bleak and bare, Our feet are worn and

wea-ry, But we will not des - pair; More hea-vy was Thy bur-then,

More des-o-late Thy way: O Lamb of God! Who

[End of 3rd verse] a - way, Give us Thy peace.
takest the sin of the world a - way, Have mer-cy up - on us. A-men.

* Last Verse, end of first line, and second line.

sor - row, Hea-vy and hard to bear;

407. Budleigh. 6.4.6.4.10.10.
T. M. Mudie.

I lift my heart to Thee, Saviour divine! For Thou art all to me, And I am Thine. Is there on earth a closer bond than this, That my Beloved's mine, and I am His? Amen.

408. St. Aelred. 8.9.3.3.
Rev. J. B. Dykes, M.A. Mus. D. By per

Fierce raged the tempest o'er the deep, Watch did Thine anxious servants keep, But Thou wast wrapped in guileless sleep, Calm and still. Amen.

409 Holley. L.M.

GEORGE HEWS.

Fervently.

410 Sherbrooke. 8.7.8.7.7.7.

W. SCHULTHES.

Moderate.

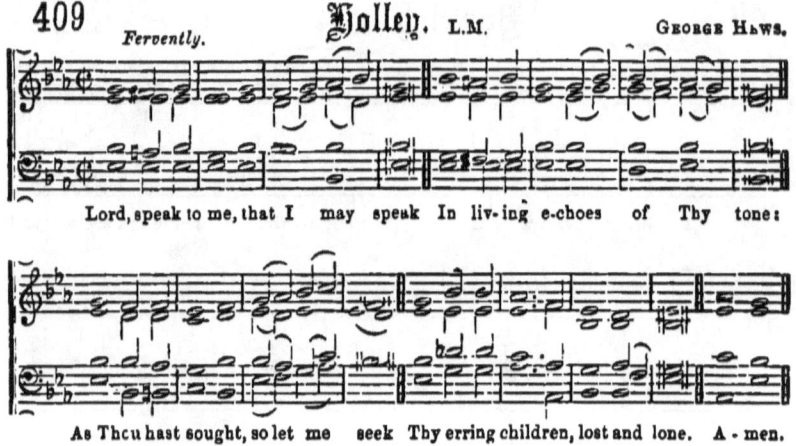

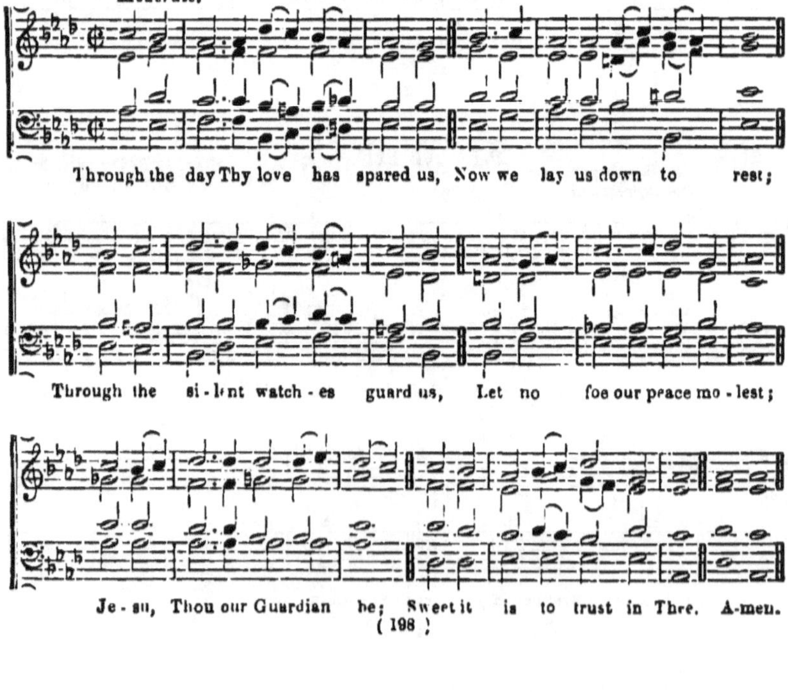

411. Lux Benigna.

Earnestly. 10.4.10.4.10.10. Rev. J. B. DYKES, M.A., Mus. D. By permission.

Lead, kindly Light, amid th'encir-cling gloom, Lead Thou me on; The night is dar', and I am far from home, Lead Thou me on. Keep Thou my feet; I do not ask to see The dis-tant scene; one step e-nough for me. A-men.

412. Cape Town.

Joyous. 7.7.7.5. Dr. F. FILITZ.

Three in One, and One in Three, Ru-ler of the earth and sea, Hear us while we lift to Thee Ho-ly chant and psalm. A-men.

413. Peniel.

Earnestly. 7.5.7.5. D. H. G. NAGELI.

Father, here we dedicate This new year to Thee, In whatever worldly state Thou wilt have us be. Not from sorrow, pain, or care, Freedom dare we claim; This alone shall be our prayer.—"Glorify Thy name." A-men.

414. Durham (St. Agnes).

Moderate. C.M. Rev. J. B. DYKES, M.A., Mus. D. By per.

O Jesus Christ, the Holy One! I long to be with Thee;
O Jesus Christ, the lowly One! Come and abide with me. A-men.

421 *With fervour.* **Sarnen.** 12.12.12.12.   L. CHERUBINI.

When thro' the torn sail the wild tem-pest is streaming, When o'er the dark wave the red light-ning is gleaming, Nor hope lends a ray the poor seamen to cher-ish, We fly to our Maker:—"Save, Lord, or we per-ish!" A-men.

422 *Earnestly.* **Aspiration.** 6.4.6 4.6.6.4.   ARTHUR SULLIVAN.
By permission, from *The Hymnary.*

Nearer, my God, to Thee, Nearer to Thee! E'en tho' it be a cross That raiseth me,

Still all my song shall be, Nearer, my God, to Thee, Nearer to Thee! Nearer to Thee! Amen.

423 Ilala. 10.10.10.10.

Moderate. From *La Feuillée.*

Bear Thou my bur-den, Thou who bear'st my sin, Both are too hea - vy,

Lord, for me to bear: Oh, take them, call them Thine; Yes, Thine tho'

mine; And give me calm re - pose in hours of care. A - - men.

424 Ellers. 10.10.10.10.

E. J. Hopkins.

By per., from the Rev. R. Brown-Borthwick's *Supp. Hy and T. Book.*

Moderate. Harm. by Arthur Sullivan.

Saviour, again to Thy dear name we raise With one accord our parting hymn of praise;

We stand to bless Thee ere our worship cease; Then lowly kneeling wait Thy word of peace Amen.

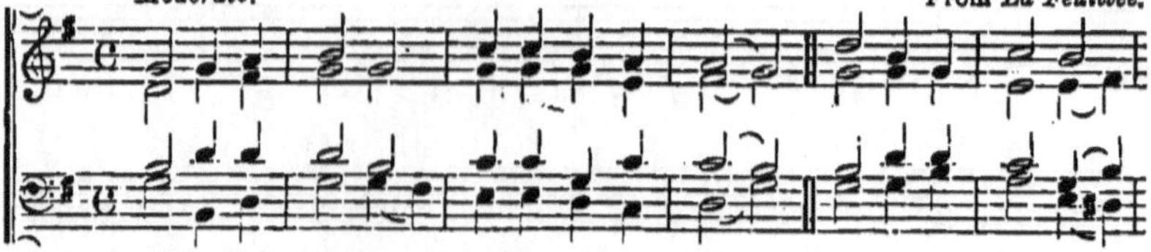

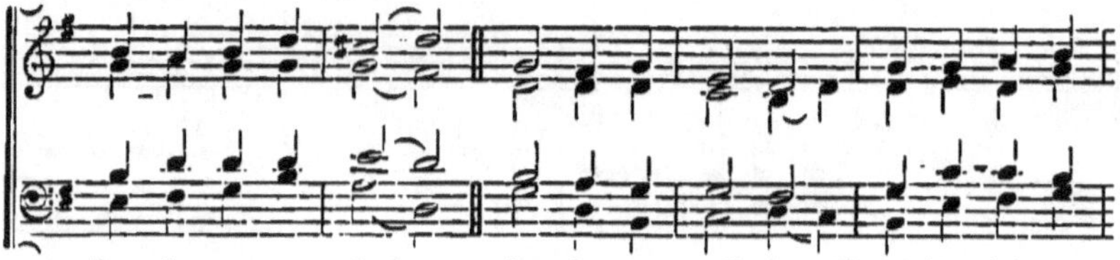

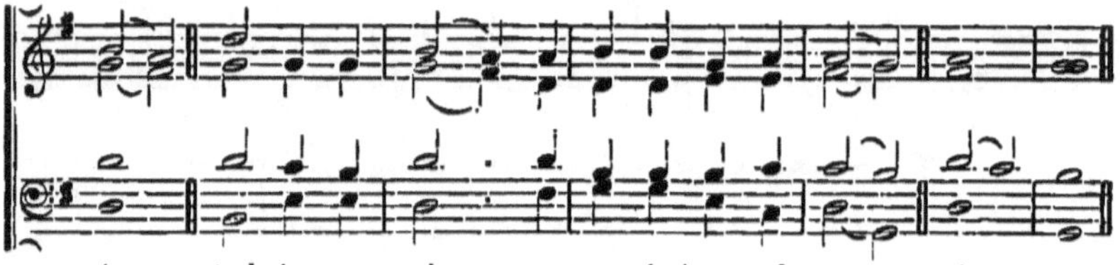

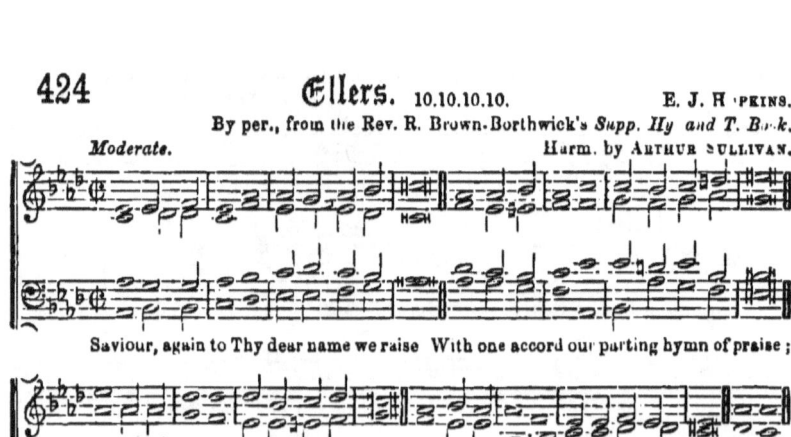

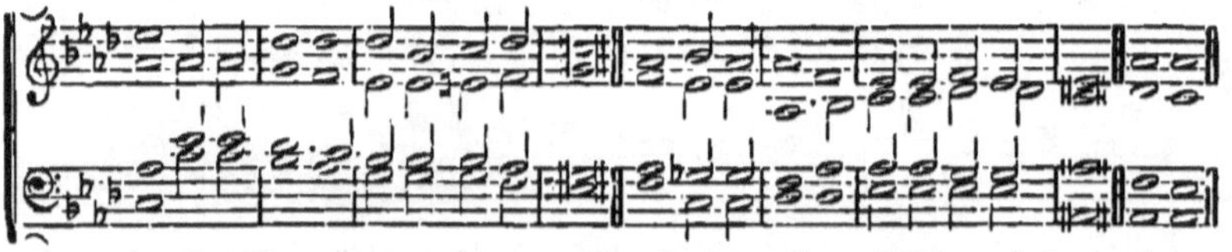

431 **Noel.** C.M.D. Arranged by ARTHUR SULLIVAN. By permission.

It came upon the midnight clear—That glorious song of old, From angels bending

near the earth To touch their harps of gold; "Peace on the earth, good will to men From

heav'n's all gracious King!" The world in solemn stillness lay To hear the angels sing. A-men.

432 **Clifton.** 8.8.8.4. (METRICAL CHANT.) W. L. REYNOLDS.

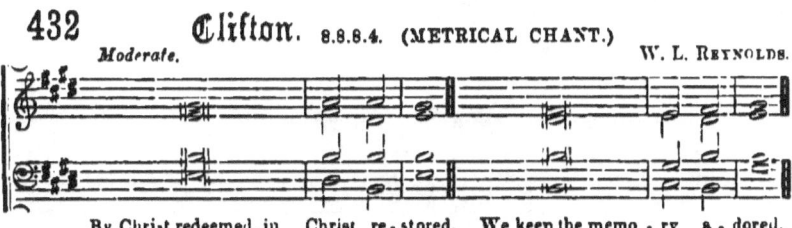

By Christ redeemed, in Christ re-stored, We keep the memo-ry a-dored,

And show the death of our dear Lord Un-til He come. A-men.

435 Maidstone. 7s, 8 or 6 lines.

W. B. Gilbert, Mus. Bac.
By permission.

Joyful.

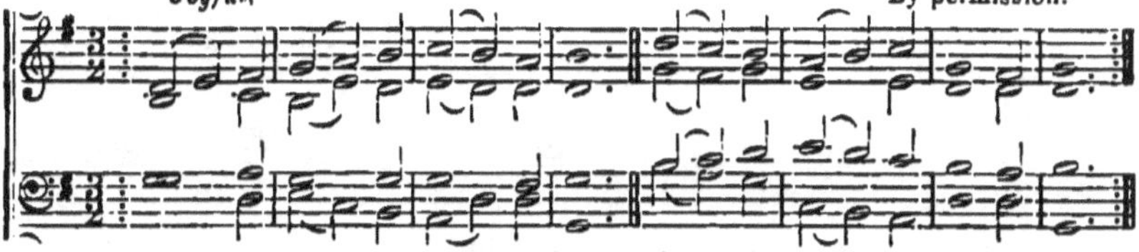

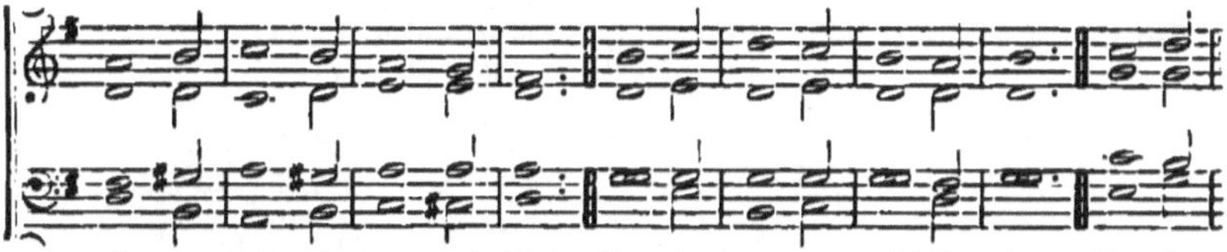

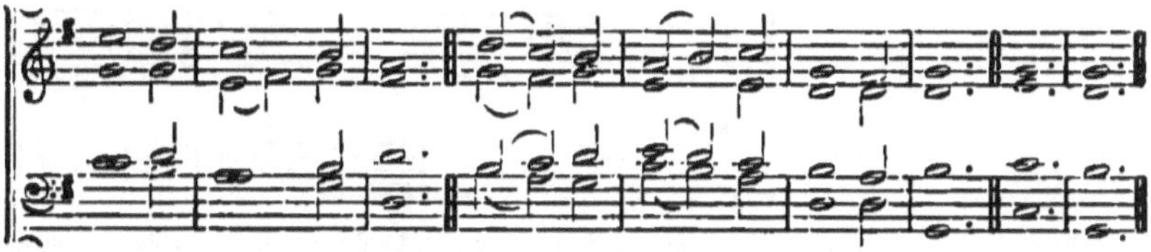

436 North Coates. 6.5.6.5.

T. R. Matthews.
By permission.

Moderate.

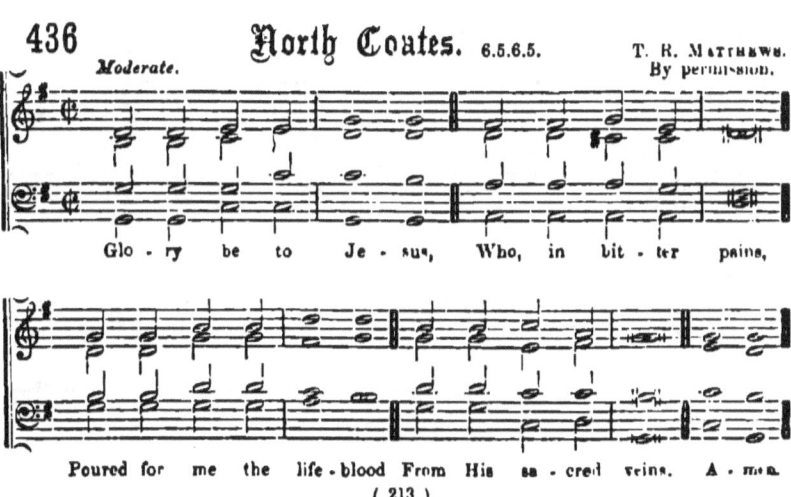

437 Labrador. 6.5.6.5.6.5.6.5.

HEINRICH OSWALD.
Arr. by Rev. P. MAURICE, D.D.

Earnestly.

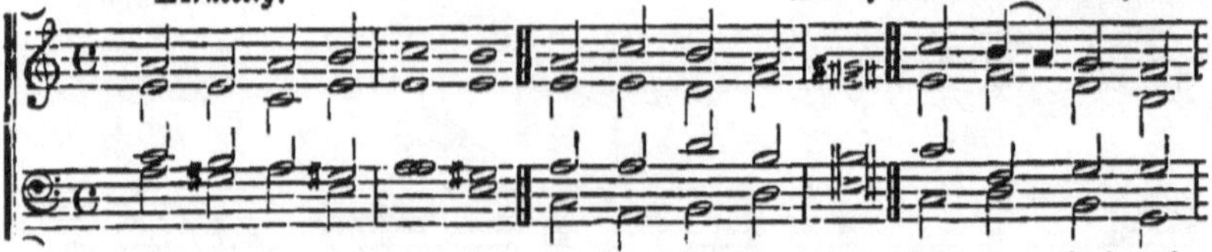

O let him, whose sor - row No re - lief can find, Trust in God, and

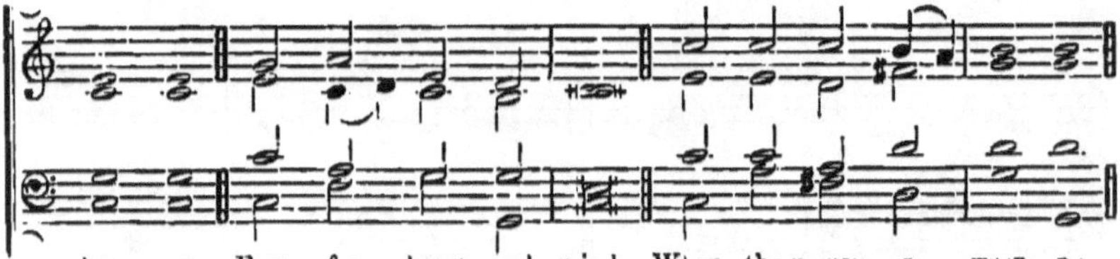

bor - row Ease for heart and mind. When the mourn - er, weep - ing,

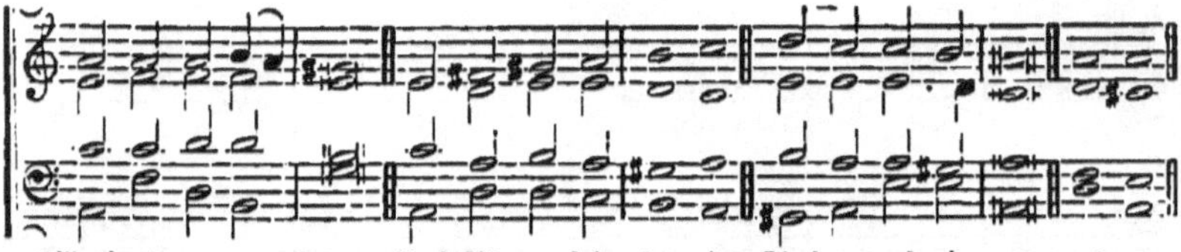

Sheds the se - cret tear, God His watch is keep - ing, Tho' none else is near. A - men.

438 Enon. 6.5.6.5.

Moderate.

FIELDEN.

Now the day is o - - ver, Night is draw - ing nigh,

Sha - dows of the ev'n - ing Steal a - cross the sky. A - men.

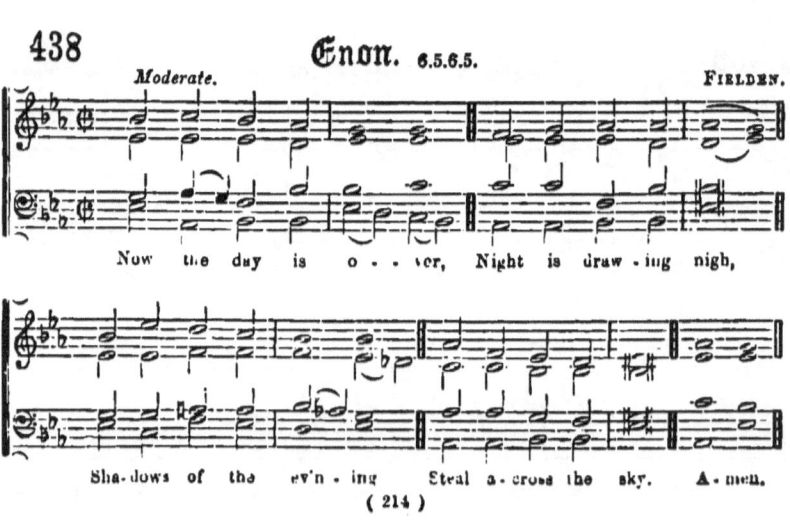

439 Ramoth. 6.5.6.5.6.5.6.5 6.5.

Joyous. R. SCHUMANN.

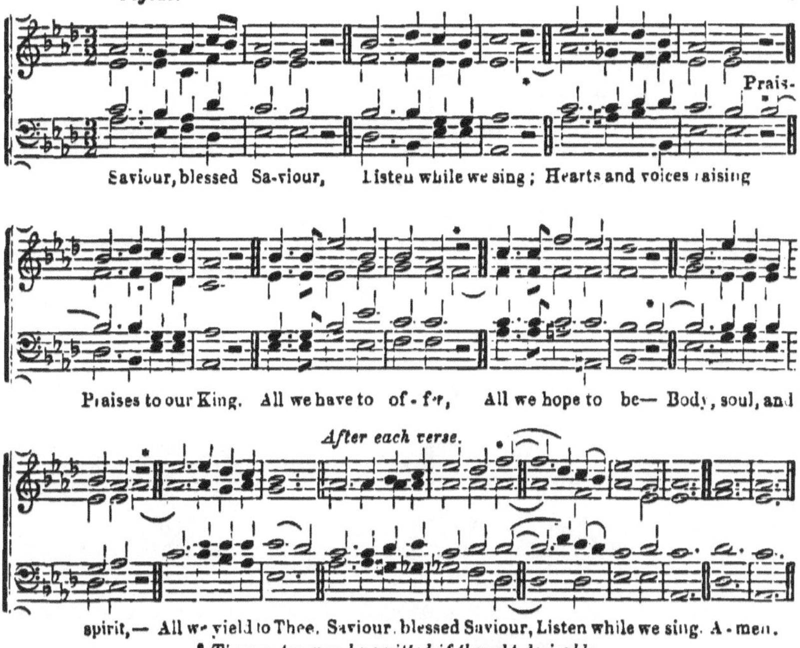

* *These notes may be omitted if thought desirable.*

440 Barton. 7.6.7.6.

Joyous. J. H. KNECHT.

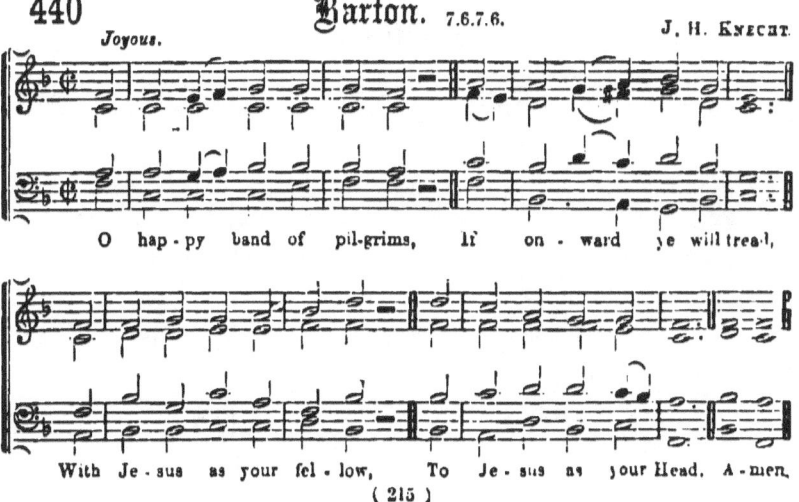

441 Stella. L.M., 6 lines.

Moderate.

O Love, who formedst me to wear The im-age of Thy God-head here,

Who sought-est me with ten-der care Thro' all my wand'rings wild and drear;

O Love, I give my-self to Thee, Thine ev-er, on-ly Thine to be. A-men.

442 Angelus. L.M.

Moderate. J. SCHEFFLER.

At e-ven, ere the sun was set, The sick, O Lord, a-round Thee lay;

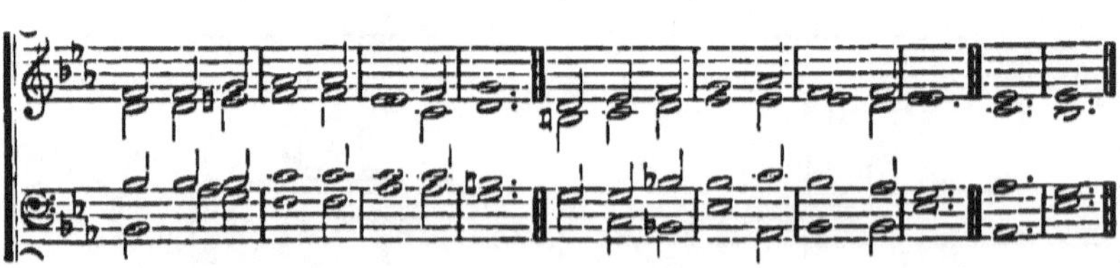

Oh, in what di-vers pains they met! Oh, with what joy they went a-way! A-men.

443. Interlachen. 8.8.8.8.8.8. (Trochaic).

Quietly.
Arranged from FERDINAND LAOS.

Hope of those that have none other, Left for life by father, mother,

All their dearest lost or taken, Only not by Thee forsaken;

Comfort Thou the sad and lonely, Saviour dear, for Thou canst only. A-men.

444. Canitz. 8.4.7.8.4.7.

Joyful.
MAROT and BEZA's Psalms, 1565.

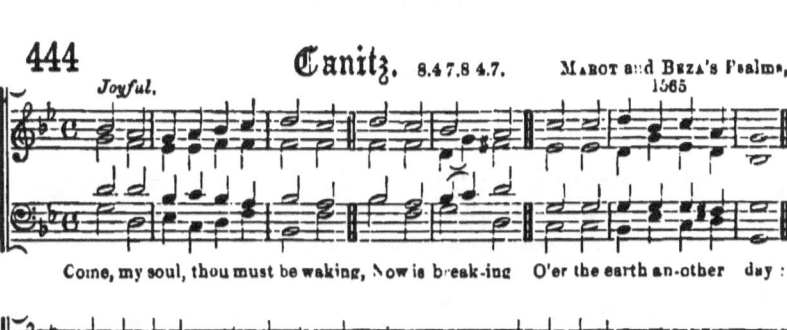

Come, my soul, thou must be waking, Now is breaking O'er the earth another day:

Come to Him who made this splendour; See thou render All thy feeble strength can pay. Amen.

(217)

SERAPHIM—*continued.*

449 Stepney. 8.7.8.7.7.7.
W. BAYLEY.

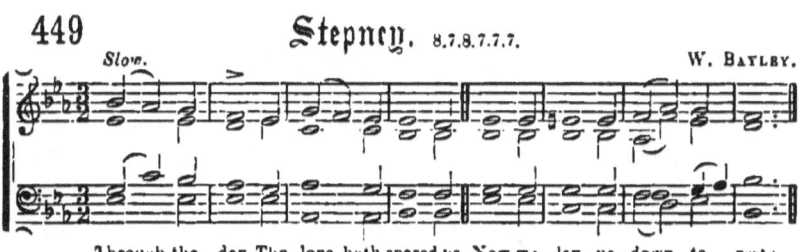

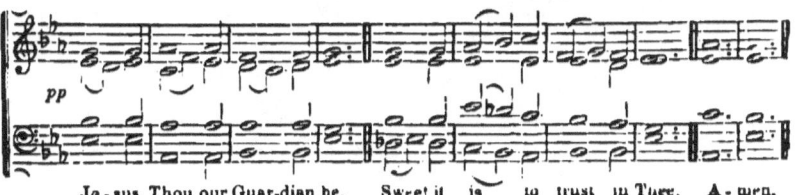

452 Ruth. 6.5.6.5.6.5.6.5.

Joyous. SAMUEL SMITH.
By permission.

Summer suns are glowing Over land and sea, Happy light is flowing Bountiful and free.

Ev'rything re-joi-ces In the mellow rays, All earth's thousand voices Swell the psalm of praise. Amen.

453 Clarence. 7 7 7.7.

Moderate. ARTHUR SULLIVAN.
By permission.

1. Win-ter reign-eth o'er the land, Freez-ing with its i-cy breath; Dead and bare the

5th and 6th verses.

tall trees stand; All is chill and drear as death. 5. But the sleeping earth shall wake,

And the flow'rs shall burst in bloom, And all nature ris-ing break Glorious from its wintry tomb. Amen.

464 **Norminster.** 7.8.7.8.7.7. JULIUS GROVE.

465 **Emmanuel.** C.M. BEETHOVEN.

466 Gennesaret. Irregular.
(FOR MISSION SERVICES.)

P. P. Bliss.

Sow-ing our seed in the morning fair, Sowing our seed in the noon-tide glare,

Sow-ing our seed in the fad-ing light, Sow-ing our seed in the solemn night;

Oh! what shall the har-vest be? Oh! what shall the har-vest be?

After each verse.
Sown in the dark - - ness or sown in the light,
Sown in the darkness or sown in the light, Sown in the darkness or sown in the light,

Sown in our weak - - - ness or sown in our
Sown in our weakness or sown in our might, Sown in our weakness or

GENNESARET—*continued.*

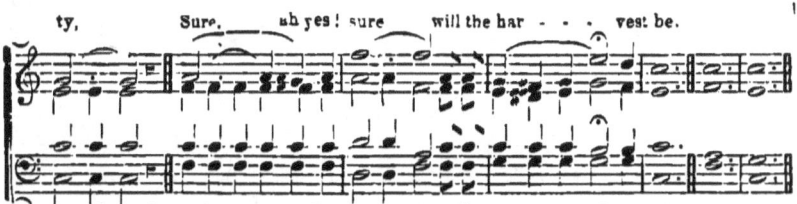

Sowing our seed by the wayside high,
Sowing our seed on the rocks to die,
Sowing our seed where the thorns will spoil,
Sowing our seed in the fertile soil;
Oh! what shall the harvest be?
Sown in the darkness, &c.

Sowing the seed of a lingering pain,
Sowing the seed of a maddened brain,
Sowing the seed of a tarnished name,
Sowing the seed of eternal shame;
Oh! such will the harvest be.
Sown in the darkness, &c.

Sowing our seed with an aching heart,
Sowing our seed while the teardrops start,
Sowing in hope till the reapers come,
Gladly to gather the harvest home;
Oh! such will the harvest be.
Sown in the darkness, &c.

467   Flabian. C.M.
Moderate.   Barber's *Psalm Tunes.*

(231)

468 Christus Consolator. 8.5.8.3.

Moderate. By permission.

Art thou wea - ry, art thou lan - guid, Art thou sore dis - tressed?

"Come to Me," saith One, "and com - ing, Be at rest."

And His side." But of thorns." Many a tear." Jor-dan past." Pass a-way." Answer, Yes." A-men.

469 Vox Dilecti. C.M., 8 lines. Rev. J. B. Dykes, M.A., Mus. D.

Moderate. By permission, from *Hymns Ancient and Modern.*

I heard the voice of Je - sus say, "Come un - to Me, and rest;

Lay down, thou wea - ry one, lay down Thy head up - on My breast."

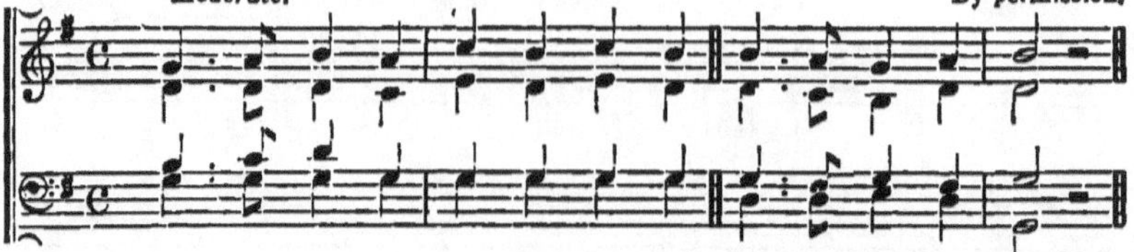

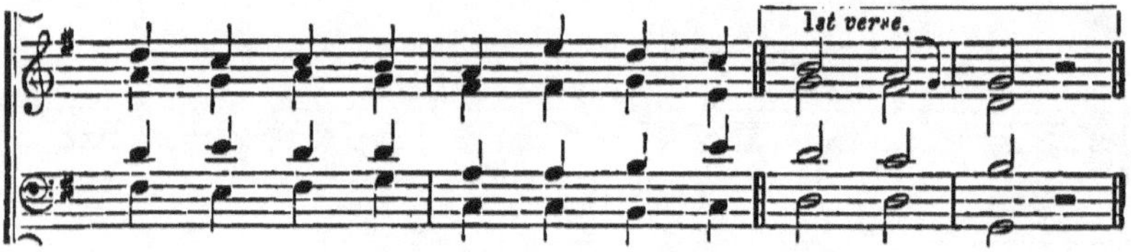

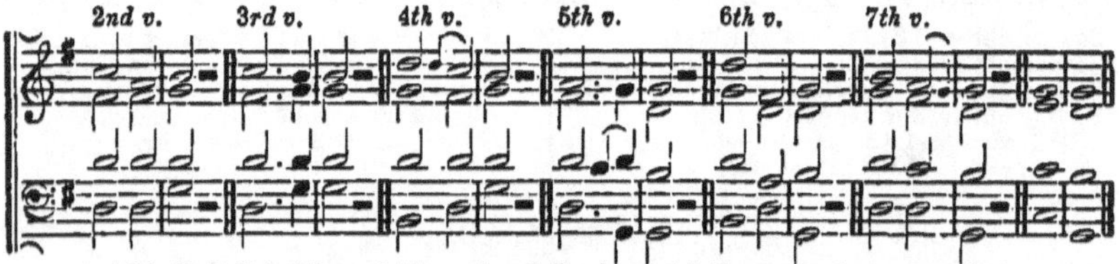

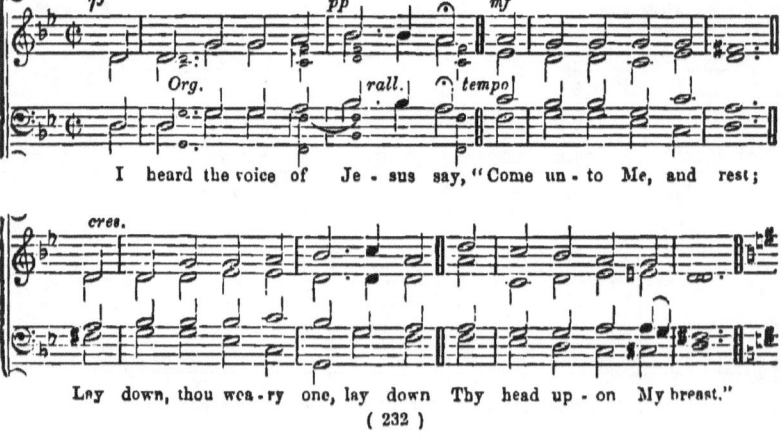

VOX DILECTI—*continued.*

470   Agatha. 6.6.6.6.6.6.6.6.   WEBER.

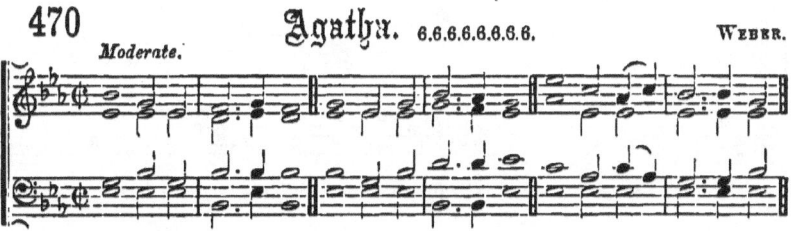

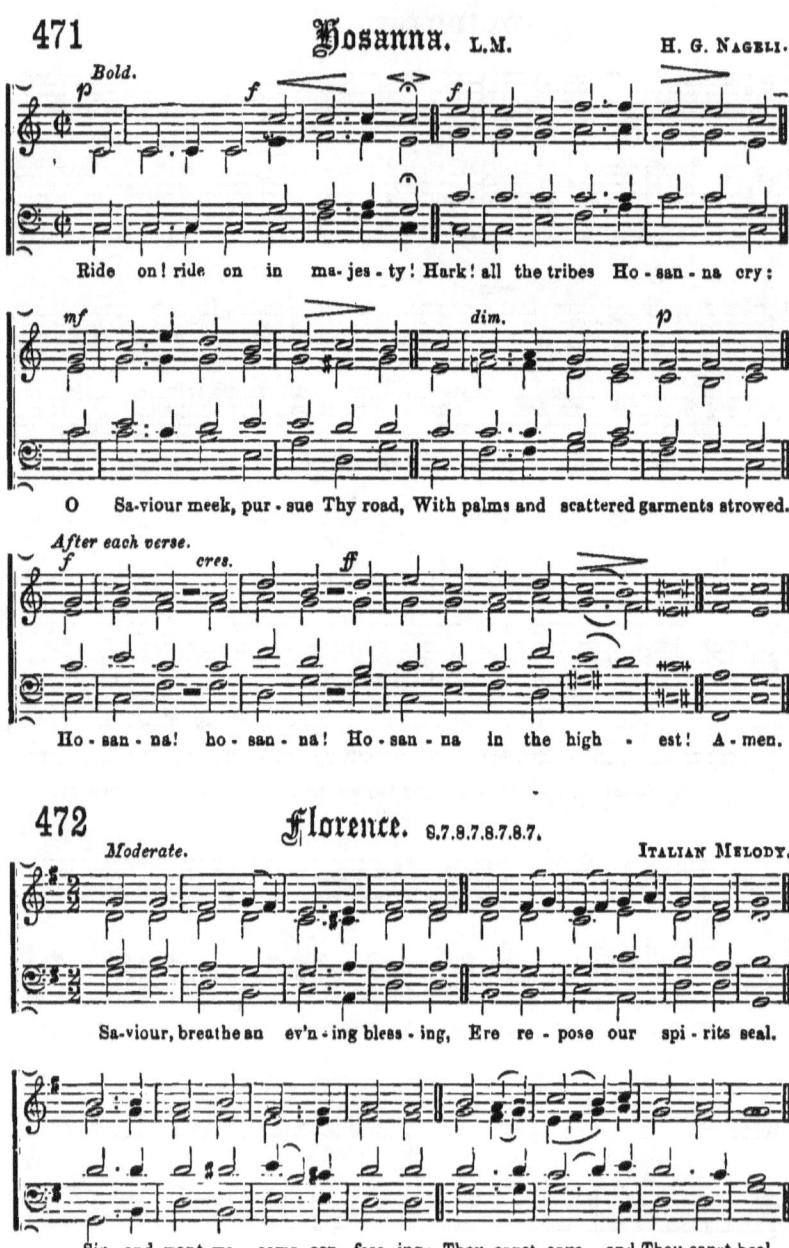

FLORENCE—*continued.*

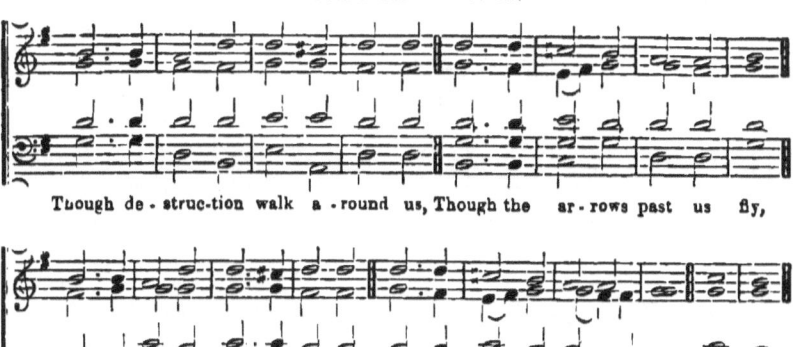

Though de-struc-tion walk a-round us, Though the ar-rows past us fly, An-gel-guards from Thee surround us; We are safe, for Thou art nigh. A-men.

473   Rutherford.   7.6.7.6.7.6.7.5.   D'URHAN.
Moderate.   Arranged from *Chants Chrétiens.*

The sands of time are sink-ing; The dawn of hea-ven breaks, The sum-mer morn I've

sighed for, The fair sweet morn a-wakes: Dark, dark hath been the mid-night, But

day-spring is at hand; And glo-ry, glo-ry dwelleth In Immanuel's land. A-men.

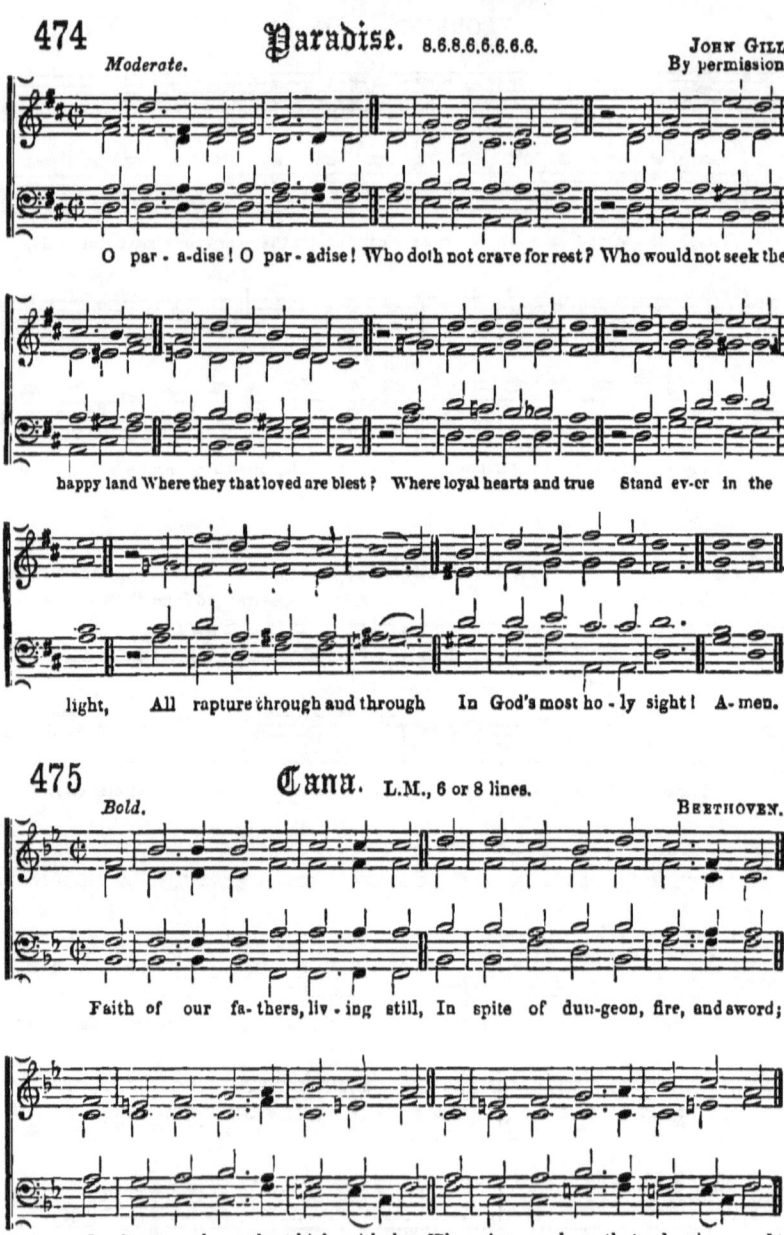

CANA—*continued.*

Faith of our fathers, holy faith, We will be true to thee till death.

Faith of our fathers, holy faith, We will be true to thee till death. A-men.

476   Greenland. 7.6.7.6.7.6.7.6.   *Lausanne Psalter.*
Joyful.   Alt. by Dr. Rimbault. By per.

Re-joice, all ye be-liev-ers, And let your lights appear; The ev'ning is ad-

vanc-ing, And dark-er night is near; The Bridegroom is a-ris-ing, And

now He draweth nigh: Up! pray, and watch, and wrestle, At midnight comes the cry. A-men.

477 Rest. L.M., 6 lines.

Dr. Stainer.
By per. of the Lond. Ch. Choir Association.

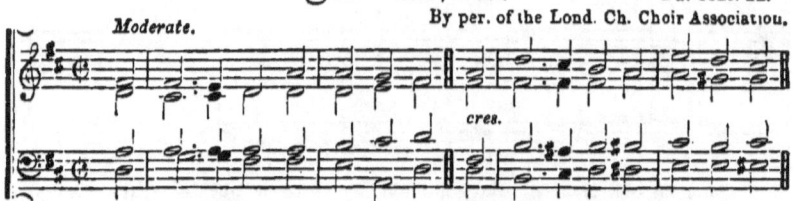

Thou hid-den love of God, whose height, Whose depth unfathomed, no man knows;

I see from far Thy beauteous light, In-ly I sigh for Thy re-pose:

My heart is pained, nor can it be At rest, till it finds rest in Thee. A-men.

478 Melanesia. L.M.

Samuel Smith.
By permission.

Up-lift the ban-ner! let it float Skyward and sea-ward, high and wide;

The sun shall light its shin-ing folds, The c.oss on which the Saviour died. A-men.

479 Scopas. 8.7.8.7.8.7.8.7.

Plaintive. — C. Hancock, Mus. Bac. By permission.

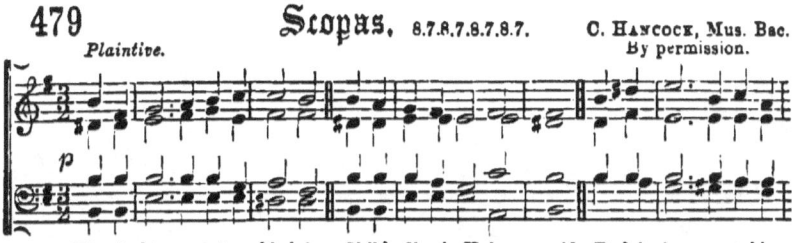

Who is this so weak and helpless, Child of lowly Hebrew maid, Rudely in a stable shelter'd, Coldly in a manger laid? 'Tis the Lord of all cre‑a‑tion, Who this wondrous path hath trod; He is God from everlasting, And to ev‑erlasting, God. A‑men.

480 Vebay. 7.7.7.

Moderate.

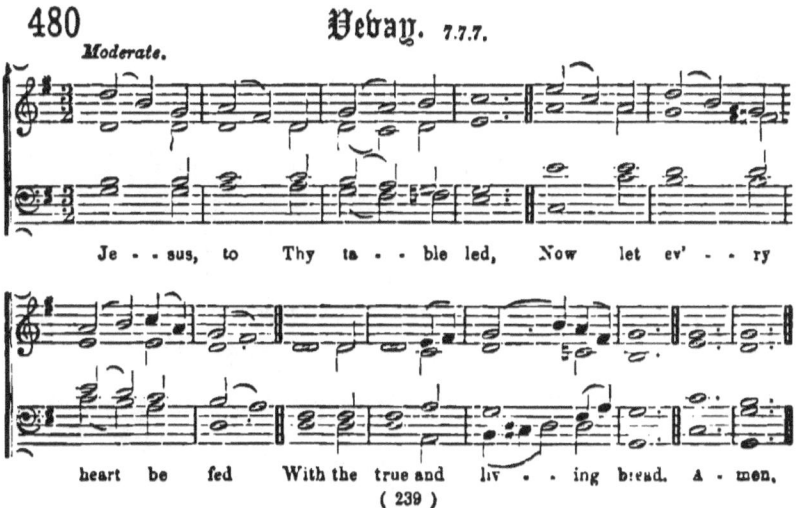

Je‑‑sus, to Thy ta‑‑ble led, Now let ev'‑‑ry heart be fed With the true and liv‑‑ing bread. A‑men.

PETERSHAM—*continued.*

483   Euroclydon. 10.10.10.10.   E. R. B.
By permission.

485 Advent. 4.6.6.4.10,10.
Bold.   J. BAPTISTE CALKIN
             By permission.

The Bridegroom comes! Bride of the Lamb, awake! The midnight cry is

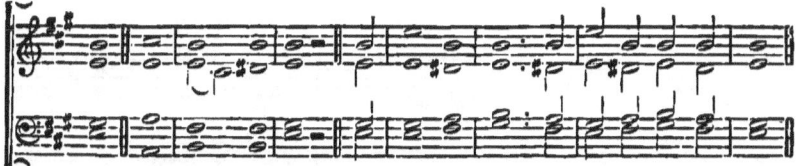

heard: Thy sleep for-sake. The mar-riage day has come; lift up thy head:

Put on Thy bri-dal robe, the feast is spread. A-men.

486 Hanford. 8.8.8.4.
Moderate.   ARTHUR SULLIVAN.
             By permission.

O Lord of heav'n and earth and sea, To Thee all praise and glo-ry be;

How shall we show our love to Thee, Giv-er of all? A-men.

(213)

487   Shalford. 7.6.7.6.7.6.7.6.6.6.9.6.

Bold.   J. A. P. SCHULTZE.

We plough the fertile meadows, We sow the furrow'd land; But all the growth and

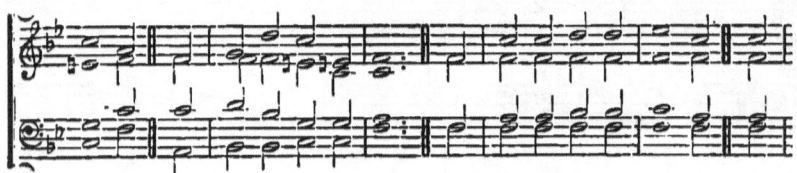

increase Are in God's mighty hand. He gives the shower and sunshine To

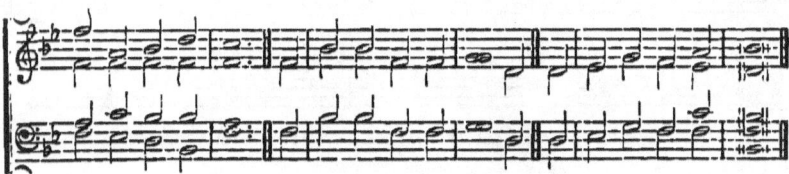

swell the quick'ning grain, The springing corn He blesses, He clothes the golden plain.

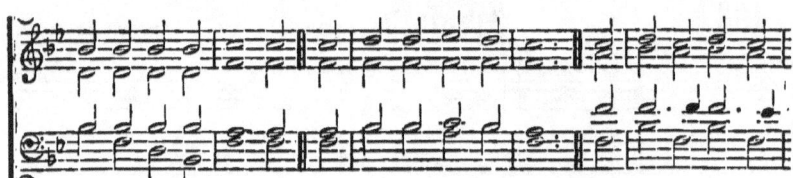

Ev'-ry bounteous blessing His faith-ful love be-stows, Then mag-ni-fy His

glorious name From whom all goodness flows, From whom all goodness flows. A-men.

491   **Elah.** 6.5., 12 lines.   From HAYDN.

On-ward, Christian sol-diers, Marching as to war, With the cross of

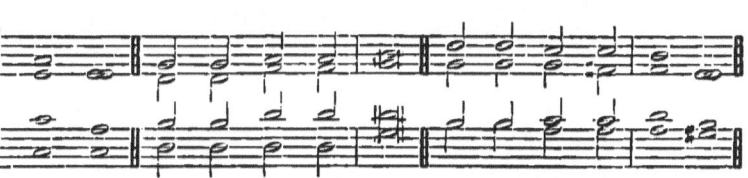

Je-sus Go-ing on be-fore. Christ, the roy-al Mas-ter,

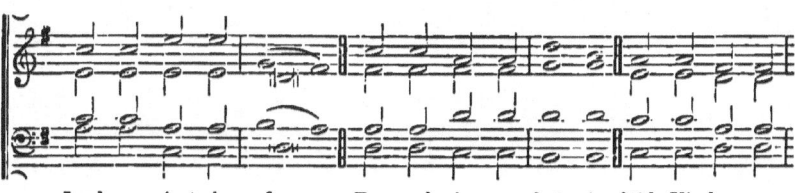

Leads a-gainst the foe; For-ward in-to bat-tle, Still His ban-ners

go. On-ward, Chris-tian sol-diers, March-ing as to war,

With the cross of Je-sus Go-ing on be-fore. A-men.

CRUCIFER—*continued.*

Per-ish ev'-ry fond am-bi-tion, All I've sought, and hoped, and known;

Yet how rich is my con-di-tion! God and heav'n are still mine own. A-men.

498 Leominster. Harm. by ARTHUR SULLIVAN.
Slowly. S.M., 8 lines. By permission.

A few more years shall roll, A few more sea-sons wane, And we shall be with

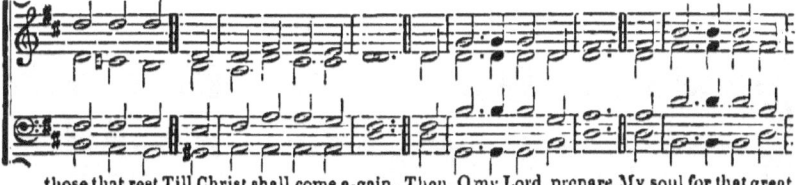

those that rest Till Christ shall come a-gain. Then, O my Lord, prepare My soul for that great

day; O wash me in Thy precious blood, And take my sins a-way. A-men.

THE ENDLESS ALLELUIA—continued.

8. Thee, the Creator of the world, with them we praise For ever, and tell out in
9. To the Eternal Son our . . . . . voi - ces sing, To Thee, O Holy Spirit,

sweet - est lays, An end - less Al - le - lu - - ia.
we will bring An end - less Al - le - lu - - ia. A - men.

531* *Earnestly.*   **Hesperus.** L.M.   H. BAKER.

Take up thy cross, the Sa-viour said, If thou wouldst my dis - ci - ple be;

De - ny thyself, the world forsake, And humbly fol - low af - ter Me. A - men.

532   The Strain upraise.
(A METRICAL CHANT.)

Dr. W. Hayes.
Adapted by Troyte.

1. The strain upraise of joy and praise, Alle- | lu- | ia. ||
   To the glory of their King, shall the ransomed | peo...ple | sing, ||
   Alle- | lu- | ia ; || Alle- | lu- | ia.

2. And the choirs that | dwell on | high, || shall re-echo | through the | sky, ||
   Alle- | lu- | ia ; Alle- | lu- | ia.

3. They in the rest of | Paradise who | dwell, ||
   The blessèd ones, with joy the | cho...rus | swell, || Alle- | lu- | ia ; || Alle- | lu- | ia.

4. The planets beaming on their | heaven...ly | way, ||
   The shining constellations | join, and | say, || Alle- | lu- | ia ; | Alle- | lu- | ia.

5. Ye clouds that onward sweep, ye winds on | pin...ions | light, ||
   Ye thunders echoing loud and deep, ye lightnings, | wild...ly | bright, ||
   In sweet con- | sent u- | nite || Your Alle- | lu- | ia.

6. Ye floods and ocean billows, ye storms and | win...ter | snow, ||
   Ye days of cloudless beauty, hoar frost and | sum...mer | glow, ||
   Ye groves that wave in spring, and glorious | fo...rests, | sing, || Alle- | lu- | ia.

7. First let the birds, with painted | plu...mage | gay, ||
   Exalt their great Creator's | praise, and | say, || Alle- | lu- | ia ; || Allu- | lu- | ia.

8. Then let the beasts of earth, with | va...rying | strain, ||
   Join in creation's hymn, and | cry a- | gain || Alle- | lu- | ia ; || Alle- | lu- | ia.

9. Here let the mountains thunder | forth so- | norous, || Alle- | lu- | ia. ||
   There let the valleys sing-in | gent...ler | chorus, || Alle- | lu- | ia.

(272)

THE STRAIN UPRAISE—continued.

10 Thou jubilant abyss of | o...cean | cry, || Alle- | lu- | ia. ||
Ye tracts of earth and conti- | nents, re- | ply, || Alle- | lu- | ia.

11 To God, who all cre- | a...tion | made, ||
The frequent hymn be | du...ly | paid : || Alle- | lu- | ia ; || Alle- | lu- | ia.

12 This is the strain, the eternal strain, the Lord Al- | migh...ty loves : ||
Alle- | lu- | ia. ||
This is the song, the heavenly song, that Christ the | King ap- | proves : ||
Alle- | lu- | ia.

13 Wherefore we sing, both heart and | voice a- | waking, || Alle- | lu- | ia. ||
And children's voices echo, | an...swer | making, || Alle- | lu- | ia.

14 Now from all men | be out- | poured, || Alleluia | to the | Lord ; ||
With Alleluia | ev...er- | more, || The Son and Spirit | we a- | dore.

15 Praise be done to the | Three in | One, ||
Alle- | lu- | ia ! || Alle- | lu- | ia ! || Alle- | lu- | ia ! || A-men.

GODESCHALCUS, A.D. 1050.
Tr. by J. M. NEALE.

533 Moderate. Sunderland. 6.5 6.5.6.6.6.5. ERSKINE ALLON.

When shall we meet a-gain, Meet ne'er to se-ver? When shall peace wreathe her chain Round us for e - ver? Our hearts will ne'er repose Safe from each blast that blows, In this dark vale of woes, Ne - ver, oh, ne - ver! A - men.

FILIUS DEI—*continued*.

Who best can drink His cup of woe, Tri-umphant o-ver pain,
Who pa-tient bears His cross be-low, He fol-lows in His train. A-men.

536 *Moderate.* **Wimbourne.** 76.76.77.77.　　C. BARNEKOV.

Mighty Quick-'ner, Spi-rit blest, Who to life didst wake me,
Wilt Thou not be-come my guest, For Thy dwell-ing take me?
Ev-er-more in me a-bide, To all truth be-come my Guide,
And for spi-rits glo-ri-fied Meet com-pan-ion make me. A-men.

BETHLEHEM EPHRATAH—continued.

"Fear not," he said (for migh-ty dread Had seized their troubled mind),

"Glad tid-ings of great joy I bring To you and all man-kind." A-men.

539 Smoothly. **Mar Saba (Hebron).** 77.77.88. JOSEPH BARNBY.

Now the la-bourer's task is o'er, Now the bat-tle-
day is past, Now up-on the far-ther shore
Lands the voy-a-ger at last; Fa-ther, in Thy pre-cious keep-ing,
Leave we now, Thy ser-vant, sleep - - ing. A - men.

560. Nocturn. 7s., 10 lines.

Sir M. Costa.
Adapted by Sir John Goss.

Fa-ther, by Thy love and power, Comes a-gain the ev'n-ing hour;

Light has van-ished, la-bours cease, Wea-ry creatures rest in peace.

Thou, whose gen-ial dews dis-til On the low-liest weed that grows,

Fa-ther, guard our couch from ill, Grant Thy chil-dren sweet re-pose.

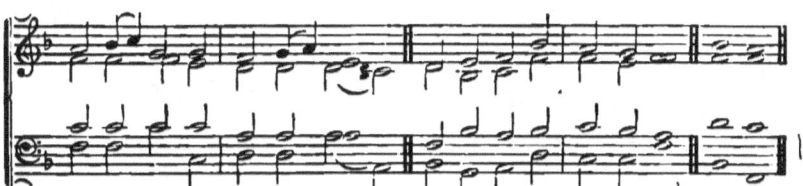

We, to Thee, our-selves re-sign, Let our latest thoughts be Thine. A-men.

567 *Bold.* **Miriam.** 65.65.65.65. T. Hastings.

Safe a-cross the wa-ters, Here in peace we stand; See the wrecks of
E-gypt Strewed a-long the sand. Safe a-cross the wa-ters,
Foes for ev-er gone, Now we march in safe-ty, God our guide a-lone. A-men.

568 *Moderate.* **St. Godric.** 66.66.88. J. B. Dykes, Mus. Doc.

One sole bap-tis-mal sign, One Lord be-low, a-bove, The
fellowship of Zi-on hath One on-ly watchword—love: From diff'rent temples
though it rise, One song as-cend-eth to the skies. A-men.

(293)

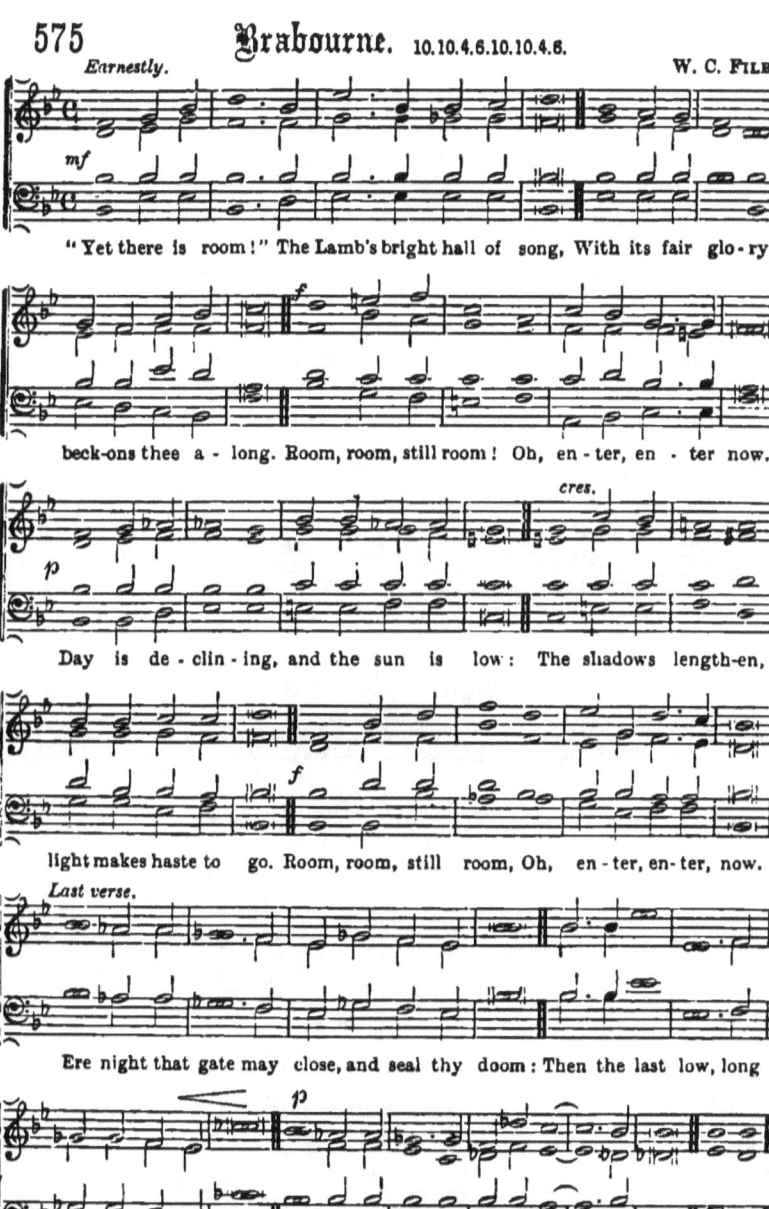

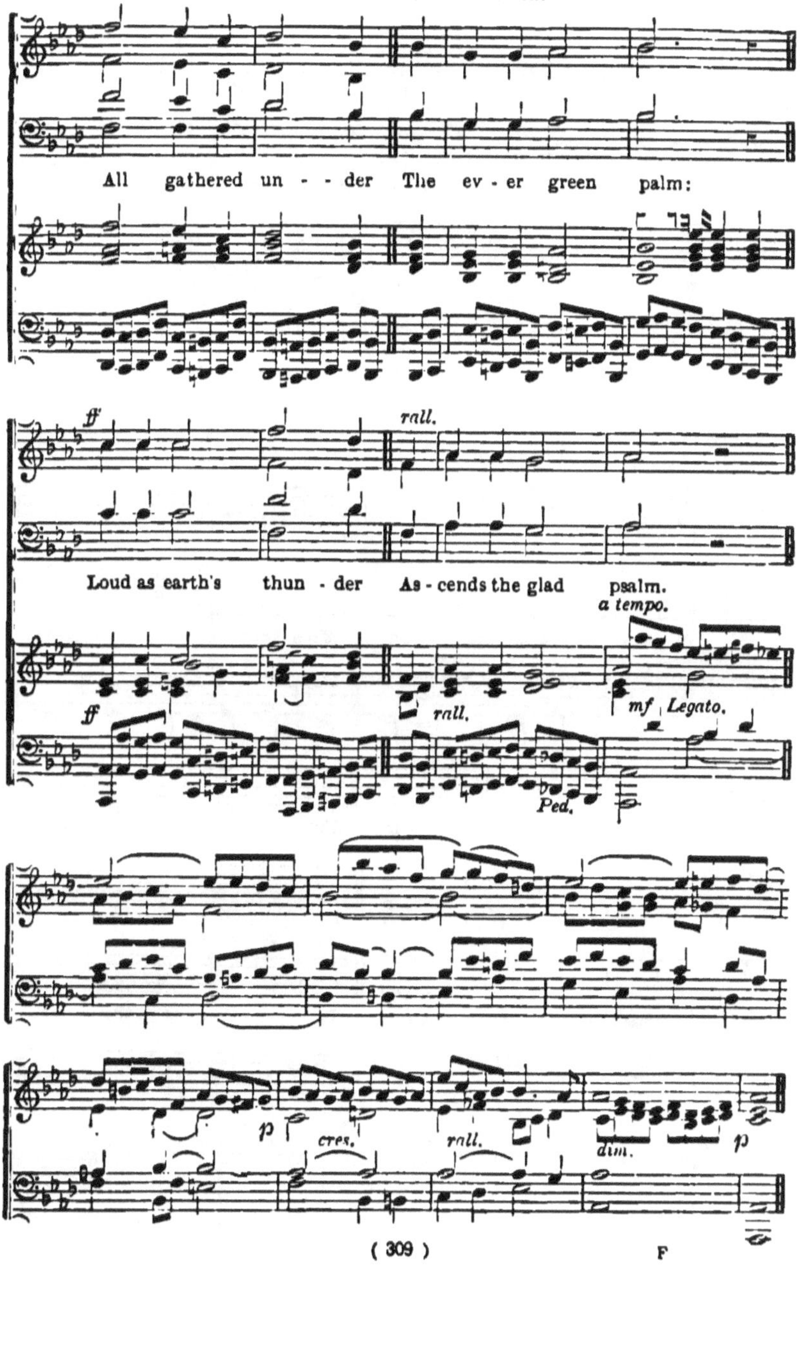

ST. CYPRIAN—*continued.*

All gathered un - - der The ev - er green palm:

Loud as earth's thun - der As - cends the glad psalm.

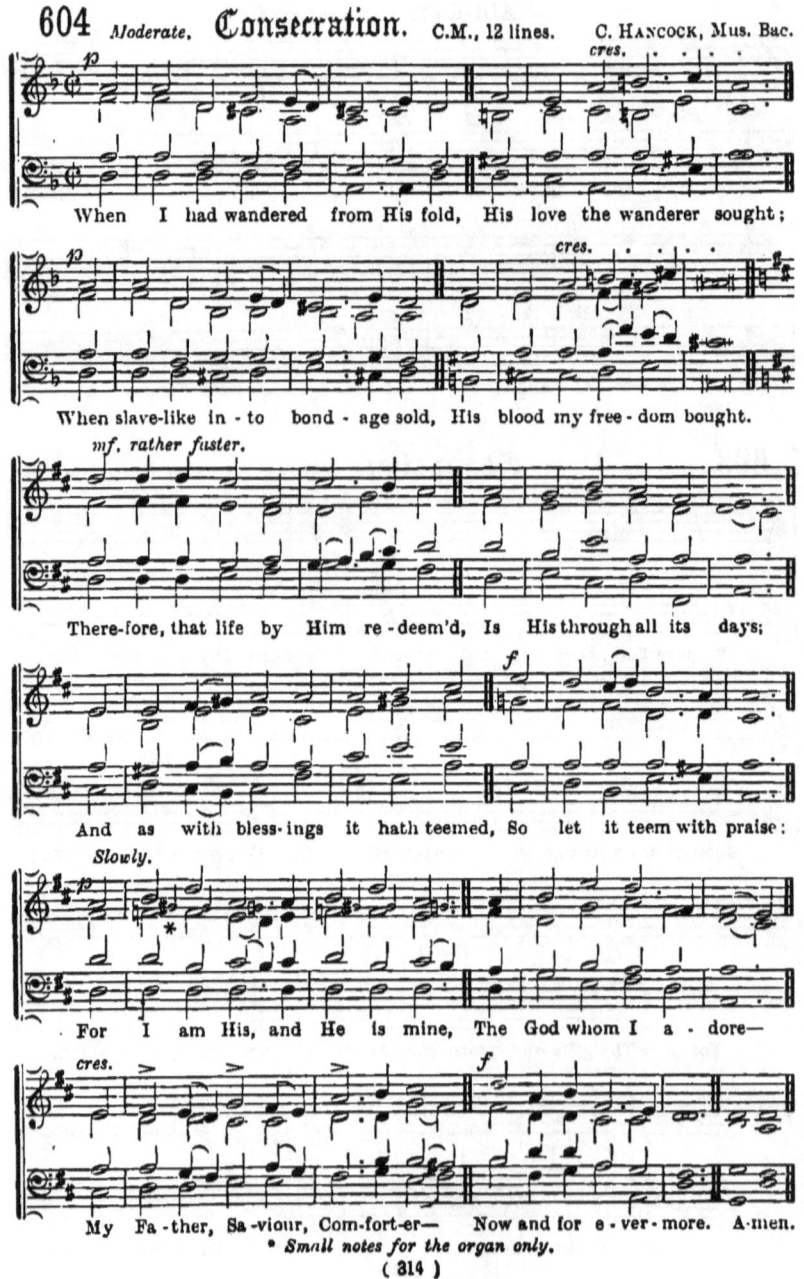

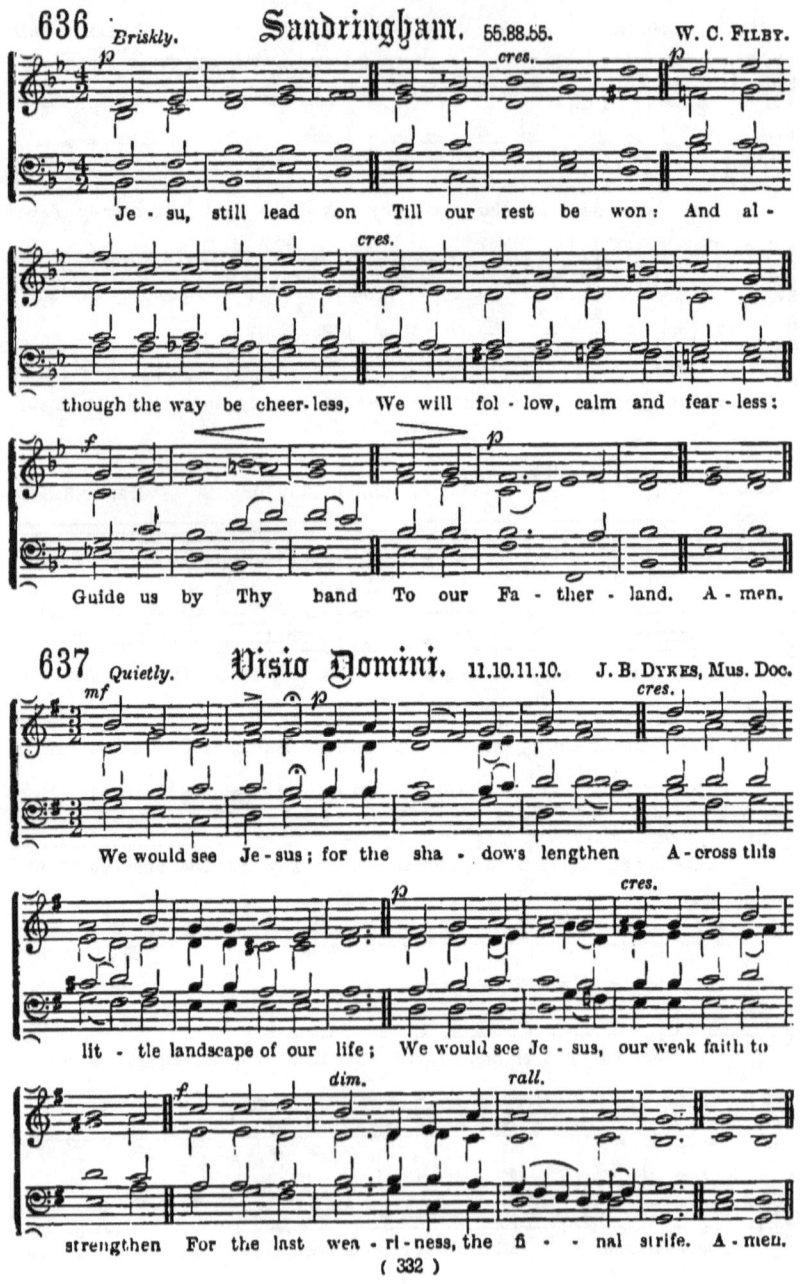

* *First verse only.*

642 *Joyously.* "Come unto Me." 76.76.76 76.

Rev. J. B. Dykes, Mus. Doc.

Note.—*Although it is suggested that the first two lines of each verse should be sung by Tenors and Basses only, yet if necessary they may be sung in Octaves by all the voices.*

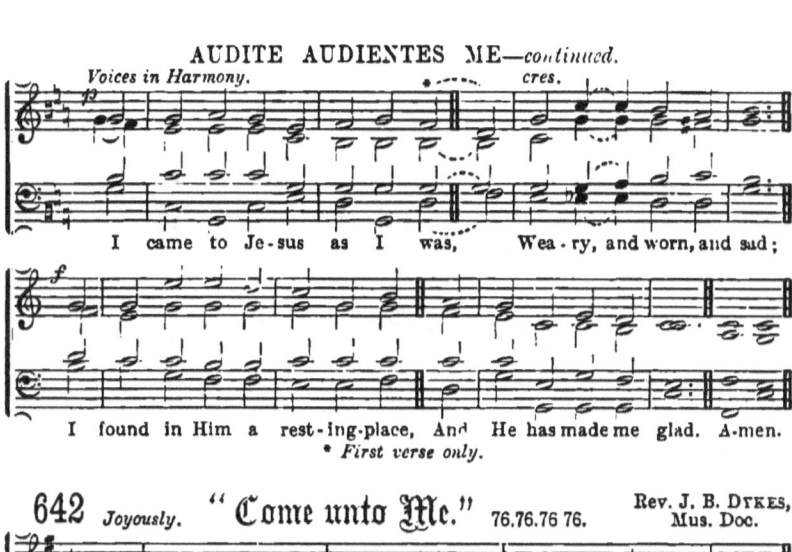

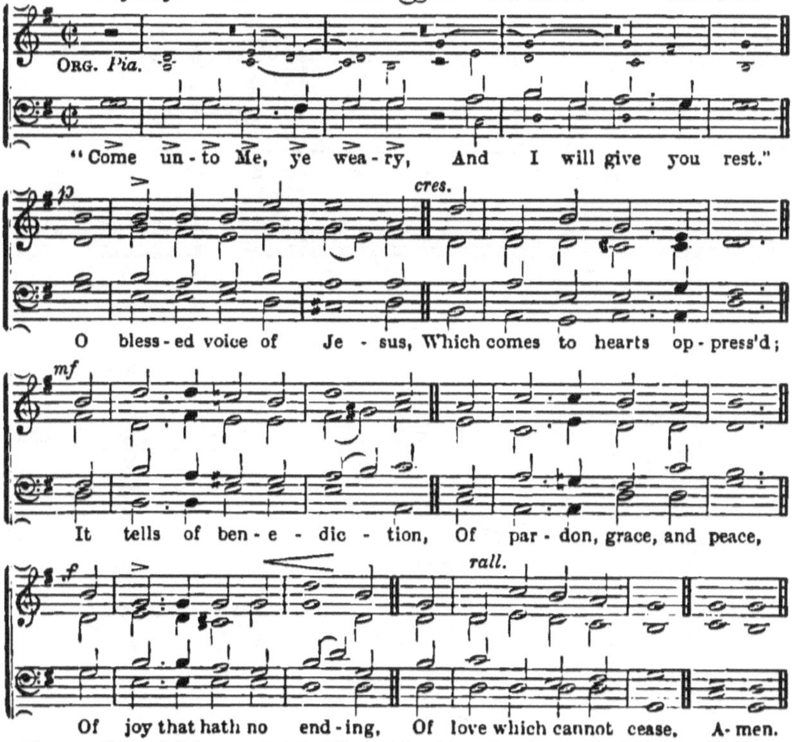

647 *Gravely.* Dies Iræ. 888. D.
Vers. 1 to 14.
Rev. J. B. DYKES, Mus. Doc.

Day of wrath! O day of mourning! See! once more the cross re-turn-ing—

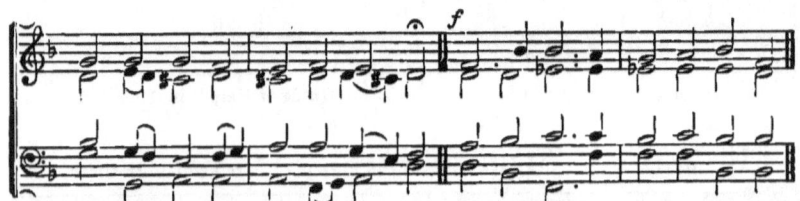

Heaven and earth in ash - es burn- ing! O, what fear man's bo-som rend-eth,

When from heaven the Judge descendeth, On Whose sentence all de - pend - eth!

With Thy fa-voured sheep, O place me! Nor a-mong the goats a - base me;

But to Thy right hand up-raise me. While the wick - ed are con-founded,

(338)

www.ingramcontent.com/pod-product-compliance
Lightning Source LLC
Chambersburg PA
CBHW032015220426
43664CB00006B/248